FEMINISM
UNDER FIRE

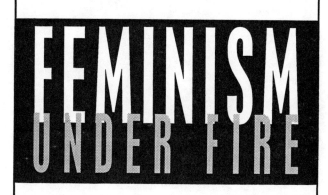

FEMINISM
UNDER FIRE

E L L E N R. K L E I N

 **Prometheus Books**

59 John Glenn Drive
Amherst, NewYork 14228-2197

Published 1996 by Prometheus Books

00 99 98 97 96   5 4 3 2 1

Library of Congress Cataloging-in-Publication Data

Klein, Ellen R.
      Feminism under fire / Ellen R. Klein.
            p.   cm.
      Includes bibliographical references and index.
      ISBN 1–57392–011–8 (alk. paper)
      1. Philosophy. 2. Feminism—Philosophy. 3. Feminism—Quine. I. Title.
HQ1190.K55   1996
305.42'01—dc20   95–35980
                                                                        CIP

Printed in the United States of America on acid-free paper

To my mother—the first feminist I ever knew,
to my father—for raising only "sons,"
with all my love.

How can you hesitate?
Risk! Risk anything!
Care no more for the opinions
of others, for those voices.
Do the hardest thing on earth
for you. Act for yourself.
Face the truth.

Katherine Mansfield
Journal (1922)

Contents

Preface

There is an appalling dearth of cool, critical analysis of the [feminist] literature.

Christina Hoff Sommers[1]

In 1984, young and naive, I entered graduate school and the world of professional philosophy. Both my professional and personal training were decidedly classical. I studied Plato and Aristotle, metaphysics and epistemology, logic and ethics; I taught undergraduate classes in logic, introduction to philosophy, and contemporary moral issues. Slowly but surely, I became aware of sexism in philosophy as it existed in classrooms, texts, and the real world. Disappointed but undeterred, I believed if I could escape from an all-male department and mingle with other women philosophers I might find professional respect and happiness.

In 1988, not as young but still naive, I entered the world of professional feminism. At a national conference on feminist philosophy and women's studies I was introduced to the many faces of feminism: radical, lesbian, Marxist, socialist, and postmodern, among others. To my horror I discovered my entire education had been "infected" by male-bias and was, at least in the eyes of my feminist comrades, illegitimate. As I went from lecture to lecture

9

being ridiculed for asking questions such as "What makes this theory an ethic?" or "What makes that epistemological account feminist?" I began to lose confidence in my professional ability as a philosopher, as well as in my personal commitment as a feminist. As a result of this experience I left the conference determined to learn as much as I could about feminist philosophy.

Shortly after the conference I was asked to teach a course entitled "Feminist Philosophy." I agreed and immediately began an intensive study of all that had been written on the subject.

The class was difficult both for myself and the students (most of whom were not philosophers and all of whom were young women who had not yet developed "feminist consciousness.") Nevertheless, we made it. Throughout the course, though, one question kept arising: How was one to distinguish *feminist philosophy, nonfeminist philosophy,* and *feminist nonphilosophy*? Interestingly, my students were asking me the very same question I myself had asked more sophisticated feminist philosophers a year earlier. While I would not ignore or dismiss the question, I still could not answer it.

Since then the question has haunted me. Fortunately, so has an answer. The solution, provided me by the most prolific feminist philosophers, was that the question cannot and indeed should not be answered; for it is impertinent for two different yet interrelated reasons. First, it suggests one is searching for a complete reductive analysis of the concept of "feminist philosophy," i.e., its necessary and sufficient conditions. Such a search is, as Alison Jaggar once stated publicly to much applause and laughter, "stupid."[2] Why so? The answer has nothing to do with classical problems of language, meaning, or the indeterminacy of translation; the question is stupid simply because *men* search for it.

The second reason concerns the presupposition of a distinction between feminism as a philosophical thesis and feminism as a political movement. Such a distinction—the divorce of theory from praxis—claim feminists, is yet another male-biased ruse designed to oppress women.

Unfortunately, these feminist responses were unsatisfying. Further questioning was in order.

After having granted feminists the historical and sociological points—that philosophy was developed almost exclusively by men and has often been used by men to oppress women—I was still inclined to ask if philosophy is *itself* essentially sexist and inherently male-biased. After all, a knife in the hands of a criminal can produce one effect, while one in the hands of a surgeon quite another. So the mere fact that the "tools" of philosophy have been abused in the past doesn't mean the tools themselves are essentially abusive.

Once again, however, I was told that the question, albeit at another level of inquiry, was illegitimate; that it presumed a distinction between tool and toolmaker and was unworthy of response.

Still undaunted, I queried, "Isn't there a distinction between philosophy and politics?" After all, can't one as a nonpartisan philosopher ask which political view is good, which ought we adopt? Isn't this question apolitical? In other words, isn't it legitimate to ask whether there is such a thing as a feminist philosophy? Or, if there is, that that philosophy may be misguided?

The answer could not be yes, for such a response would entail what is being resisted, that there is, in fact, a distinction between feminism and philosophy. Yet the answer could not be no, for such a response would lead, correctly, to an indictment of dogmatism. The answer had to be—and was—that such questioning was evidence of my corrupt (male) nature.

I began to believe that if such questions are ruled illegitimate, then feminism (as theory or politics) has descended to dogma. This notion struck at the very core of my being—as a philosopher, a teacher, and a responsible belief-holder. It struck me as nothing less than dangerous. No claim should be unreproachable, no theory or political view so pristine that it should be immune to challenge. Thus I was moved to expose feminism to the philosophical method of critical analysis and put feminism to the test. It was time to put *feminism under fire.*

I tried to write the book in such a way that would allow its reading by nonphilosophers while remaining true to philosophy's methods of critical analysis. That is, I attempted to combine rigorous argument—not too bogged down in scholarly minutia—with provocative prose.

Although many of my more accomplished male colleagues found my interest in such a project to be nothing more than a waste of time, and many of my female colleagues warned me of the possible backlash (to what academic feminists may themselves see as backlash), I persevered. Courage, more than political acumen, has always been my strong suit.

I would like to thank Mr. Steven L. Mitchell and Ms. Mary A. Read for their insightful comments and editorial expertise, and Dr. Richard Campbell for his forthright comments and criticisms. I would like to also thank Dr. Christina Hoff Sommers, Dr. Kristin Shrader-Frechette, and Dr. Susan Haack for their comments and criticisms on earlier versions of this work. I would like to give special thanks to Dr. Alice Perrin, Dr. Carole Klein-Bolitho, Dr. James Bell, Dr. Andrea M. Weisberger, Dr. Brian Striar, Dr. David Fenner, Dr. Ed Erwin, and Athena for their philosophical insights with respect to this work and their continual support of all of my endeavors. To the students who were especially helpful in my feminist philosophy courses—Alyssa Calhoun, Melissa Caputo-Goslin, David Cross, Richard Davis, Amy DeRocher, Jill DiBerardino, Katrina Finley, Keith Fisher, Jennifer Jeakle, Judith Julian, Chris Kennedy, Daniel Leigh, Jr., Diana Moxley, Dana Robison, Michael Veber, and Alexandra Wrigley—my sincerest gratitude. To Dr. P. Kurtz: Thank you for this opportunity. Finally, I would like to thank Mr. Phillip James Perea for both his hard work on the manuscript and undying love for me.

Notes

1. Christina Hoff Sommers, "The Feminist Revelation," *Social Philosophy and Policy* 8, no. 1 (1989): 158.
2. Alison M. Jaggar, "How Can Ethics Be Feminist?" Explorations in Feminist Ethics: Theory and Practice. Duluth, Minnesota, October 7–8, 1988.

Introduction

What Is Feminist Philosophy?

By woman's philosophy I mean philosophical work (i.e., discussion of traditional philosophical issues) that arises from, explicitly refers to, and attempts to account for the experience of women.

Nancy J. Holland[1]

[F]eminist philosophy seeks a new space in which women can write and think as women and not as men's imperfect counterparts or approximations. . . . In short, a feminist philosophy could accept its position as historically grounded in patriarchal texts; yet its future involves a movement beyond this history. It would no longer be confined to women's issues . . . but be free to range over any issue. What makes it feminist is not its object but its perspective.

Elizabeth Grosz[2]

What is feminist philosophy? What distinguishes it from feminist nonphilosophy on the one hand, and nonfeminist philosophy on the other? Furthermore, what distinguishes "feminist philosophy" from "woman's philosophy"? The point of these questions is not to quibble, nor is it to develop *sharp* distinctions, i.e., necessary and sufficient conditions. To do so would be "stupid,"[3] for such is the evil men do, right?

Not so fast! While a search for a complete reductive analysis of any

13

term or concept may be misguided, it is not so simply *because* men do it. First of all, *all* men do not. For example, Ludwig Wittgenstein seemed to have been after a much less precise notion of concepts, something more like a "family resemblance." The true goal is to develop some kind of working definition of "feminist philosophy" so that we can determine if it ought to be adopted by the philosophical community at large.

If one is loyal to the philosophical method, then one should remain committed to the idea that whatever feminist philosophy is it must be *definable* to a degree sufficient to allow for robust critical examination of the concept. In the interest of illuminating feminist philosophy, I propose to do just that. (I beg nonanalytics and antianalytics to forgive my perspicacity.)

Within the framework of women's philosophy presented above there exist at least three subcategories of feminist philosophy: philosophers, varieties, and topics.

One way to distinguish feminist philosophy from nonfeminist philosophy on the one hand, and feminist nonphilosophy on the other, is through a study of individual philosophers. Under this rubric, feminist philosophy has as its main object of inquiry female *philosophers, writers, or thinkers.* They may be ancient or contemporary, existentialist or Marxist, but they share biology. In this vein a study of male philosophers would not be particularly feminist. However, once the distinction is carved in such a way, it is best merely to incorporate feminist philosophy as a part of women's philosophy.

Another way to distinguish feminist philosophy from nonfeminist philosophy is to focus at a metalevel on feminism itself, specifically the many different *varieties* of feminism (Marxist, radical, postmodern, and the like).[4] In this context differences and similarities among the alternative feminisms are examined. This method of distinguishing feminist philosophy, like the method above, makes it a subcategory of women's philosophy.

A third possible point of distinction is to focus on *topics* that are of special interest to women, for example, questions about the morality of abortion, pornography, or preferential hiring. Feminist philosophy here refers to articles and books that discuss what has often been called "sex/gender issues." Although I believe the sex/gender dichotomy is a distinction without a difference,[5] I will honor the literature and its belief that " 'women' and 'men' are not simply biological or simply sociological categories."[6] I will use the term 'gender' only in conjunction with the term 'sex' (for example, 'sex/gender'). Once again, then, this notion of feminist philosophy is subsumed quite easily under the rubric of women's philosophy, i.e., garden-variety philosophy which, incidentally, happens to primarily involve, or be of primary interest to, women.

I believe none of these subcategories, insofar as they fit into the overarching category of women's philosophy, are really "philosophy." Philosophy must be more than simply a description of the lives of specific women, their political and/or social struggles, or the political role certain contemporary moral issues play in women's lives.[7] To qualify as philosophy, more is needed.

With respect to the first category—philosophers—a research project involving what a particular woman wrote, what theories she espoused, what political and personal pressures she was under, and so forth, is not philosophy proper. Philosophy is not biography; it must transcend description. Philosophy must be normative, or at least prescriptive, if not fundamentally evaluative of moral and epistemic worthiness. To rank as philosophy, theories must be advanced or rejected, and they must be so for good *reasons*.

The same problem holds true for those who claim the study of the varieties of feminism is philosophical. Although the various theories are discussed and contrasted, they are always assessed solely in terms of *instrumental* value: the value they hold in bringing about specific goals, primarily the empowerment of women. However, since philosophy must be fundamentally normative it needs at some point to question the goodness of the goals themselves. Anything less is intellectually dishonest and, in the final analysis, anathema to philosophy.

In terms of the variety category, to meet the standards of philosophy not only instrumental questions (such as which of the various feminist trends achieves the greatest amount of empowerment for women), but questions concerning the goodness of their goals must be attended. Insofar as philosophers ascribing to this branch of women's philosophy do not take this challenge, they are blowing dogmatic—politics qua philosophy.

The third category of women's philosophy, topics, is problematic for a slightly different reason. The "topics" to which I refer include: "special moral issues in women's liberation,"[8] "problems of gender inequality,"[9] and, more generally, *gender issues*, such as preferential hiring, pornogra-

phy, and abortion. Under this heading it is falsely assumed that with respect to moral issues the concept of 'woman' essentially denotes a gender construct, something purely sociological as opposed to a purely biological construct. It is assumed that there are such things as gender
issues and that such concerns are genuinely philosophical.

That the concept of 'woman' can be subdivided into the concepts of
'gender' and 'sex' allows for classifications like feminine women, masculine women, feminine men, and masculine men, and, I presume, other
imaginative concoctions such as feminine masculine men and women.
This in itself is not problematic.[10] But with respect to applied ethics—
preferential hiring, pornography, abortion, and other issues—it seems
nothing less than sophistry to pass over the lean meat of moral issues. A
further exploration of this point via the above referred contemporary
moral issues may be instructive.

The issue of preferential hiring is either one which should be taken
seriously by all philosophers,[11] both men and women, and is, therefore,
not a peculiarly woman's issue; or is one of concern only to women precisely because they are women, regardless of their particular software
(masculine women, feminine women). In other words, there's really no
need conceptually to slice 'woman' into sex and gender components.

No need, that is, unless one is searching for evidence of, for example,
workplace sexual discrimination in a way to ensure discovery. For instance, if a woman claims no experience with sexual discrimination,
"gender feminists"[12] can proclaim she is not a *real* woman but one gendered "masculine." Circularly, the fact that she never experienced discrimination is evidence for her masculine woman status.

Unfortunately, the gender/sex distinction allows for this kind of non-
sense. Academic women who criticize feminism are said to have been
genderized masculine (by, for example, the fraternity of philosophy), and
even nonacademic "nonfeminist sentiment is conveniently seen as the
product of socialization that has educated women to subordinate roles."[13]
Nonacademic women have yet to reach consciousness. Gender-envy explains anything and everything.

Questions over the ethical nature of pornography raise another source
of skepticism concerning the sex/gender dichotomy. Whether pornography
ought (ought not) to be regulated is a moral issue in and of itself.

First, it is debatable that *pornography* harms at all.[14] Men (and women) hurt women; some of them are pornography users, some are not. Moreover, many women claim to enjoy it; some women philosophers even argue its virtues.[15]

Second, if pornography is fundamentally harmful, it is unclear that the harm is caused to women alone. Women are not the only persons depicted in pornographic material; a great deal of pornography centers around men.[16] Therefore, genderwise, pornography is an equal opportunity enterprise.[17]

Of course, feminists could argue that the oppressed man, for example, a male pornographic model for a male audience, is oppressed precisely because he is gendered feminine. The evidence for this label is, again circularly, that he is oppressed via the medium of pornography.[18] Once again, the use of gender only delegitimizes evidence and detracts from the serious sociological question, Does pornography depersonalize? and the more serious philosophical question, Ought one ever do that which depersonalizes another? Hence, the pornography issue is not even a sex issue, let alone a gendered one.

The same is true about the abortion issue.[19] I am at a loss to see how the important moral question about the value of the life of a fetus (be that fetus male or female) and its relative value to other persons[20]—its mother or father—is a sex or gender issue. Judith Jarvis Thomson's violinist example makes exactly this point.* The question about the rights and obligations of the person (regardless of sex) to another possible person seems sex/gender neutral. Turning this difficult and deeply philosophical issue into a "woman's issue" trivializes philosophical questions about personhood, individual rights, and human values. It's not that politics and philosophy can't intermarry, but politics must always take philosophy's surname: political philosophy, not philosophize politically.

---

*In this example, Thomson imagines that someone is unwillingly abducted and surgically hooked up to a famous violinist. Since the violinist is dependent on the other person (the sex/gender of both parties is irrelevant) for, surprisingly, a period of only nine months, the reader is to put herself in the shoes of the abductee and decide what her moral duty is: Should she discontinue the life support to the violinist and reclaim her original lifestyle or stay hooked up for the next nine months? Judith Jarvis Thomson, "A Defense of Abortion," *Philosophy and Public Affairs Quarterly* 1, no. 1 (Fall 1971): 47–66.

In light of the above, I claim that little of what has been done under what I am calling women's philosophy is in any interesting way philosophical. This is quite clear with respect to the categories of philosophers and varieties, but it is also true of topics. Once these important moral issues are brought under the auspices of women's issues (via the subheading "gender issues"), they in fact engender misguided data collection and politicize important philosophical foundations and contemporary moral issue applications.

Women's philosophy, though seriously feminist, is at best only *incidentally* philosophical.

Now I realize some feminists would disagree with the manner in which I have distinguished the discussion of women as philosophers—their role in society and their "special" interest in certain moral issues—from the doing of philosophy. They might claim such a distinction is, itself, sexist. Although I disagree with the criticism, I will take it seriously, since the claim itself is at least truly philosophical.

Additionally, many feminists may claim that what I call philosophy—a method of critical analysis that attempts to make normative, unbiased judgments based on reason and objective evidence—does not really exist at all.[21] 'Reason' does not deliver to us "a single objective truth"[22] because "objectivity, the 'ostensibly noninvolved stance',"[23] "is the male epistemological stance . . . we see a male-created truth and reality, a male point of view, a male-defined objectivity."[24] The only explanation for why it has been privileged by the philosophical tradition for so long is that men recognize the conflict "many women experience between Reason and femininity."[25] Philosophy is nothing special, it is just one of the many politics, and "the full dimensions of the maleness of Philosophy's past are only now becoming visible."[26] The point of all this is to recommend that *traditional science, philosophy of science, and epistemology ought to be abandoned and that feminist science, philosophy of science, and epistemology ought to be put in its place.*

This two-part metaphilosophical claim is normative, philosophically interesting, and worthy of special attention. This is what should properly be called "feminist philosophy."

This book will focus on feminist philosophy as it is defined above, what I call "second-generation feminism." That is, what follows will focus on attempts by feminist philosophers to do philosophy: to criticize and replace more traditional methods of science, philosophy of science, and epistemology with concepts and constructs that are not essentially male-biased. Although much work has been done in the areas of ethics[27] and aesthetics,[28] this work is ultimately grounded in the work done in philosophy of science and epistemology. It is these later areas alone in which I will concentrate.

Incidentally, all of the criticisms of traditional science or classical* epistemology addressed in my work are espoused by women. It seems in order for the critique to count as feminist it must be generated by a woman. I say this because the works of, for example, Paul Feyerabend and Richard Rorty are critical of traditional philosophy of science but are not (ordinarily) considered to be feminist, while the works of Sandra Harding, also critical of traditional philosophy of science, are. Apparently, if you are not a woman criticizing the tradition, with the express intent of empowering women, then what you are doing, though philosophical, is not peculiarly feminist.

Chapter 1 will show that the case against traditional science and philosophy of science, that they are essentially male-biased, has not been made. As such, the *need* to replace traditional science and philosophy of science is unwarranted. In addition, I will argue that even if traditional science and philosophy of science needed to be dismantled or dismissed, it ought not to be replaced by a feminist science or philosophy of science. For doing so is not only antiscience, it is bad for women.

Chapter 2 will demonstrate that the case against classical epistemology, that it is essentially male-biased, has also not been made. As such, the *need* to replace classical epistemology is unwarranted. In addition, I will argue that even if classical epistemology needed to be dismantled or dismissed, it ought not to be replaced by a feminist epistemology. The difficulties in developing a peculiarly feminist epistemology

---

*I use the term 'classical' here to denote what has generally been thought of as the epistemological corpus since Plato. I use this term, as opposed to 'traditional', however, to connote something that is fundamental to everything that follows, the way that classical ballet or music is fundamental to jazz and other modern forms, without being oppressive. Therefore, by 'classical' I mean both historically and fundamentally classic.

are similar to those with respect to the development of a special brand of feminist science, except, ultimately, more problematic.

Chapter 3 will look at what I am calling the Relativism Question in Feminism. I will examine the claims made by a number of feminists that their feminist accounts of philosophy of science and epistemology are not relativistic, and argue that they cannot escape relativism's grip. I will then discuss the positions of the few feminists who embrace relativism, along with the logical and pragmatic problems such accounts entail.

Chapter 4 is a first look at the recent trend of feminists to embrace naturalized accounts of epistemology. I first outline the contemporary debate between the naturalist and the nonnaturalist. I then give a very brief introduction into the work of W. V. Quine, the man who put naturalism on the philosophical map and the one whose work is appealed to by two feminists, Louise Antony and Lynn Hankinson Nelson, who argue that Quinian naturalism is a viable and important position for contemporary feminism.

Chapter 5 more precisely examines the work of W. V. Quine. I will both give a fuller—albeit a beginner's—account of Quine's program in order to fill in any gaps in chapter 4, as well as remain true to my belief that Quine's account must be taken as a whole. In addition, I will suggest that Quine has not made the case that we ought to naturalize epistemology. This chapter is the most technical and may be skimmed or skipped over by anyone wishing to avoid such specifics or, of course, experts on Quine.

Chapter 6 takes up where chapter 4 left off in examining the real point of challenging naturalism, Quinian or otherwise: Is it good for women? I first analyze a recent attempt by Jane Duran to develop a Naturalized Feminist Epistemology. I then demonstrate that her attempt fails and that no account of naturalized epistemology is particularly helpful to the feminist cause.

Chapter 7 switches from the theoretical to the practical. I will take a look at some recent attempts to put the above epistemic commitments to work in the academy through the publication and teaching of philosophy. I will argue that the commitments by what Christina Hoff Sommers calls "academic" or "gender" feminists have been articulated in policies that have harmed the academy and its students.

In the Conclusion I will challenge the feminist supposition that "the personal is the political," i.e., that everything, even philosophy, is merely politics. I will suggest that at the very least philosophy and politics are conceptually distinct and therefore a peculiarly feminist approach to anything is not above normative challenge. I conclude by claiming that an 'is'/ 'ought' distinction, along with the classical philosophical methods of analysis with respect to science, philosophy of science, epistemology, and pedagogy are compatible with, and necessary for, the empowerment of women. .

Notes

1. Nancy J. Holland, *Is Woman's Philosophy Possible?* (Savage, Md.: Roman and Littlefield, 1990), p. 1.

2. Elizabeth Grosz, "Philosophy" in *Feminist Knowledge: Critique and Construct,* ed. Sneja Gunew (New York: Routledge, 1990).

3. Alison M. Jaggar, "How Can Ethics Be Feminist?" Exploration in Feminist Ethics: Theory and Practice. Duluth, Minnesota, 1989.

4. See, for example, Rosemary Tong, *Feminist Thought* (Boulder, Colo.: Westview Press, 1989).

5. A discussion about the UN's World Conference on Women in Beijing, on "Morning Edition," National Public Radio, August 29, 1995, emphasized the fact that not one of the leading participants knew how to define 'gender'. In Maggie Humm, *Dictionary of Feminist Theory* (Hertfordshire, UK: Wheatsheaf, 1989), "gender" is defined as: "A culturally shaped group of attributes and behaviors given to the female or to the male. Contemporary feminist theory is careful to distinguish between sex and gender." Nothing more is given as a standard definition.

6. Lynn Hankinson Nelson, *Who Knows? From Quine to a Feminist Empiricism* (Philadelphia: Temple University Press, 1990), p. 320, n.11.

7. This would more properly be categorized as women's' history. This topic could then be broken down into the study of specific epochs, e.g., Emilie M. Amt, *Women's Lives in Medieval Europe* (New York: Routledge, 1993), in which some of the women chronicled are quite philosophical.

8. Sharon Bishop and Marjorie Weinzweig, eds., *Philosophy and Women* (Belmont, Calif.: Wadsworth, 1979), p. v.

9. Janet Kouranay, James Sterba, and Rosemary Tong, eds., *Feminist Philosophies* (Englewood Cliffs, N.J.: Prentice-Hall, 1992), p. 2.

10. Actually an empirical scientist like Dr. Maryanne Baenninger in her empirical research on cognitive differences between men and women uses the term "sex-related" to describe any empirical findings. See, for example, Maryanne Baenninger and Nora Newcombe, "Environmental Input to the Development of Sex-Related Differences in Spatial and Mathematical Ability," *Learning and Individual Differences* 7, no. 4 (1995): 363–79.

11. See, for example, Alan H. Goldman, *Justice and Reverse Discrimination* (Princeton, N.J.: Princeton University Press, 1979).

12. See, e.g., Christina Hoff Sommers, "Do These Feminists Like Women?" *Journal of Social Philosophy* 21, no. 2 (Fall/Winter 1990): 66–74.

13. Christina Hoff Sommers, "The Feminist Revelation," *Social Philosophy & Policy* 8, no. 1 (1990): 150.

14. One argument that claims that pornography is essentially harmful is made by Melinda Vadas, "A First Look at Pornography/Civil Rights Ordinance: Could Pornography Be the Subordination of Women?" *Journal of Philosophy* 89, no. 4 (1987): 487–511. Others, for example, claim that this can't be the case since examples of pornography *by* women would be too problematic. See, for example, Stephanie Rothman's film, *Group Marriage.*

15. See, e.g., Sandra Schuh, "A Closer Moral Look at Pornography," paper presented at the Florida Philosophical Association, 1990.

16. See, for example, "Men's Pornography: Gay vs. Straight," *The Problem of Pornography,* ed. Susan Dwyer (New York: Wadsworth, 1995).

17. The claim that pornography is, in our society, nonetheless more harmful to women is made by Ann Garry, "Pornography and Respect for Women," *Social Theory and Practice* 4 (Summer 1978): 395–442.

18. Christina Hoff Sommers has pointed out that even "nonfeminist sentiment is conveniently seen as the product of a socialization." Sommers, "Feminist Revelation," p. 150.

19. See, for example, Lewis M. Schwartz, *Arguing About Abortion* (Belmont, Calif.: Wadsworth, 1992).

20. I realize that some feminists claim that even the concept of what constitutes a person is determined by male-bias. See, e.g., Holland's *Is Women's Philosophy Possible?*

21. This is a paraphrase of the only "noncontroversial" definition of 'philosophy', aside from "thinking about thinking" given in Ted Honderich, ed., *The Oxford Companion to Philosophy* (New York: Oxford University Press, 1995), pp. 666–70.

22. Genevieve Lloyd, *The Man of Reason,* 2d ed. (Minneapolis: University of Minnesota Press, 1993), p. ix.

23. Catharine MacKinnon, "Feminism, Marxism, Method and the State: An Agenda for Theory," *Signs* 7 (1982): 538.

24. Ruth Bleier, *Science and Gender: A Critique of Biology and Its Theories on Women* (New York: Pergamon Press, 1984), p. 196.

25. Lloyd, *Man of Reason,* p. x.

26. Ibid., p. 108.

27. See, e.g., the *APA Newsletter on Feminism* 90, no. 2 (Winter 1991): 86–99, for a number of good articles and a comprehensive reading list on this topic.

28. See, e.g., the *APA Newsletter on Feminism* 89, no. 3 (Spring 1990): 69–83, for a number of good articles and a comprehensive reading list on this topic.

1

The Feminist Critique of Science

What we [feminists] are doing, is comparable to Copernicus shattering our geocentricity, Darwin shattering our species-centricity. We are shattering andro-centricity, and the change is as fundamental, as dangerous, as exciting.

Elizabeth Minnich[1]

I, for one, am embarrassed when I hear feminist theorists compare themselves to Copernicus or Darwin.

Christina Hoff Sommers[2]

As a philosopher and a woman I find it difficult to accept my colleagues' claim that the academy is stricken with "sex/gender oppression," and that the remedy is to "go feminist." In this chapter I will demonstrate that science and its method, both of which require a commitment to objectivity, have not been shown to be essentially male-biased. Furthermore, I will suggest that once 'objectivity' is abandoned, that which remains does not serve the fairer sex well.

Engaging Objectivity

Sandra Harding, a leading authority on feminist philosophy of science, attempts to argue that philosophers of science and scientists have underestimated "the pervasiveness of gender relations" and have "false beliefs about the natural sciences."[3]

She wishes to dismantle such false beliefs in order to expose "the natural sciences as a social phenomenon and, consequently, to appreciate the relevance of feminism to the content and logic of research and explanation."[4] In other words, Harding attempts to expose (allegedly) traditionally held beliefs about science—primarily that *science is objective*—as false so as to demonstrate that gender relations in the sciences matter. More to the point, Harding claims that science at this time is not only *not* objective, but is male-biased as well.

To achieve her goal, Harding discusses what she calls "six false beliefs" held by contemporary scientists and philosophers of science. The six false beliefs are:

(1) "Feminism is about people and society: the natural sciences are about neither; hence, feminism can have no relevance to the logic or content of the natural science."[5]

(2) "Feminist critics claim that a social movement can be responsible for generating empirically more adequate beliefs about the natural world. But only false beliefs have social causes. Whatever relevance such critics have to point out the social causes of false beliefs, feminism can not generate 'true beliefs.' "[6]

(3) "Science fundamentally consists only of the formal and quantitative statements that express the results of research, and/or science is a unique method. If feminists do not have alternatives to logic and mathematics or to science's unique method, then their criticisms may be relevant to sociological issues but not to science itself."[7]

(4) "Applications of science are not part of science proper. So feminist criticism of the misuses and abuses of the sciences (such as of the proliferation of dangerous reproductive technologies) challenge only public policy about science, not science itself."[8]

(5) "Scientists can provide the most knowledgeable and authoritative explanations of their own activities, so sociologists and philosophers (including feminists) should refrain from making comments about fields in which they are not experts."[9]

(6) "Physics is the best model for the natural sciences, so feminist social science analyses can have nothing to offer the natural sciences."[10]

At the heart of the sextet is the first "false belief," which has at its heart the rejection of science's objectivity. (I will discuss this first and most essential "false belief" last, since I believe it grounds all the others.)

FALSE BELIEF NO. 2

This "false belief" is that "feminist critics claim that a social movement can be responsible for generating empirically more adequate beliefs about the natural world. But only false beliefs have social causes. Whatever relevance such critics have to point out the social causes of false beliefs, feminism can not generate 'true beliefs.' "[11] According to Harding, "conventionalists," i.e., the enemies of feminism, argue that good science is not effected by social causes; it is, in fact, objective.

The problem with the concept of 'objectivity' will be discussed in detail below via the first "false belief." For now, though, it is important to point out that Harding has drawn a number of illegitimate conclusions concerning what traditional science believes about itself and what traditional philosophers of science believe about science.

Essentially, Harding builds a straw account. Clearly, no scientist or philosopher of science would propose that *no* social science finding could be *relevant* to our *explanations* of how the best hypotheses arise and gain legitimacy. As a matter of fact, it is precisely to the social scientist we turn when we want this kind of information, e.g., statistics on who said what when. History, sociology, psychology, and the like, are the appropriate sciences to consult when one wants to ascertain what social/psychological forces allow hypotheses (good and bad) to come to the fore of the scientific community.

It is important to note, however, that nothing follows from this about the judging of the goodness or badness of the hypotheses themselves. To claim that an hypothesis *ought* to be labeled good science does not entail that a mystical, arbitrary exercise be performed on claims we wish to christen 'objective'. Good science aims to take any hypothesis, regardless of how it was formed, regardless of the social conditions that surrounded its birth, and determine its worthiness. Part of this determination requires that the hypothesis was, in fact, developed respectful of objectivity. 'Objectivity' is not merely a label but an essential test to determine the goodness of the hypothesis itself.

Harding has conflated where she should have juxtaposed: at the Hans Reichenbachian distinction between the "context of discovery" and the "context of justification."[12] The point the natural scientist (and the philosopher of science) presses is not that phlogiston theory* and Nazi science were more a product of their societies and histories than electromagnetism or the contemporary laws of physics, but that the former and not the latter were unable to withstand criticism once the condition of objectivity was applied. Once, for example, the supposition grounding Nazism—that Jews are inferior—was dropped, the hypotheses on which it was built was without justification. Without the benefit of anti-Semitic colored glasses, evidence disappeared. This is not the case for contemporary laws of physics, for which evidence has over time, regardless of observer, maintained its verisimilitude.[13]

Of course, some scientists claim there is something about the 'context of discovery' that allows for cases of good science, e.g., Sir Alexander Flemming's discovery of penicillin, J. D. Watson's discovery of the double helix, or even Friedrich August Kekulé's discovery that benzene, at the atomic level, is shaped like a ring—but not cases of bad science. The individuals mentioned, having been real scientists, used a sense of intuition all along, which has been developed by the methods of good science—mainly a commitment to critical analysis and unbiased evidence. The Nazis doctors, on the other hand, having been better racists than they

---

*The phlogiston theory stated that there was an actual substance, phlogiston, which played a role in the combustion of every material. At one point, given the empirical finding that some substances weighed more while others weighed less after being burnt, it was suggested, in order to save the belief in phlogiston, that phlogiston had a negative weight.

were scientists, either never had this type of intuition to begin with or squelched it under the weight of prejudice.

Therefore, if one separates the 'context of discovery' from the 'context of justification' one can see the reasons, i.e., causes, for developing a theory that had no epistemic weight. One can then also see why certain theories are maintained regardless of standpoint.

Some feminists find the discovery/justification distinction itself to be problematic.[14] Harding is one. She claims that one need not "make a sharp distinction between the 'context of discovery' and the 'context of justification'."[15] But at issue is not whether one *must*, but whether one *should*; that one *should not* is not directly argued. It is suggested that the distinction, like all dichotomies, is "especially problematic in that they posit exclusionary constructs, not complementary or interdependent ones that could shade into one another or function as 'mixed modes' rather than absolutes."[16] Little else is offered.

What is further suggested is that the desire to dichotomize at all, combined with the "devaluation of the 'context of discovery' "[17] once the dichotomizing is achieved, is one of many "androcentric biases that enter science in the form of problematics."[18] I contend that while the male-biased nature of science is precisely what is at issue, Harding's faint attempt to dispel the distinction simply by charging it with male-bias begs the question. (Harding herself acknowledges the conceptual legitimacy of the discovery/justification distinction when she accuses it of playing a part in the androcentric biasing of science.[19])

For the sake of fairness, however, let us look at two well-known arguments for the untenability of the Reichenbachian distinction: Thomas Kuhn's[20] and Harold Brown's.[21] Although these arguments do not rest on the charge of male-bias, they nonetheless fail.

Kuhn, according to Harvey Siegel, claims the context of discovery/context of justification distinction is illegitimate for three interconnected reasons:

> The first centers on what Kuhn calls the "context of pedagogy," which is significantly distinct from the more familiar contexts. An important feature of science pedagogy is the tendency, Kuhn argues, to oversimplify the decisions, including decisions concerning theory choice, that scientists actually make. Therefore, to the (considerable) extent that philosophers of

science take crucial experiments to be typical reason-providers for scientific decisions, they have in mind a highly misleading picture of actual scientific decision making.

Kuhn offers [another] reason for doubting Reichenbach's distinction. This reason depends on Kuhn's claim that "subjective factors" are an ineliminable element of a scientist's decision to adopt a scientific theory.[22]

Both criticisms, Siegel correctly points out, merely presuppose, not demonstrate, the illegitimacy of the distinction.

That is, with respect to the first criticism, if we deny the distinction between discovery and justification, the history of "crucial experiments" takes on an undeserved epistemic status. This, however, is precisely the point of maintaining it.

With respect to the second criticism, the response is similar. After all, why is it that "subjective factors" are ineliminable from our theory adoption? Is this a fact of our weak psychologies or something inherent in the scientific theory itself? If the former, this does not speak to the goodness of the distinction itself, only our inability to maintain it. If the latter, however, then Kuhn is clearly begging the question once again, for if the context of discovery is kept distinct from the context of justification then one could simply agree with him. Yes, we *adopt* theories in accordance with subjective factors, but we only *maintain and nurture* theories that have been born out by evidence. Brown's criticism does not fare much better. He claims that

> when we credit Galileo or Newton or Einstein or Bohr with having made scientific discoveries, we only consider those hypotheses which they had good reasons for entertaining to be discoveries. The context of justification is thus part of the context of discovery and no sharp line can be drawn between discovery and justification.[23]

This is clearly an equivocation on the term 'discovery'. When adherents of the distinction talk about the "context of discovery" they mean precisely the acceptance of theory prior to testing. Once a theory is tested it has entered the "context of justification" so at the very least there is a chronological distinction that needs to be recognized. More substantively, to use the former construct in such an overarching way misconstrues Reichenbach's account.

Further, our crediting big scientific names with only discovering their "good" theories is not an epistemic distinction but a historical failing. "We want, for instance, to be able to distinguish between theories we reject, theories we are agnostic about, theories we think are worthy of further pursuit, theories we accept as plausible, theories we take to be true, and so on."[24] Brown's definition of 'discovery'—which actually entails a meaningful justificatory component—makes his rejection of the distinction moot.

With respect to the above, then, it has not been demonstrated that False Belief No. 2 is, in fact, held by scientists or philosophers of science. Furthermore, given that the Reichenbachian distinction is still intact, that which is maintained by science (and philosophy of science)—that the determination of the goodness of scientific hypotheses is something that is to meet the criterion of objectivity—has not been shown to be false. The genetic fallacy* has been avoided.

One could, sympathetically, claim that perhaps all that Harding was saying was that "yes, there is a discovery/justification distinction, but not one that will do the work that was originally intended, namely to allow what occurs in the context of justification not to be shaped by what occurs in the other context. Harding can, therefore, concede the distinction but deny its point."[25]

But this finesse does not work. If Harding is really making a distinction without teeth, then why bother? Either she believes the distinction maintains itself, and at least does the work of pointing to a conceptual difference, or she does not. If she believes that the two contexts are distinct, i.e., maintain distance from the genetic fallacy, then we have no beef. If she does not, or if she believes that the distinction exists but is irrelevant, then my criticisms above hold.

FALSE BELIEF NO. 3

Another presumption involves the notion that science is fundamentally expressible only in the formal system of mathematics and that there "can

---

*The genetic fallacy "consists in evaluating a thing in terms of its earlier context and then carrying over that evaluation to the thing in the present." T. Edward Damer, *Attacking Faulty Reasoning: A Practical Guide to Fallacy-Free Arguments* (Belmont, Calif.: Wadsworth, 1995).

appear to be no social values in results of research that are expressed in formal symbols."[26] Harding argues two main points. First, formal statements are never truly formal, for they "require interpretation in order to be meaningful."[27] The second point has to do with science, not as formalizable in a metamathematical sense, but formalizable in the sense there is one thing (out of all the scientific methods history has informed us of) that can be called *the* scientific method.

These two points are completely separate: the first has to do with the nature of scientific hypotheses, the second with the nature of science itself.

Harding's objection to the fact that formal systems require interpretation in order to be meaningful will not be debated here. I will simply concur, they need not. However, I will say it is unclear what bearing this allowance has on her overall agenda to prove the nonobjectivity of science. Simply stating that formal language needs interpretation, i.e., needs meaning, does not in and of itself entail that that meaning will be biased. And certainly it does not entail that it will be male-biased. The suppressed premise Harding seems to be implying is that objectivity and interpretation are incompatible notions. Such an assumption, however, begs the question and is false. One can, at least in principle, give an objective interpretation.[28]

The second part of the claim—that no one has ever determined what is "unique about the scientific method"[29]—is buttressed by argument. Harding maintains, in chorus with other feminists, that if there is "no single correct scientific methodology,"[30] no one thing which is essential to all things that history has called the "scientific method," then traditional scientists (and philosophers of science) have no leg to stand on in their claim that science is objective. This is non sequitur. Just because there is not one "single correct" method does not mean that there are no correct methods, or methods that are better than others.

Most of the evidence given for Harding's claim comes from the general study of science, and the history and sociology of science. She says that "for one thing different sciences develop differently. . . . Philosophers and other observers of science have argued for centuries over whether deduction or induction should be regarded as primarily responsible for the great moments in the history of science."[31]

Aside from the fact Harding has "oversimplifie[d] a complex history"[32] as well as what it is really like to "muck in" real science,[33] "the fact that scientists [or philosophers of science] do not consciously practice [or acknowledge] a formal methodology is very poor evidence that no such methodology exists,"[34] let alone that it *ought not* to be developed. Once again, the prescriptive aspect of the scientific method must not be given short shrift.

I will not attempt to defend the claim that there is a specific scientific methodology, however. My reasoning here is twofold. One, Harding admits a serious candidate for the single criterion essential to all science, the adoption of a certain "critical attitude."[35] This, in general, is good enough for me. However, and this is my second reason, although I agree that a "critical attitude" is essential to the scientific method, I do not think it can or should be thought of as discrete. Operationalized, yes. Strictly definable in terms of its necessary and sufficient conditions? Why bother?

The scientific method, if one wants to call it that, "can and should be characterized generally, as consisting in, for example, a concern for explanatory adequacy . . . ; an insistence on testing . . . ; and a commitment to inductive support. . . ."[36] Nothing more is needed to defeat Harding's pessimism and nothing more is needed to start science on its way.

In sum, *the* scientific method may be any number of procedures, as long as they maintain a commitment to unbiased evidence, i.e., objectivity.

Insofar as Harding believes scientists and philosophers of science are searching for a *unique* procedure essential to science, she is again constructing a straw account. Furthermore, this (general) account of the scientific method is intended to be normative, not descriptive. Therefore, the historical evidence Harding brings to bear, namely, that "[t]he history of science shows that scientists and science communities again and again make unjustified assumptions and that they are loath to examine critically the hypotheses in whose plausibility they have invested considerable time, energy, and reputation,"[37] is beside the point.

Without denying the adequacy of Harding's historical account, I fail to recognize what it has to do with the original claim about scientific method and its critical stance. The original claim is meant to be normative, not merely descriptive. As such, it attempts to prescribe how one ought to act if she wants to do good science. She ought act in such a way as to adopt theories with an eye toward truth, criticizing and abandoning theories in the wake of compelling counterevidence. How scientists actually behave is not the point. Harding misses the important distinction between the normative and the descriptive, between the philosophy of science and the history of science. In the final analysis, Harding has not compelled the belief that a (general) method underlying science is nonexistent.

FALSE BELIEF NO. 4

The fourth "false belief" to which Harding claims scientists and philosophers of science fall prey is the idea that we can sharply distinguish between (pure) science and technology. She believes that if such a distinction could be made, it would be clear that science can oppress no one, only its products can. Harding states that since we cannot make this distinction, science cannot be separated from its products. And if science is only its products, and its products really affect people—specifically they comfort white men and afflict everyone else—then science is just as heinous as its product.

This equivocation of 'science' and 'technology' is nothing less than Harding engaging in political propaganda. No one seriously considers science qua methodology—a critical, unbiased attitude adopted when testing hypotheses in the face of evidence—to be *completely* reducible to technological production.

First of all, not all sciences even aim at production; some aim simply to understand phenomena that naturally occur, e.g., astrophysics. Second, some sciences that have such an aim have yet to actually produce anything, e.g., artificial intelligence; some technology has been developed incidentally to the projects of traditional science; and some science/technology, though developed with the intent to politically disadvantage women, ends up in the long run being quite advantageous. For example, with respect to the history of gynecology, an applied science littered with examples of heinous and atrocious acts on the part of male scientists and physicians, one of the products, safe effective birth control, has been downright liberating.

The point is that even if one takes seriously the link between technology and science, the two areas are, nonetheless, conceptually distinct. Harding, in order to make her case against traditional science and this "false belief," must deny conceptual distinctness and this is precisely what she has not done.

FALSE BELIEF NO. 5

If scientists do indeed possess this "false belief"—that "scientists can provide the most knowledgeable and authoritative explanations of their own activities, so sociologists and philosophers (including feminists) should refrain from making comments about fields in which they are not experts"—then I agree with Harding: they ought not. I must agree, not because I believe nonexperts should not be making noise but because I believe in the expertise of philosophers. The kinds of questions we address (for example, queries about the normative nature of evidence, the kind of commitment we owe to evidence and why) are precisely the type of things which fall, properly, in the philosopher's bailiwick.

I fail to see, though, how exposing this belief helps Harding in the case against traditional science. Certainly, this criticism does not tell against traditional philosophy of science. At best, this criticism, if answered by scientists with the appropriate actions, would allow Harding's feminist account of science, *along with the more traditional accounts,* to be taken seriously by the community of working scientists. It does not, however, win her the day.

FALSE BELIEF NO. 6

One of the more interesting claims Harding maintains is that scientists and philosophers of science hold False Belief No. 6—that is she thinks scientists (and philosophers of science) believe falsely that "physics is the best model for the natural sciences."[38]

According to Harding, this is a false belief because it is based on the supposition of a sharp demarcation between the social ("soft") and natural ("hard") sciences. Again, if the distinction is dismantled, if it can be shown that "everything scientists do or think is part of the social world,"[39] then it can be shown that feminist criticisms of science—specifically that science is male-biased—must be taken seriously.

Alas, Harding offers no case at all here. Instead, she appeals to the fact that once the community of scientists and philosophers of science realize they have been worshipping False Belief No. 1—that science is "objective and value-free"[40]—they will come to their senses. They will realize there is no distinction between the social and natural sciences, that feminism has demonstrated sexism in the social sciences, and therefore, mutatis mutandis, there is sexism in the natural sciences, as well. But "precisely how sexist attitudes infect, indeed *distort*, the body of ideas now generally recognized as giving a cogent view of the physical world at the level addressed by physicists,"[41] does not emerge from her writings. Furthermore, it has been argued by accomplished scientists that Harding "doesn't know anything about physics"[42] and that "Harding's success in establishing a reputation as a major thinker on science and epistemology would be incomprehensible in an age less determined to celebrate difference at all costs."[43]

Harding aside for the moment, some feminists have waged a slightly different war against physics. Instead of claiming that physics is just another social science, they have attempted to use physics-evidence to make a point about objectivity, or the lack of it, in science. That is, they use the traditional belief in the legitimacy of physics, as the hardest of all hard sciences, to demonstrate that science is not as objective as it might seem. The evidence hallmarked is, of course, quanta.

One feminist claims that "Heisenberg's 'uncertainty principle' suggests that not even physical objects are inert in and untouched by observational processes."[44] Another refers to the "notable breakdown of confidence in modes of 'objectivist' inquiry even among its proponents. The criteria constituting objectivity are subject to stringent criticisms from within even the most 'objective' of knowledges—particularly theoretical physics (since the advent of Heisenberg, Einstein, and the principle of uncertainty . . .)."[45]

In other words, these feminists suggest that subatomic physics supplies us with hard evidence that there really are no such things as scientific "facts." This evidence ostensibly demonstrates that science is simply not objective.

To use the findings of particle physics in this way is a gross misinterpretation. First, the laws of physics articulated by the Heisenberg uncertainty principle obtain in only the most limited venue: when subatomic particles that go into eigenstate, i.e., superposition.* The principle, therefore, applies to very little of what we would call science. Few scientific hypotheses, theories, or investigations—including most of biology and chemistry—depend on any knowledge of these particles. Feminist criticisms of science, on the other hand, neither began with, focused on, nor are limited to, the work done in theoretical physics. Their critical agenda against the concept of 'objectivity' is much more sweeping.

Second, once 'observation' is added to some subatomic system, i.e., when the wave is collapsed, the reality that is created is as objective as the xx chromosomes in a woman's DNA. In other words, there is a sense in which we create the reality by "observing" the wave, but once this occurs there is no question about the facts of the matter.

Finally, even if every observer creates her own reality, there is no reason to believe that those realities differ. More specifically for this argument, there is no reason to believe that they differ consistently with, and with respect to, one's sex/gender. There is no evidence that every woman physicist would view plutonium decay both identically with every other woman and differently from every man. Subatomic particles seem to misbehave for everyone, male and female.

In the final analysis, it does not seem to be the case that the evidence gleaned from particle physics lends much weight to feminist criticisms of science and their loyalty to some notion of a male-biased conception of 'objectivity'. But it is with the concept of 'objectivity', specifically demonstrating its androcentrism, that feminists must continue to work if their cry against traditional science and philosophy of science is to be heard. This then brings us back to what Harding calls False Belief No. 1.

FALSE BELIEF NO. 1

False Belief No. 1—that science is not objective and value-free—is Harding's real complaint and it is at the heart of "false beliefs" numbers

---

*In laymen's terms, a subatomic particle in superposition acts like a wave and has, at this time, no values—no position and no momentum.

2, 3, 4, and 6. (I do not include No. 5 because I fail to see how the falsity of No. 5—that philosophers, including feminists, should refrain from making comments about fields in which they are not experts—helps her make her case against the objectivity of science.)

False Belief No. 1 is also the serious point of contention for all other feminist critiques of science and I will, therefore, devote more attention to its analysis.

The upshot of my criticisms is that the feminist contention that science is not objective and value-free, which is central to most feminist criticism of science and philosophy of science, caricatures traditional science; dismisses what is essential to any serious empirical account, i.e., evidence; and undermines the political goals of feminism.

Objectivity Under Siege[46]

The concept of 'objectivity' is articulated in a number of ways by a number of different feminists working in science criticism. For Ruth Bleier and Catharine MacKinnon, for example, 'objectivity' is synonymous with a "value-free stance,"[47] and the "noninvolved stance,"[48] respectively. Evelyn Fox Keller claims the objectivist ideology proclaims "disinterest,"[49] a formulation similar to Jean Grimshaw's understanding of 'objectivity' as "impartiality."[50]

Some feminists go so far as to claim the desire for 'objectivity' is merely male fantasy. Susan Bordo,[51] for instance, argues that the Cartesian desire/obsession for objectivity is an expression of anxiety over separation from the organic female universe, and thus constitutes an intellectual flight from the feminine, and a desire for control.[52] In general, then, 'objectivity' is simply "pernicious."[53]

THE TWO FACES OF HARDING'S CONCEPTION OF OBJECTIVITY

Sandra Harding understands the concept of 'objectivity' in two disparate ways. The first is in terms of what has been known in the literature as the traditional notion of 'objectivity', which, as stated by a number of feminists (above), is synonymous with an attempt to achieve "value-free, impartial, dispassionate research."[54] The second is less conventional and, interestingly, at odds with the first.

Via a "feminist standpoint"[55] Harding has "appropriate[d] and redefine[d] objectivity,"[56] claiming that objectivity "is not maximized through value-neutrality."[57] Instead, she claims that "feminist standpoint theory can direct the production of less partial and less distorted beliefs."[58] The former traditional notion of objectivity she calls "weak objectivity"; the latter she calls "strong objectivity."

The traditional notion is pegged as "weak," for it conceptualizes value-neutrality in a way that is at once too narrow and too broad. It is too narrow, according to Harding, because it tends to identify and eliminate "*only* those social values and interests that differ among the researchers and critics who are regarded by the scientific community as competent to make such judgments."[59] Such selective elimination of bias is, itself, biased. She fantasizes:

> If the community of "qualified" researchers and critics systematically excludes, for example, all African Americans and women of all races, and if the larger culture is stratified by race and gender and lacks powerful critiques of this stratification, it is not plausible to imagine that racist and sexist interests and values would be identified within a community of scientists composed entirely of people who benefit—intentionally or not—from institutional racism and sexism.[60]

The traditional, i.e., "weak," concept of objectivity is, according to Harding, also too broad,

> for it requires the elimination of all social values and interests from the research process and the results of research. It is clear, however, that not all social values and interests have the same bad effects upon the results of research. Some have systematically generated less partial and distorted beliefs than others.[61]

Harding suggests that feminist values are one such case.

Because of the above, Harding recommends that scientists (and philosophers of science) stop looking for "weak" objectivity; instead, they should concentrate on trying to achieve the "strong" variety. The muscular notion of objectivity extends "the notion of scientific research to include [the] systematic examination"[62] of one's "cultural influences . . . cultural agendas . . . background assumptions . . . auxiliary assumptions . . . [and even] the macro tendencies in the social order."[63]

In the final analysis, "weak" objectivity is represented by the traditional notion—value-free, noninvolved, impartial, and/or disinterested stance—expressed in one or all of these ways by any number of philosophers throughout the years. "Strong" objectivity—the emancipatory variety—is vintage Harding.

INTERPRETATIONS OF OBJECTIVITY

In what follows I will examine both the "weak" and "strong" notions of 'objectivity'. I will show that the "strong" account is too obviously biased and political to take seriously as a target for criticism from either traditional or feminist camps. I will show that the "weak" concept, fleshed out in terms of value-free or noninvolved stance—what I will call "weak no. 1"—caricatures the traditional concept of objectivity held by most scientists and philosophers of science and therefore need not be defended against feminist criticism. The "weak" concept of objectivity, expressed in terms of impartiality or disinterest—what I will call "weak no. 2"—accurately reflects the sentiments of most scientists and philosophers of science; but the criticisms leveled against this interpretation are not sufficient to support the claim that science is itself sexist.

Objectivity as Emancipatory

Harding's attempt to articulate an account of "strong objectivity" is most salient in the following passage: "The paradigm models of objective science are those studies explicitly directed by morally and politically emancipatory interests—that is, by interests in eliminating sexist, racist, classicist, and culturally coercive understandings of nature and social life."[64] This attempt, I believe, has already been thoroughly criticized by Kristin Shrader-Frechette.[65] Therefore, I will only point out the relevant passage in her critique of Harding. Schrader-Frechette states that because

> Harding is not employing the term 'objectivity' in its ordinary sense . . . her
> use is question-begging both because she has not defined it, and because
> this sense of the term is highly stipulative . . . [that is] she does not explain
> how scientific work becomes more objective by being directed by moral and
> political *interests* . . . how work expressing moral and political *values* lays
> claim to objectivity.[66]

Since this critique, however, Harding has attempted to alter her response to meet this objection. In her more recent article, "Starting from
Women's Lives," Harding claims that "maximizing objectivity requires
critically examining not only those beliefs that differ between individuals . . . but also those that are held by virtually everyone who gets to
count as inside the 'scientific community'."[67]

With this interpretation of objectivity I have no objection,[68] although I
fail to see what is provocative or particularly feminist. On the one hand, it
seems simply to restate that which has been claimed all along by many traditional scientists and philosophers of science, 'objectivity' as community
consensus.[69] On the other hand, depending on how we count "who gets to
count," 'objectivity' can be interpreted as sexist, one way or another. In her
most recent work, however, Harding returns to her more radical (1986) account of 'objectivity', claiming that "research is socially situated, and it can
be more objectively conducted without aiming for or claiming to be value-
free";[70] that "research projects [should] use their historical location as a resource for obtaining greater objectivity";[71] and that "starting off research
from women's lives will generate less partial and distorted accounts. . . ."[72]

In the final analysis, her later position is not fundamentally different
from her original, provocative stance. And, like Shrader-Frechette, I cannot begin to see how starting from any moral or political bias, including
the primacy of "women's lives," makes science *more* objective. Such a
clearly biased starting point is, at best, irrelevant with respect to, for example, the study of quarks, and, at worst, no less insidious than the os-
tensive male biases already in place.

Harding must either develop this unusual account of objectivity more
fully or retreat to one of the more ordinary approaches described above.
Until she has done this, her account is neither worthy of criticism from
traditional scientists and philosophers of science, nor deserving of defense by feminists.

Objectivity as Value-Free

The form of feminist argument against "weak objectivity no. 1"—a value-free stance—is quite simple: A value-free stance is *essential* to the scientific method; the desire to achieve a value-free stance is an *androcentric* goal; therefore, "science is a masculine project."[73] Unfortunately for the feminists, this first premise is false—a value-free stance is not essential to science or the scientific method—and hence the second premise, even if true, speaks to a straw account.

Again, the wave/particle problem, along with the Heisenberg discoveries, are cited by feminists as evidence that, even for modern science, there is no such thing as 'objectivity'. As I have argued above, this is a philosophical misinterpretation of empirical evidence. But even if this were not a complete misinterpretation of quantum phenomena, one can certainly recognize that "nature is no longer at arm's length"[74] and yet consistently believe that science is objective. As Stephen Toulmin has pointed out:

> We now realize, [that] the interaction between scientists and their objects of study is a *two*-way affair. . . . Even in fundamental physics, for instance, the fact that subatomic particles are under observation will make the influence of the physicists' instruments a significant element in the phenomena themselves . . . the scientific observer is now—willy-nilly—also a *participant*.[75]

This, though, as stated above, is more an acceptance of intersubjectivity than of subjectivity. The latter would be going too far. Toulmin has not changed what is essential to the concept of 'objectivity': its commitment to unbiased evidence. He has merely restructured the traditional concept to acknowledge that we can no longer treat *any* objects (be they people or electrons) in *purely* objectified ways. This is a denial of naive scientific realism, not an acceptance of subjectivism.

Such restructuring does not depend on interpreting the concept of 'objectivity' via a value-free stance; instead, it maintains the spirit of the traditional concept of 'objectivity' by stressing the desire and attempt to remain unbiased. The feminist critics of objectivity seem to confuse the true belief that the scientist must realize that her position sometimes makes her both observer and observed, with the false belief that her position as scientist means that her *contextuality* cannot be overcome. She can still do good, i.e., unbiased, science.

Examples of not-quite-value-free-but-nonetheless-unbiased acts abound. They occur, for example, when we adjudicate philosophical disputes at conferences, moderate philosophical analyses in the classroom, or evaluate the work of our students. To quote Toulmin again:

> In all these cases, to be objective does not require us to be *un*interested, that is, devoid of interests or feeling; it requires us only to acknowledge those interests and feelings, to discount any resulting biases and prejudices, and to do our best to act in a *dis*interested way.[76]

Feminist criticism which is aimed at objectivity *qua* a value-free stance—value-neutrality, noninvolvedness, or disinterestedness—simply misses the point.

Objectivity as Disinterest

Some feminist critics of science and scientific methodology do in fact address the concept of "weak objectivity no. 2" in its more sophisticated form—via the notion of a disinterested or unbiased stance. Nonetheless, they still claim the traditional concept of 'objectivity' is male-biased. Two different kinds of criticisms are offered.

The first focuses on a hermeneutical rendering of the texts of science as androcentric; the second focuses on the fact that "humans cannot be impartial or objective recorders of the world."[77] Both are problematic.

The Hermeneutical Fallacy*

The first criticism focuses on the fact that 'objectivity' has been genderized male, while 'subjectivity' has been genderized female. Both concepts are creations of an overarching "phallocentric discourse."[78]

Such generalization is obvious (to many feminists) from several different avenues: feminist historical interpretation, literary criticism, and

---

*By "hermeneutical" I mean, simply, the interpretation of a text.

psychoanalysis, to name a few. It is claimed that there are ways to " 'read science as a text' [which] reveal the social meanings—the hidden symbolic and cultural agendas—of purportedly [disinterested] claims and practices."[79] What the text has demonstrated is that science is "inextricably connected with specific masculine . . . needs and desires."[80]

This kind of "metaphor mongering"[81] is illegitimate. For one thing it has no textual support. The quotation above, for example, cites the texts of other feminist critics of science as support (e.g., "see Keller"), offering no specific pages, just whole texts. These texts in turn supply spotty evidence. To use Keller again as an example, when you peruse her book you find that she cites a number of other feminist critics of science who also claim to have textual evidence of male-bias in science, but has herself cited the work of only one male scientist, Francis Bacon. His use of sexist metaphor is, according to Keller, exhibited in passages like, "let us establish a chaste and lawful marriage between Mind and Nature. . . . It is Nature herself who is to be the bride, who requires taming, shaping, and subduing by the scientific mind."[82] Such passages, being so metaphorical and ambiguous could have any number of interpretations.

Moreover, no modern scientists are cited and even the outdated comments of Bacon are seen as less insidious when modified by his claim that "for man is but the servant and interpreter of nature . . . nor can nature be commanded except by being obeyed."[83] Little else is given to support this kind of claim.

But even if the list of Bacon-like metaphors was enormous, it could not do the work feminists need done. The logic is simple: such evidence presupposes precisely what is being challenged, namely, that the concept of a 'disinterested stance' in traditional science is male-biased. To adopt an androcentric interpretation without offering some justification for such an adoption is to beg the question.

But what kind of justification could be offered? This is yet another problem with the account, for any appeal to evidence is problematic. Evidence is empirical and, hence, to some degree or other, the bailiwick of science. For feminists to attempt to defend their claim that there is male-bias in traditional science by appealing to evidence—a concept defined within traditional science—is self-defeating.

No Such Thing as Objectivity

The hermeneutical "reason," however, is not the only justification feminist critics supply for rejecting the traditional notion of objectivity. Their other, stronger claim posits that one can never act in a disinterested way.

Why not? Why is it that "human beings cannot be impartial or objective recorders of their world?"[84] Is this a fact about the frailness of human psychology or the logical outcome of the epistemological fact that there is no disinterested stance to be had?

The Psychological Point

If feminist critics of science mean the former, then their claim, reminiscent of the psychological egoists' claim that 'Human beings can never act except in their own best interest', is in the same kind of trouble. As an empirical thesis it is either false, e.g., Mother Teresa, or unfalsifiable and, therefore, empty.[85]

With respect to the claim that 'Human beings can never act in a disinterested way', the argument against it follows suit: as an empirical thesis it is either false, e.g., when we rationally *decide*, not merely arbitrarily *choose*, which of our students ought get an "A," or unfalsifiable, hence the claim is vacuous.

James F. Harris makes an additional connection between ethical egoism and feminist criticisms of science.

> If ethical egoists really believe that people generally are selfish and ought to act in ways of furthering their own self-interests, then it seems they ought never to tell anyone about their theory since it would be against their own self-interests to have everyone else acting on an enlightened basis of such a theory. Also, an intelligent ethical egoist would not publicly announce his or her commitment to egoism since then other people would be placed on guard against the egoist. Similarly, if the feminists who advocate feminist science are right, if they really believe that they are right about the influence of general social and cultural values on the level of SC2 (contextual values) upon the nature of scientific inquiry on the level of SC1—[science community 1, the "object level"], then surely they ought not to publicly advocate their position in a male-dominated [science] society.[86]

To do so would find them being blackballed. It seems that feminists, like egoists, must keep their thesis, if true, to themselves.

The Epistemological Point

The psychological interpretation is probably not what feminist critics have in mind. The point is not that there are shortcomings in the human psychological mechanism which prevent one from being disinterested, but that, despite one's best intentions, there is no unbiased stance to be had. If the only stance is a biased stance then, given science and its history of male-domination, this bias translates into the fact that the male-stance is the only stance.

I am not sure if feminists who criticize science really would claim that if there is this psychological problem, that it is equally endemic to both men and women. If they say both, then feminism itself becomes one of many biases forced by one's psychological make-up. If they say that women suffer from this problem less than men, they would have to support this claim. But where could unbiased evidence for this kind of bias possibly come from?

Feminists against traditional science, however, do not directly argue for the claim that there is no unbiased stance to be had. Instead, ironically, they appeal to male authority: e.g., Thomas Kuhn. Feminists, following Kuhn, claim that the "Kuhnian strategy of arguing that observations are theory-laden, theories are paradigm-laden, and paradigms are culture-laden: [demonstrates that] there are and can be no such things as . . . objective facts."[87] Without objective facts, there can be no objective, i.e., unbiased, stance.

Of course, relying on Kuhn leaves an important question open for debate: Is he right?

Although a thorough discussion of Kuhn's arguments against the notion of 'objectivity' would fall outside the scope of this book, suffice it to say that, at best, there is a vast body of philosophical literature claiming he has *not* made his case against objectivity.[88]

Briefly, Kuhn's use of 'incommensurability'—which means theories from two different paradigms cannot be compared and therefore rationally adjudicated—is at the heart of his version of relativism. Because of this,

his account of relativism is caught between the horns of a dilemma. Either the thesis, on the one hand, truly embraces incommensurability or it does not. If the former, then Kuhnian relativism is provocative, for it entails unintelligibility; if the latter, it entails the promise of objectivity and is, therefore, benign. As Israel Scheffler has pointed out, "objectivity requires simply the possibility of intelligible debate over the comparative merits of rival paradigms."[89]

Although it is not clear that Kuhn himself actually supports the radical reading of the incommensurability claim, it is certain the feminists cannot simply rest on their Kuhnian laurels. Steven Yates, for example, believes that Kuhn rejects the radical reading citing Kuhn's "Commensurability." He claims that Kuhn's ideas are actually quite similar to Scheffler's and that their real difference lies in the rhetoric and not the substance of their work. Yates therefore argues that "there is nothing for the feminists to exploit in any accurate reading of Kuhn; they simply do not understand him."[90]

The point is that even if Kuhn is interpreted to be a radical incommensurabilist, feminist critics of traditional science must take the body of criticisms of Kuhnian and, therefore, their own relativism seriously. If on the other hand Kuhn is not a radical incommensurabilist, then these particular feminist arguments against the traditional notion of 'objectivity' cannot be Kuhn-dependent. In either case, it seems, the feminists will have to develop a Kuhnian-free attack on objectivity.

At this point it is important to mention that the feminists have not made their case against 'objectivity' and, therefore, traditional scientists and philosophers of science need not reject their own projects in lieu of feminist ones. It is just as important to admit that this does not mean science—the way it is practiced by specific scientists and philosophers of science (in the laboratory, classroom, and publishing house)—is not sexist. There are certainly inequalities in these arenas. However, these are not issues that challenge what is *essential* to science and its methodology.

Parenthetically, some interesting examples from sociobiology, genetics, and the social sciences are given by Lynn Hankinson Nelson in her recent book *Who Knows? From Quine to a Feminist Empiricism,* see especially chapters four and five. What is noteworthy is that she admits no one has yet presented any real evidence of sexism in the hard sciences, especially physics. Nelson's feminist take on this dearth of evidence is to remain hopeful, claiming that the future will hold the answer about the sexism of physics, and we're not dead yet![91]

Furthermore, feminists must realize this lack of evidence against the (essential) male-biased nature of science is a blessing, for it is precisely by way of scientific (objective) evidence that sexism in the sciences is exposed.[92] Feminists without objectivity are feminists without evidence of sexism.

FEMINISM AND SUBJECTIVISM

Feminists who deny objectivity are stuck with subjectivism, whether they invoke Kuhn or not. And subjectivism—the belief that any knowledge (in this case scientific knowledge) is restricted to the sensory, affective, and volitional states of the knowing subject, i.e., every object apprehended is created by the apprehender,[93] some specific apprehender—creates havoc for feminists.

The difficulties stem from the fact that subjectivism with respect to scientific knowledge, as opposed to some kind of intersubjectivism, is merely a form of Protagorean relativism. Needless to say, Protagorean relativism comes with its own logical and pragmatic baggage. Its problems and implications for feminism, as well as those of more sophisticated forms of relativism, will be discussed in chapter 3.

For now, however, we need to look at what is underlying the philosophical feminists' critiques of traditional science: the male-biasedness of classical epistemology.

Notes

1. Elizabeth Minnich, "Friends and Critics: The Feminist Academy," Keynote Address, *Proceedings of the Fifth Annual GLCA Women's Studies Conference*, November 1979.

2. Christina Hoff Sommers, "Do These Feminists Like Women?" *Journal of Social Philosophy* 21, no. 2 (Fall/Winter 1990): 66.

3. Sandra Harding, *Whose Science? Whose Knowledge?* (Ithaca, N.Y.: Cornell University Press, 1991), p. 78.

4. Ibid., p. 77.

5. Ibid., p. 79.

6. Ibid., p. 81.

7. Ibid., p. 83.

8. Ibid., p. 88.

9. Ibid., p. 93.

10. Ibid., p. 97.

11. Ibid., p. 81.

12. Hans Reichenbach, *The Rise of Scientific Philosophy* (Berkeley: University of California Press, 1959). The distinction states that there is a fundamental difference between the way we come to discover scientific hypotheses from the way we verify them. The point is to allow for the various ways in which scientists actually have discovered hypotheses—given to us from the history of science—which are often mystical or bizarre, from the ways in which these hypotheses are later confirmed. The point is to maintain a commitment to scientific rationality in the light of its outrageous history.

13. The "problems" surrounding quantum physics will be discussed below.

14. See, e.g., Sandra Harding, "Why Has the Sex-Gender System Become Visible Only Now?" in *Discovering Reality: Feminist Perspectives in Epistemology, Metaphysics, Methodology and Philosophy of Science,* ed. S. Harding and M. Hintikka (Dordrecht, Holland: Reidel, 1983); Alison Jaggar, *Feminist Politics and Human Nature* (Totowa, N.J.: Rowman and Allenheld, 1983); and, most recently, Helen E. Longino, *Science as Social Knowledge* (Princeton, N.J.: Princeton University Press, 1990), pp. 64–65.

15. Harding, *Whose Science?* p. 40.

16. Lorraine Code, *What Can She Know? Feminist Theory and the Construction of Knowledge* (Ithaca, N.Y.: Cornell University Press, 1991), p. 29.

17. Harding, *Whose Science?* p. 209.

18. Ibid., p. 40.

19. Ibid.

20. Thomas Kuhn, *The Essential Tension* (Chicago: University of Chicago Press, 1977). Longino depends almost exclusively on Kuhn's account in her discussion and rejection of the context of discovery/context of justification distinction.

21. Harold I. Brown, *Perception, Theory and Commitment* (Chicago: Precedent Publication, Inc., 1977).

22. Harvey Siegel, *Relativism Refuted* (Dordrecht, Holland: Reidel, 1987), pp. 62–66.

23. Brown, *Perception*, p. 130.

24. Siegel, *Relativism Refuted*, p. 106.

25. Richard Campbell, informal discussion.

26. Harding, *Whose Science?* p. 84.

27. Ibid.

28. If this is not acknowledged, the move to relativism, if not skepticism, is swift and sure. See chapter 3.

29. Harding, *Whose Science?* p. 85.

30. Ruth Bleier, *Science and Gender: A Critique of Biology and Its Theories on Women* (New York: Pergamon Press, 1984), p. 4.

31. Harding, *Whose Science?* p. 85.

32. John Chandler, "Androcentric Science? The Science Question in Feminism," *Inquiry* 30 (1987): 329. Chandler is actually criticizing Harding's account of the history of science from her *Science Question in Feminism*, but I believe this criticism still holds true for *Whose Science?* as well.

33. Dorothy E. Smith, "Commentary on Sandra Harding's 'The Method Question,' " *APA Newsletter* 88, no. 3 (1989): 44.

34. Peter Brian Medawar, *Induction and Intuition in Scientific Thought* (Philadelphia: American Philosophical Society, 1969), p. 9.

35. Harding, *Whose Science?* p. 86.

36. Harvey Siegel, "What Is the Question Concerning the Rationality of Science?" *Philosophy of Science* 52 (1985): 528.

37. Harding, *Whose Science?* p. 86.

38. Ibid., p. 97.

39. Ibid., p. 99.

40. Ibid., p. 79.

41. Paul R. Gross and Norman Levitt, *Higher Superstition: The Academic Left and Its Quarrels with Science* (Baltimore: The Johns Hopkins University Press, 1994), p. 130.

42. Ibid., p. 129.

43. Ibid., p. 126.

44. Lorraine Code, "Taking Subjectivity Into Account," in *Feminist Epistemologies*, ed. L. Alcoff and E. Potter (New York: Routledge, 1993), p. 36.

45. Elizabeth Grosz, "Bodies and Knowledge: Feminism and the Crisis of Reason," in *Feminist Epistemologies*, ed. L. Alcoff and E. Potter, p. 192.

46. Much of this has been adopted from E. R. Klein, "Criticizing the Feminist Critique of Objectivity," *Reason Papers* 18 (Fall 1993): 57–70.

47. Bleier, *Science and Gender*, p. 4.

48. Ibid., p. 538, n.2.

49. Evelyn Fox Keller, *Reflections on Science and Gender* (New Haven, Conn.: Yale University Press, 1985), p. 12.

50. Jean Grimshaw, *Philosophy and Feminist Thinking* (Minneapolis: University of Minnesota Press, 1986), p. 83.

51. Susan Bordo, *The Flight to Objectivity* (Albany: State University of New York Press, 1987), and Susan Bordo, "The Cartesian Masculinization of Thought," in *Sex and Scientific Inquiry*, ed. S. Harding and J. F. O'Barr (Chicago: University of Chicago Press, 1987), pp. 247–64.

52. Nancy Tuana, Review of *Sex and Scientific Inquiry*, ed. S. Harding and J. F. O'Barr, *APA Newsletter on Feminism* 89, no. 2 (1990): 62.

53. Helen Longino, "Can There Be a Feminist Science?" in *Women, Knowledge and Reality*, ed. A. Garry and M. Pearsall (London: Unwin Hyman, 1984), p. 212.

54. Harding, *Whose Science?* p. 143.

55. Sandra Harding, *The Science Question in Feminism* (Ithaca, N.Y.: Cornell University Press, 1986); "The Instability of the Analytical Categories of Feminist Theory," in *Sex and Scientific Inquiry*, ed. S. Harding and J. F. O'Barr; *Whose Science?*; and "Starting from Women's Lives: Eight Resources for Maximizing Objectivity," *Journal of Social Philosophy* 21 (1991): 140–49.

56. Harding, *Whose Science?* p. 134.

57. Harding, *Science Question*, p. 249.

58. Harding, *Whose Science?* p. 138.

59. Ibid., p. 143.

60. Ibid.

61. Ibid., p. 144.

62. Ibid., p. 149.

63. Ibid.

64. Harding, *Science Question*, pp. 249–50, n.7.

65. See also Chandler, "Androcentric Science?"

66. Kristin Shrader-Frechette, Review of *The Science Question in Feminism* by Sandra Harding, *Synthese* 76 (1988): 444.

67. Harding, "Starting from Women's Lives," p. 149.

68. I have little objection for there is no reason that one cannot maintain a commitment to traditional notions of 'objectivity' while walking in the large grey area between hard scientific realism and soft idealism.

69. See, for example, the works of Merleu Ponty, C. S. Peirce, Hans Reichenbach, Karl Popper, and Larry Laudan.

70. Harding, *Whose Science?* p. 159.

71. Ibid., p. 163.

72. Sandra Harding, "Rethinking Standpoint Epistemology: 'What Is Strong Objectivity?' " in *Feminist Epistemologies*, ed. L. Alcoff and E. Potter, pp. 49–82.

73. Harding, "Starting from Women's Lives," p. 177, n.5.

74. Stephen Toulmin, "The Construal of Reality: Criticism in Modern and Postmodern Science," in *The Politics of Interpretation*, ed. W. J. T. Mitchell (Chicago: University of Chicago Press, 1983), p. 112.

75. Ibid., p. 103.

76. Ibid., p. 112.

77. Harding, *Science Question*, p. 83, n.6.

78. Drucilla Cornell and Adam Thurschell, "Feminism, Negativity, Intersubjectivity," in *Feminism as Critique*, ed. Seyla Benhabib and Drucilla Cornell (Minneapolis: University of Minnesota Press, 1987), p. 143.

79. Harding, *Science Question*, p. 23, n.7.

80. Ibid., p. 23.

81. Gross and Levitt, *Higher Superstition*, p. 116.

82. Keller, *Reflections on Science*, p. 36.

83. Ibid.

84. Grimshaw, *Philosophy and Feminist Thinking*, p. 83.

85. See the criticism of psychological egoism by James Rachels, *The Elements of Moral Knowledge* (New York: McGraw-Hill, 1986) and *The Right Thing to Do* (New York: McGraw-Hill, 1989).

86. James F. Harris, *Against Relativism* (LaSalle, Ill.: Open Court, 1992), p. 184.

87. Harding, *Science Question*, p. 102.

88. Just to name a few: W. H. Newton-Smith, *The Rationality of Science* (London: Routledge and Kegan Paul, 1981); Israel Scheffler, *Science and Subjectivity* (Indianapolis: Bobbs-Merrill, 1967); Harvey Siegel, *Relativism Refuted*; Carl R. Kordig, *The Justification of Scientific Change* (Dordrecht, Holland: Reidel, 1971); and James F. Harris, *Against Relativism*.

89. Israel Scheffler, "Vision and Revolution: A Postscript to Kuhn," *Philosophy of Science* 39 (1972): 369.

90. Steven Yates, 1992, personal telephone correspondence.

91. Lynn Hankinson Nelson, *Who Knows? From Quine to a Feminist Empiricism* (Philadelphia: Temple University Press, 1990), pp. 249–54.

92. A similar point is made by Susan Haack, "Science 'From a Feminist Perspective,' " *Philosophy* 67 (1992): 5–18.

93. This definition is adopted from Herman Hausheer, "Epistemological Subjectivism," in *Dictionary of Philosophy*, ed. D.D. Runes (Totowa, N.J.: Littlefield, Adams and Co., 1962), p. 303.

2

The Feminist Critique
of Epistemology

Epistemology made by professional philosophers of the mainstream [is] one
of the more arcane and esoteric artifacts of men. . . . [I]ts very neutrality
masks the facts of its derivation from and embeddedness in a specific set
of interests: the interest of a privileged group of white men.

Lorraine Code[1]

Epistemology, at least at it is classically conceived, is the study of knowledge. Contemporary epistemologists attempt to give accounts of what
knowledge is. Given that all of our beliefs do not hold the same epistemic
weight, the job of the epistemologist is to articulate a way of discrimi-
nating, of choosing only those beliefs that are *good* enough to be called
knowledge. Epistemic goodness is at its heart, at least classically speaking, a thoroughly normative notion and has primarily been discussed in
terms of some commitment to reasons—empirical or logical.

At the heart of the feminist epistemological project, a component of
which is essential to the feminist science program discussed in chapter
1, is the belief that the classical accounts of epistemology, with their fundamental commitment to the normative notions of 'reason' and 'rationality,' are androcentric.

This chapter attempts to demonstrate that epistemology has not been shown to be simply an "artifact used in the interest of men," i.e., that it is essentially male-biased, and, therefore, that the call to "go feminist" in epistemology is premature.

Pre-Feminist Epistemology

Historically, in the Academe, males have predominated. Feminists, appropriately, resented this apparent injustice and attempted to balance the scales. Unfortunately, many women still have not reached parity. This empirical fact may prompt the feminist to query, Why?

Two possible explanations arise from this observation. One is that women, at least some women, do not deserve equality: they are not smart enough or strong enough or aggressive enough to grab it. The other is that the game is inherently unfair: it is not that women are inferior players, but that the game is rigged such that only men can win.

In her 1982 book, *In A Different Voice*, Carol Gilligan, one of the most widely read and quoted academic feminists, holds to the second explanation. With respect to the particular topic of moral knowledge, she cites evidence[2] which she believes demonstrates that men rig the game of moral agency in their own favor. We are told that by traditional—i.e., male—standards women, more often than not, make immature and poor moral decisions. With this evidence, it seems justified to deny women moral power—as judges, members of government, professors, etc.—because they could not make decisions as well as men.

Gilligan challenged the legitimacy of this evidence and its oppressive practical implications. She asks this general question: Are women incapable of moral knowledge—the kind of knowledge that values universalizability (as opposed to contextuality) and privileges reason (over emotions)? or, Do women merely appear incapable because there is something wrong with the criteria for determining what counts as moral knowledge itself? After all, she points out, these criteria were invented by men and have often been used by men to oppress women. Her answer, naturally, was to reject the moral inferiority of women.[3] She then proceeded to suggest that it was the criteria, not the women, which needed fixing.

The assumption that women can and do have moral knowledge led to the birth of "feminist ethics." At precisely the same moment, feminist epistemology was born. Even though Gilligan uses the term 'epistemology' only once,[4] once seems to have been enough. Since then feminist epistemologists from all areas of academe have flocked to Gilligan's island; and to this day, many remain there, marooned.

Common to all of these feminist theorists is their foundational assumption that women have knowledge—that they are competent knowers in all areas from ethics to science—and, moreover, that if that knowledge is not accepted, respected, properly compensated, etc., by men, the desiderata for knowledge must be fundamentally male-biased.

Although this seems like a reasonable deduction, at a more fundamental level it is not, nor *can* it be. It is unreasonable not because the post-Gilliganite feminists use faulty evidence or fallacious reasoning (although this seems also to be the case[5]), but because they challenge the very notion of having *good* evidence and *valid* reasons.

This challenge to the classical account of knowledge—whether it can be applied to moral, scientific, or philosophical reasons—is at the heart of feminist epistemology. The challenge falls into two distinct but interconnected stages: (1) characterizing the classical account of epistemology, demonstrating that these characteristics are fundamentally male-biased, and (2) urging those who are convinced to make the appropriate nonsexist, antisexist changes, i.e., develop *feminist epistemologies*.

I propose that: (1) the account of classical epistemology developed by most feminists is a caricature, (2) the evidence of male-bias leveled against such accounts is built on shaky historical and hermeneutic/psychoanalytic grounds, and (3) given that the feminists have both caricatured the classical account of epistemology and offered inadequate support for their charge of male-bias, epistemologists ought not abandon classical epistemology. In addition, I will suggest that the very idea of a feminist epistemology is misguided and ought to be resisted at all cost.

Reason and Rationality

THE FEMINIST CHARACTERIZATION OF CLASSICAL EPISTEMOLOGY

There are as many different charges against classical epistemologists as
there are feminists working in the field, so I will not list all of them here.
There are certain themes, however, which dominate the feminist epistemological corpus. Classical epistemology has been damned most often for
having privileged reason: (1) for having taken an approach to reason as
"theorizing . . . divorced from the body,"[6] (2) for maintaining the "belief
that knowers can and should be self-sufficient,"[7] and (3) for attempting
to "obtain epistemic certainty."[8]

CLASSICAL EPISTEMOLOGY IS MALE-BIASED

The second step is to show that the privileging of reason, in the ways described above, is a male phenomenon[9] and that "the feminine has been
associated with what [reason] transcends, dominates, or simply leaves behind,"[10] i.e., 'emotion'.

Feminist Epistemology

Using the evil, i.e., male, method of dichotomization[11] feminists have
claimed that feminist epistemology should: (1) accept that "our emotions
are epistemologically indispensable,"[12] (2) realize "that subjectivity and
the specificities of cognitive agency can and must be accorded central
epistemological significance,"[13] and (3) believe that epistemological
"contextualization is related to and dependent upon bodily awareness of
context through senses."[14]

Now it is important to realize that the "incorporation of emotions
into epistemology," recognizing the "importance of the subjective stance"
and the "contextualization of knowledge in the body," are all theories
which predated feminist criticism. Plato, Hegel, and Hume, respectively,
advocated theories similar to these. As such, it is not clear what is particularly feminist or even womanly about them.

Furthermore, nowhere in the feminist literature is there a positive account given of why anyone ought to incorporate these theses into their epistemology, let alone why all women or feminists should. The literature is, however, strewn with accounts of why people (especially women) should view classical epistemology as essentially male-biased.

Going Feminist

So what exactly is a feminist epistemology? Alas, there are few positive accounts. This is partly due to the fact that few of the feminists who claim that there is a feminist epistemology are philosophers and fewer still are epistemologists. Much of what is being called epistemology is too "metaphorical and vague"[15] to do any serious philosophical work. In part it is also due to the fact that once existing "male" epistemology was dismissed, "the question of where feminist knowledge should situate itself"[16] arose. Answering the question, "From where does it [feminist epistemology] derive an authority or legitimacy which is *not* constructed by the prevailing structures of knowledge?"[17] becomes a serious problem. "For as Archimedes had to stand somewhere [to place the fulcrum so that he could move the earth], one has to assume something in order to reason at all."[18] Unfortunately for the most radical feminist critics of classical epistemology, what is usually assumed for one to *reason at all* is that there is such a thing as rationality—at its bare bones an unbiased commitment to evidence (via traditional concepts of objectivity) and logical consistency—which is precisely what is being challenged by feminists as male-biased.[19]

Unfortunately, all that the literature offers is a number of negative accounts of 'male' epistemology and the feminist critiques they have sparked.

Criticisms

De-Caricaturing the Classical Account

Has classical epistemology privileged reason? Yes and no. While some philosophers have, not all maintain such an agenda. There are contemporary philosophers of science, for example, Paul K. Feyerabend, who have not. In his books, appropriately entitled *Against Method*[20] and *Farewell to Reason*,[21] Feyerabend offers challenges to reason and the scientific method. Even the father of "reason privilege," Plato, is being defended as feminist by some philosophers who claim his fundamental epistemic commitment was to that aspect of the soul which housed the emotion of love, not the faculty of reason.[22]

However, even those epistemologists who do privilege reason do not exalt the notion as necessarily "divorced from the body" (for example, all the empiricists up to and including Quine). Nor is it a commitment to a concept of reason that entails that "knowers can and should be self-sufficient."

Epistemologists have always exposed their ideas to oral and written comments and criticisms. Even Descartes (I choose Descartes because he is often blamed for the "psychotic" desire for "private, abstract thought"[23]) who sat alone in his armchair did not sustain his philosophical life solipsistically. He corresponded with men (and women) about his ideas and published work.

Finally, the classical epistemologist's supposed "desire for certainty" is hyperbolized. Not all epistemologists sought, or are seeking, foundations. Descartes, again, often cited as the creator of this ostensibly misguided account, may have been after incorrigible beliefs. But incorrigibility is a hallmark of "mental" beliefs, beliefs about one's own mental states; they are not a characteristic of scientific beliefs, beliefs about the world. The true impetus behind classical epistemology is, and always has been, the desire to justify beliefs about the world. Further, those of us who do classical epistemology[24] do not at all insist that such foundations be infallible.

This brings us to the real question: "Is classical epistemology committed to objectivity—the belief that there are at least some 'facts of the matter' which exist independently of the knower?" Again, yes and no. Certainly there are those (male) philosophers throughout the history of (Western) philosophy who were not so inclined. (Feminists and nonfeminists alike usually cite Hegel as a case in point.) But those of us who are committed to objectivity are not hopelessly devoted to the desire for a "value-free stance." We recognize that the relationship between knower and object is a "two-way affair";[25] however, it is a union which requires a chaperone. Not everything believed by the knower about the known is knowledge. It is consistent to admit that there are values inherent in our objective theory making, for example, the desire to get to true or justified beliefs, without sharing the feminist paranoia about male-bias.

Is the Classical Account Male-Biased?

Perhaps even an accurate account of classical epistemology is not worth criticizing; perhaps *any* commitment to reason is sexist. To find out, a closer look at feminist criticisms of objectivity and reason is needed.

There are two kinds of arguments feminists level against even the most modest classical account. One I call 'psychoanalytic', the other 'historical'. Together they are meant to demonstrate the inherently sexist nature of classical epistemology.

The Psychoanalytic Attack

The psychoanalytic evidence for the male-biased nature of epistemology is hallmarked by the work of Susan Bordo,[26] but has its roots in the work of other psychoanalytic feminists such as Dorothy Dinnerstein,[27] Jane Flax,[28] and Evelyn Fox Keller.[29] It is important to note that some of these feminists realize that many people will not share their "confidence in the value of psychoanalytic theory as a tool"[30] in reworking fundamental epistemological concepts. Still, they plod on.

Bordo, for example, argues that the epistemological desire for objectivity is really the psychotic "flight from the feminine."[31] As Lorraine Code points out:

> Bordo focuses on the images of anxiety, confusion, and separation which permeate Descartes's *Meditations,* prompting him to develop strategies to preserve himself from vertigo. . . . For Bordo, Cartesian objectivism is of a piece with, and indeed consequent on, a seventeenth-century "flight from the feminine." Rationalists and empiricists were of one mind, she maintains, in their conviction that the essential epistemic task (both practical—in empirical science—and theoretical) was to tame " the female universe." Ideal objectivity is the *masculine* epistemological stance that a knower must adopt if this project is to be carried out successfully. . . . To develop

this detachment, a knower had to neutralize all traces of emotional unruliness and of the 'female' mystery that such unruliness implies.[32]

However, after having reached some strong skeptical conclusions, Descartes went into an "epistemological panic."[33] Certainty was neither in his mind, nor, certainly, in the "world as female flesh."[34] Descartes, according to some feminists, transfers all certainty to a god's-eye view, and "a masculine God"[35] at that.

According to Bordo:

> A new theory of knowledge, thus, is born, one which regards all sense experience as illusory and insists that the object can only be truly known by the perceiver who is willing to purge the mind of all obscurity, all irrelevancy, all free imaginative associations, and all passionate attachments. . . . A new world is constructed, one which all generality and creativity fall to God the spiritual father rather than to the female flesh of the world. For Plato and Aristotle, and throughout the Middle Ages, the natural world had been "mother"—passive, receptive, *natura naturata* to be sure, but living and breathing nonetheless. Now, in the same brilliant stroke that insured objectivity of science—the mutual opposition of the spiritual and corporeal—the formerly female earth becomes inert *res extensa*: dead, mechanically interacting matter.
>
> "She" becomes "it"—and "it" can be understood. Not through sympathy, of course, but by virtue of the very *object*-ivity of the "it." At the same time, the world of separateness—[male children are forced to wrench themselves from their mothers in order to be appropriately socialized]—is healed through the denial that there ever was any union: for the mechanists, unlike [John] Donne, the female world-soul did not die; rather, the world *is* dead. There is nothing to mourn, nothing to lament. Indeed, the new epistemological anxiety is not over loss but is evoked by the memory or suggestion of union: empathic, associational, or emotional response obscures objectivity, feeling for nature muddies the clear lake of the mind. The otherness of nature is now what allows it to be known.[36]

The Cartesian desire for certainty is a "flight from the feminine" caused by "anxiety over 'separation from the organic female universe of the Middle Ages and Renaissance.' "[37]

The psychoanalytic attack begins by arguing that the desire for objectivity and the commitment to reason grow out of a sickness suffered by men, a malady which all men acquire because of the cultural pressure to separate from their mothers. It is then suggested that such desires, having been developed in sickness, must themselves be sick. A need for healthier, i.e., women's, epistemic desires emerges.

Fallacies

First, this kind of psychoanalytic evidence is terribly weak. On the one hand, it cannot speak to an entire tradition, nor to the essential concepts which have been sustained throughout that tradition's development. These kinds of things cannot be so analyzed; only individuals can suffer from these stresses and even then I believe that the evidence is at best ad hoc.

Unfortunately, most feminists have neither the luxury nor the inclination to claim it is only the sickness of particular individual men that is responsible for sexism. Given that feminists have no desire for such a dismissal—since they want to claim that it is the entire enterprise of epistemology that is sexist, and that they do not have the luxury of such evidence—and given that they so often claim that the sex/genderizing of important epistemological concepts is entrenched in the surrounding culture, these critics are left with the unhappy conclusion that psychoanalysis (with its dubious science of individuals) is even more suspect when applied to entire societies and cultures.

Counterevidence

Second, any attempt to speak to the entire culture would render the thesis false. I, for one, though a woman, attempt to achieve objectivity and seriously value reasons and rationality—and I am not the only woman who does so. Feyerabend, on the other hand, though a man, does not. What should psychoanalytic feminists do with such contemporary pieces of counterevidence? If they take them seriously, it hurts their empirical thesis; if they do not take them seriously, however, it still injures their claim. Empirical theses are like that: Evidence matters. Given that empirical evidence is used to construct the psychoanalytic theory to begin with, those bits of evidence that do not fit the theory must be taken seriously.

Weak Cause and Effect

Third, even if there was no counterevidence, and even if it did speak to an entire society or culture collectively, such mass psychosis that compels everyone to neurotically long for epistemic certainty and dichotomizing, mind/body dualism does not damn the epistemological enterprise itself. For one thing, simply because such beliefs follow from, for example, irrational infantile fears of estrangement from one's mother, does not mean that such beliefs are, in fact, irrational. "It would commit the genetic fallacy to argue that beliefs caused in a certain way are false because of their causal origins."[38] For another, once epistemology is viewed not as a caricature of Descartes, but, correctly, as a method of critical analysis committed to logical consistency and evidence, little of the psychoanalytic character of its content is relevant. The spirit of rational thinking always triumphs over fetishism and psychopathology.

In other words, aside from the genetic fallacy, little follows from this cause-and-effect account of knowledge. Furthermore, classical epistemologists often make an epistemically analogous dichotomy to the one above via the scientific context of discovery/context of justification distinction discussed above. That is, they distinguish between *how* a philosophical thesis is acquired and its *justificatory status,* i.e., whether it is worthy of our belief. It may be that these theories are the product of sick male minds. But no matter. It does not follow that simply because something was developed by a sick male mind that what is developed is, in fact, sick. Not every meal Julia Child cooks is worth eating and not every theory developed by the Nazis is necessarily wrong.

Caricature

Fourth, chastising all classical epistemology as a product of "masculinist hubris"[39] solely in terms of the Cartesian desire for epistemic certainty builds a straw account. Few classical epistemologists claim there exists a "monolithic Reason."[40] Still fewer claim that epistemic certainty is a desideratum. Again, as stated above, most classical epistemologists, even some contemporary foundationalists, are fallibilists. Although they may believe one can develop the general criteria for determining the justifica-

tory status of our beliefs, they believe neither that there is only one criterion for all time nor that their account of it is indubitable or incorrigible.

Inconsistent with Political Goals

Finally, these accounts depend on a specific preestablished bias in the
reading of the text. One can, if she chooses, find male-bias in the same
places one finds penis-envy or self-centeredness, i.e., *everywhere.* If one
adopts a certain hermeneutic approach to the corpus of Western epistemology entailing that one read the texts as male-biased, then male-bias
will abound. Clearly, feminists need to make the case not that in putting
on their feminist glasses everything turns a more masculine shade of
male, but that one ought put on such glasses at all.

Historical Attack

The Case

The work usually cited as evidence of the historical male-bias of epistemology is *The Man of Reason.* In this book, Genevieve Lloyd describes
the symbolic historical associations of maleness with the ideals of Reason, and femaleness with "what rational knowledge transcends, dominates, or simply leaves behind."[41] In Code's words, "Lloyd's point . . . is
that in spite of explicit avowals to the contrary (by such philosophers as
Augustine and Descartes), Reason nonetheless persists as an ideal that
incorporates attributes valued as masculine and is defined in terms of
them. That incorporation is accomplished by suppressing traits that are
devalued because of their associations with 'the feminine'."[42]

The important point about Lloyd's argument is that it suggests that the
remedies usually offered for women's indifference to, and difficulties
with math, logic, and the like, are wrongly conceived. It is not, Lloyd suggests, women's *mis*-perception that there is a conflict between reason
and femaleness; rather, women who perceive this conflict are perceiving
a deep philosophical problem, not a myth or a superficial social or linguistic bias. Neither are they victims of personal psychological "hang-
ups" or biases, or of biological destiny. Reason, according to Lloyd, has

been *defined* as the antithesis of that which is female, by virtue of the meanings of the terms. So on Lloyd's account the woman who perceives a conflict between reason and female identity, and who acts on this belief, is in fact behaving rationally.[43]

Unfortunately, Lloyd did *not* demonstrate any of this.[44] All of the evidence built in her corpus is weak, a very important point given that this particular work is heavily cited by most feminists critical of classical epistemology.[45]

Criticisms

Although Lloyd begins her book with some grand claims about how the "maleness of the Man of Reason . . . is no superficial linguistic bias,"[46] that "*The Man of Reason* tried to avoid treating the maleness of reason as a 'mere' metaphor,"[47] and that our "trust in a Reason that knows no sex has been largely self-deceiving,"[48] her book never demonstrates this. She does not even show that an "exclusion or transcending of the feminine is built into past ideals of Reason."[49] At best her book demonstrates that certain philosophers, for example, Philo (hardly one of the "big boys"), were sexist; not that Reason is.

In fact, Lloyd herself concedes the weakness of her position. She demonstrates, for example (fairly I believe), that Plato's concept of Reason (a concept which most epistemologists take much more seriously than they do Philo's) is not male-biased.[50] The same is true of other big names in the history of epistemology: Descartes, whose method he believed was "accessible to women,"[51] and Kant, who does not even "explore the possibility of a sexual differentiation."[52]

Most importantly, though, Lloyd specifically states that regardless of what she has demonstrated, she wants to make clear that even if she had demonstrated that past conceptions of Reason have been imbedded with male-bias, she does not believe that anything particularly feminist about epistemology follows from this. That is, she does not think "that what is true or reasonable varies according to what sex we are."[53] She concludes that "philosophers can take seriously feminist dissatisfaction with the maleness of Reason without repudiating either Reason or Philosophy."[54] The Man of Reason may be male but, according even to Lloyd, rationality is still sex/gender neutral.

In the final analysis, by the time Lloyd is through with her own historical and hermeneutic romp, little is left that is provocative. Epistemology remains, by her own lights, still committed to reason (not *Reason*) and is left unscathed. It is unclear then why so many post-Lloydian feminist critics of epistemology,[55] rationality, or reason make comments similar to the following:

> A recent example of feminist critique which confirms the foregoing analysis of the way dichotomies function in the history of Western philosophy is Genevieve Lloyd's *The Man of Reason: 'Male' and 'Female' in Western Philosophy*. Lloyd's careful analysis of the history of conceptions of reason aims to demonstrate that 'the maleness of the Man of Reason . . . is no superficial linguistic bias.' Rather, she argues, the latent conceptual connections between reason, masculinity, truth and the intellect, on one hand, and sense, femininity, error and emotion, on the other, are so entrenched and pervasive in the history of philosophy that they virtually prohibit women from reason.[56]

In short, they seem intent on making epistemic mountains out of linguistic mole hills.

Feminist Epistemology Revisited

To be fair to these feminist critics of reason, however, one must acknowledge the spirit of their position. It is not so much that classical epistemology is sick as much as 'historically' it has misrepresented itself as that which is desired by all persons, including women, without ever taking seriously the epistemic desires of women. If this is true, the next step might be to ask: What do women desire epistemically? Ironically, feminist critics of classical epistemology claim that women desire what male history has *supposedly* always said that women desire (I say "supposedly" because even the most cited piece of historical evidence, Lloyd's *The Man of Reason*, is noncommittal with its evidence and clearly states Lloyd's commitment to reason): a theory of knowledge which is juxtaposed to men's, one that privileges emotion and is committed to subjectivity.

Although one can read the history of philosophy in such a way as to be able to "associate"[57] "maleness" with reason and objectivity, and "fe-

maleness" with emotion and subjectivity, one need not. Even Lloyd believes this. One could, for example, read the texts the way I read them—
as gender neutral. The real question is: How *ought* one "read" the text
and judge the concepts of reason and objectivity? Should nonsexist and
antisexist philosophers reject the privileging of these concepts on the
grounds that they are male and that all attempts to ground epistemology
on them are sexist?

Such 'ought' questions, and the need to answer them, bring us to the
third and final criticism of past attempts to dismantle classical epistemology, a criticism that also leads me to believe that *any* attempt to develop a feminist account is doomed.

At first blush it would seem that one *should* reject sexist epistemologies. But what kind of 'should' is this? Is it a 'should' that can be answered
with an appeal to reasons or evidence? If yes, then what need is there for
feminist critique in the first place? What, that is, is provocative and
new? If no, however, then to what could these feminist critics appeal in
order to defend their philosophical theories, or more importantly, their political goals?

The problem is that when what is being questioned are the foundations required for challenge itself—namely, our commitment to reason—
then it is unclear what can possibly count as a worthy response. Responses cannot be grounded in just any belief, or left defenseless. They
must be developed with a commitment to evidence and, at the very least,
the avoidance of contradiction. Responses not dependent on reason cannot be reasonable.

Given that separating out the reasonable from the unreasonable is at
the heart of any epistemological project, there can be no feminist epistemology. What is peculiarly feminist about "feminist epistemology" is not
particularly epistemic; and what is epistemic is not particularly feminist.

FEMINIST BUT NOT EPISTEMIC

As characterized above, "feminist epistemology" is easy to identify. It is
brightly characterized by notions which insist both that the content of
Western philosophy, specifically, the notions of 'reason' and 'rationality',
and its form (the process of critical analysis) be essentially male-biased.

Certainly one may accuse me of unfairly exaggerating the feminist critical account, by even calling it "*the* feminist critical account," but what is one to do with some of the outrageous claims set in print? Taking them seriously seems to be the only responsible thing to do.

Lloyd, for example, claims that "our trust in a Reason that knows no sex has been largely self-deceiving";[58] that "rationality has been conceived as transcendence of the feminine."[59] Nancy J. Holland states that all of contemporary analytic philosophy is committed to a "self-definition that identifies it as necessarily men's philosophy."[60] Lorraine Code writes that "mainstream epistemology masks the facts of its derivation from and embeddedness in a specific set of interests: the interests of a privileged group of white men."[61] Finally, Karen J. Warren points out that numerous feminist philosophers have maintained "the hypothesis that mainstream Western conceptions of reason and rationality are distinctively male or have masculine perspectives."[62] (Some feminists have even suggested there is a peculiarly "woman's way of knowing."[63])

These comments, though I believe unjustified, are at least provocative and certainly feminist, if one views feminism as "a political movement for social change."[64] Nevertheless, theses of this kind cannot be taken seriously *as epistemology*, for they are, ultimately, intolerant of criticism. I find it awkward to have to extol the virtues of criticizability to sister philosophers who, like myself, encourage it in our classrooms and embrace it in our scholarship; so I will resist the temptation. Instead, I would like to point out that the vice of fundamentalism, racism, sexism, and the like, is its dogmatism, its defiant self-ordained immunity from the ravages of logic and evidence.

Therein lies the philosophical dubiousness of feminism. Legitimate epistemology must be committed, at some level, to logic and evidence. I say "at some level," for I want to allow for the *philosophical* criticism of epistemology (at least specific epistemologies). For any epistemology to consistently live up to its own ideals, every one of its theses (although not all at once) must be criticizable—even, at some level, the method of critical analysis itself. Unfortunately, radical feminist claims like those offered above suffer the same syndrome as their fundamentalist counterparts: they cannot countenance rational challenge. How can one epistemically criticize claims or offer reasons why a position is incorrect if *the*

commitment to reasons is itself viewed as "male" and, therefore, illegitimate? (Alison Jaggar, for example, once viewed the commitment to reason as "the pretension of a distinctively masculine intellect."[65]) When
criticism is intolerable, epistemology (and maybe even philosophy as a
whole) becomes, in principle, impossible.

The quotation by Code, along with the genre of hypotheses summa-
rized by Karen Warren, are also protected, though only incidentally. For
although these claims are not in principle impossible to criticize, they are,
for all practical purposes, shielded. For who could criticize? Certainly no
man. All such words and methods would be dismissed out of hand as gender infected. Furthermore, any woman who criticizes feminism using reason and the basic ("masculine") methods of analysis would just as quickly
be dismissed. Criticism becomes impossible. What looks like epistemology is not, in any important sense, epistemic.

Therefore, although those feminists who seriously oppose classical
epistemology proudly ask for nothing less than "the abandonment of philosophy altogether,"[66] and although, as I have argued, this view is misguided, I believe it is, nonetheless, worth discussing.

FEMINIST PHILOSOPHY IS NOT PARTICULARLY FEMINIST

Recent critics of my work[67] claim I have mischaracterized the feminist account of epistemology. I have been told that today's feminists do not reject reason or analysis, and certainly not philosophy altogether. Unfortunately, there seems to be little scholarly evidence of such apostasy.
Nevertheless, for the sake of argument I will assume feminists no longer
believe the commitment to reasons and the method of critical analysis to
be essentially male-biased.

But what now? What of interest is left? What remains that is peculiarly feminist in "feminist epistemology"? If all along feminists were simply making standard criticisms about the Western philosophical tradition's concept of 'reason' and its devotion to analysis—e.g., that 'reason'
is too narrowly defined, that 'reason' should be broadened to incorporate
emotions, that devotion to analysis is harmful to society—then they must
wait their turn in the 2,500-year corpus of such critiques. Certainly, they
should get behind those critics whose works predated theirs and who are

still alive, e.g., Jacques Derrida and Richard Rorty.[68] If this is all that "feminist epistemology" wants to say, then it is saying nothing new, and certainly it is saying nothing particularly helpful to women. Without the call to deconstruct classical epistemology in the name of gender-bias, and without the call to restructure it in the name of female empowerment, "feminist epistemology" may maintain its philosophical integrity, but only at the cost of losing its political punch.

The lack of a peculiarly feminist aspect to "feminist" epistemology is even more apparent in the work of those feminists committed to saving epistemology from their sisters' more radical claims by unearthing feminist veins in nearly every traditional thesis, from Platonic Realism to Quinian Empiricism. Unfortunately, if these more moderate feminists are successful, not only will they have demonstrated that epistemology (and maybe even philosophy) does not need feminism, they will have shown that feminism does not even need women. Surely, this is no way to run a political campaign.

"Feminist epistemologists" are caught between the horns of a dilemma. Insofar as their position is provocative and politically potent in its criticism of reason and analysis, it is dogmatic and therefore not properly epistemic. Insofar as their position retreats from its sex/gender stance, it ceases to play its essential political role. It seems that there really is no such thing as a feminist epistemology.

A good thing perhaps. If the goal of developing a feminist epistemology is to empower women, then the feminist epistemological project, based ultimately on its criticisms of reason and objectivity, must be abandoned. Feminists have been successful in making their fight against sexism precisely because they have offered *evidence* of oppression. Feminists have been successful in making their case against further injury precisely because they have argued against injustices, i.e., offered reasons why such practices must cease. If feminists, in the name of developing a feminist epistemology, give up their commitments to the same criteria for evidence and methods of reasoning that have taken them this far, they will not only lose the ground they have gained, they will implode. Without commitments to objectivity and reason, one is well within her rights to view evidence of sexist practices as evidence *only* for feminists, to view women's rational claims for justice and power as, dare I say, hysterical.

In the final analysis, feminist epistemology is neither feminist nor epistemic. Theoretically, it cannot help to develop a viable theory of knowledge; practically, it cannot help to empower women.

Feminist epistemologists must believe in the phoenix. They must believe they can continue to cast classical epistemology onto the pyre and that something peculiarly feminist and epistemic will arise from the ashes. Unfortunately, the fire has caused all that is feminist and epistemic to go up in smoke.

Summary

The feminist critics discussed above have not been able to make their case against classical epistemology. Insofar as feminist epistemologists have viewed the concept of 'reason' or 'rationality' as being committed to certainty, they have built a straw account. Insofar as they claim to have evidence, psychoanalytic and historical, that 'reason' is a male-biased notion, their case is both inconclusive and dependent on the very point that it is being used to substantiate, that epistemology is essentially male-biased.

In addition, it seems the very act of repudiating classical epistemology—with its commitment to logical consistency and an unbiased account of evidence—leaves the feminists standing on shaky ground. They cannot seriously criticize the classical accounts (without being charged with self-refutation), nor can they, minus a foundation, begin to build their own feminist accounts.

Notes

1. Lorraine Code, *What Can She Know? Feminist Theory and the Construction of Knowledge* (Ithaca, N.Y.: Cornell University Press, 1991), pp. ix–x.

2. Empirically speaking, which is outside the scope of this book, Gilligan has been seriously discredited by Carol Tavris, *The Mismeasure of Women* (New York: Simon and Schuster, 1992).

3. The moral superiority of women is sometimes assumed to be what Gilligan really intended to demonstrate. Furthermore, it is important to note that one could *both* deny Gilligan's *way* of delegitimizing the evidence—via its underlying methodology—and still show that the evidence is illegitimate, i.e., empirically unsound.

4. Carol Gilligan, *In a Different Voice* (Cambridge, Mass.: Harvard University Press, 1982), p. 173. (There are 174 pages in the book.)

5. See note 3.

6. Jane Duran, *Toward a Feminist Epistemology* (Savage, Md.: Rowman and Littlefield, 1991), p. 88.

7. Lorraine Code, *What Can She Know? Feminist Theory and the Construction of Knowledge* (Ithaca, N.Y.: Cornell University Press, 1991), p. 110.

8. Duran, *Toward a Feminist Epistemology*, p. 25.

9. See, e.g., the articulation by Rosemary Tong, *Feminine and Feminist Ethics* (Belmont, Calif.: Wadsworth), p. 70, and Alison M. Jaggar, "How Can Philosophy Be Feminist?" *APA Newsletter on Feminism* (April 1988): 6.

10. Genevieve Lloyd, *The Man of Reason* (London: Methuen, 1984), p. 2.

11. "It is worth remarking on the fact that one of the feminist criticisms of masculinist thought has frequently been its tendency to think in dichotomies; the very setup of these theoretical dyads is already androcentric." Duran, *Toward a Feminist Epistemology*, p. 107.

12. Alison M. Jaggar, *Feminist Politics and Human Nature* (Totowa, N.J.: Rowman and Allenheld, 1983), p. 163.

13. Code, *What Can She Know?* p. 4.

14. Duran, *Toward a Feminist Epistemology*, p. 254.

15. Ibid., p. 108.

16. Sneja Gunew, "Feminist Knowledge: Critique and Construct," in *Feminist Knowledge: Critique and Construct*, ed. S. Gunew (New York: Routledge, 1990), p. 25.

17. Ibid.

18. Myra Jehlen, "Archimedes and the Paradox of Feminist Criticism," in *The Signs Reader: Women, Gender and Scholarship*, ed. E. Abel and E. K. Abel (Chicago: University of Chicago Press, 1983), p. 70.

19. I realize that feminist critics of rationality are now backpedaling, claiming that they had no desire to repudiate logic and evidence. There are two problems with this, however. One is that if this is not what they are doing then I see little that is new or provocative. The other problem is their incendiary comments to the contrary. These points are developed further below.

20. Paul Feyerabend, *Against Method* (London: Verso, 1975).

21. Paul Feyerabend, *Farewell to Reason* (New York: Verso, 1987).

22. See, e.g., Lloyd, *Man of Reason*, pp. 18–22, and Nancy Tuana, Review of *Sex and Inquiry*, edited by Sandra Harding and J. F. O'Barr, *APA Newsletter on Feminism* 89, no. 2 (1990): 114.

23. Code, *What Can She Know?* p. 5. See also, Rosie Braidotti, "Feminisim and Modernity," *Free Inquiry* 15, no. 2 (Spring 1995): 24–28.

24. See, e.g., Jaegwon Kim, "What Is Naturalized Epistemology?" and Harvey Siegel, "What Is the Question Concerning the Rationality of Science?" *Philosophy of Science* 52 (1985): 517–37.

25. Stephen Toulmin, "The Construal of Reality: Criticism in Modern and

Postmodern Science," in *The Politics of Interpretation,* ed. W.J.T. Mitchell (Chicago: University of Chicago Press, 1983), p. 103.

26. Susan Bordo, *The Flight to Objectivity* (Albany: State University of New York Press, 1987), and "The View from Nowhere and the Dream of Everywhere: Heterogeneity, Adequation and Feminist Theory," *APA Newsletter* 88, no. 2 (1989): 19–25.

27. Dorothy Dinnerstein, *The Mermaid and the Minotaur: Sexual Arrangements and Human Malaise* (New York: Harper and Row, 1977).

28. Jane Flax, "The Conflict between Nurturance and Autonomy in Mother-Daughter Relationships and within Feminism," in *Women and Mental Health,* ed. E. Howell and M. Bayes (New York: Basic Books, 1981), pp. 51–69, and "Political Philosophy and the Patriarchal Unconscious: A Psychoanalytic Perspective on Epistemology and Metaphysics," in *Discovering Reality: Feminist Perspectives on Epistemology, Metaphysics, Methodology and the Philosophy of Science,* ed. Sandra Harding and Merrill Hintikka (Dordrecht, Holland: D. Reidel Publishing, Co., 1983), pp. 245–81.

29. Evelyn Fox Keller, *Reflections on Science and Gender* (New Haven, Conn.: Yale University Press, 1985), and "Feminism and Science," in *Women, Knowledge and Reality,* ed. A. Garry and M. Pearsall (London: Unwin Hyman, 1984), pp. 175–88.

30. Keller, *Reflections on Science and Gender,* p. 73.

31. Susan Bordo, "The Cartesian Masculinization of Thought," in *Sex and Scientific Inquiry,* ed. S. Harding and J. F. O'Barr, pp. 247–64.

32. Code, *What Can She Know?* pp. 50–51.

33. Duran, *Toward a Feminist Epistemology,* p. 90.

34. Nancy J. Holland, *Is Woman's Philosophy Possible?* (Savage, Md.: Rowman and Littlefield, 1990), p. 53.

35. Ibid.

36. Bordo, "Cartesian Masculinization," pp. 260–61.

37. Karen J. Warren, "Male-Gender Bias and Western Conceptions of Reasons and Rationality," *APA Newsletter* 8, no. 2 (1989): 48–53.

38. John Chandler, "Feminism and Epistemology," *Metaphilosophy* 21, no. 4 (1990): 372, 377.

39. Bordo, "View from Nowhere," p. 21.

40. Mary E. Hawkesworth, "Knowers, Knowing, Known: Feminist Theory and Claims of Truth," *Signs* 14, no. 3 (1989): 556.

41. Warren, "Male-Gender Bias," p. 49, quoting Lloyd, *Man of Reason,* p. 2.

42. Code, *What Can She Know?* p. 118.

43. Ruth Ginzberg, "Feminism, Rationality and Logic," *APA Newsletter* 88, no. 2 (1989): 35.

44. It has been pointed out that even if *Lloyd* did not demonstrate the sexism inherent in the philosophical corpus on reason, there is "plenty of historical evidence for it in literature and philosophy," appealing to Schopenhauer, Kierkegaard, and Nietzsche. I challenge this. If such textual evidence were so available and obvious,

Lloyd would have chosen it. Given that along with the usual cast of characters—Plato, Descartes, and Hegel—she chose to spend a chapter on Philo, I believe she did the best she could given the history. My claim, below, is that it just wasn't good enough.

45. See, for example, Moira Gatens, *Feminism and Philosophy: Perspectives on Difference and Equality* (Indianapolis: Indiana University Press, 1991); Jean Grimshaw, *Philosophy and Feminist Thinking* (Minneapolis: University of Minnesota Press, 1986); Elizabeth Grosz, "Philosophy," in *Feminist Knowledge: Critique and Construct*, ed. Sneja Gunew (New York: Routledge, 1990); Lorraine Code, "Taking Subjectivity into Account," in *Feminist Epistemologies*, ed. L. Alcoff and E. Potter (London: Routledge, 1993), and *What Can She Know?*; Margaret Atherton, "Cartesian Reason and Gendered Reason," in *A Mind of One's Own: Feminist Essays on Reason and Objectivity*, ed. L. Antony and C. Witt (Boulder, Colo.: Westview Press, 1993).

46. Lloyd, *Man of Reason*, p. ix.

47. Ibid.

48. Ibid. (1st ed.), p. x.

49. Ibid., pp. 37, 108.

50. The lack of male-bias in Plato has been demonstrated by many feminists since then. See, e.g., Patricia Ward Scaltsas, "Is There Time to Be Equal? Plato's Feminism," *APA Newsletter* 90, no. 1 (1990): 108–10.

51. Lloyd, *Man of Reason*, p. 48.

52. Ibid., p. 67.

53. Ibid., p. viii.

54. Ibid., p. 109.

55. See the list of authors and works in note 46.

56. Gatens, *Feminism and Philosophy*, pp. 94–95.

57. Warren, "Male-Gender Bias," p. 49, and Code, *What Can She Know?* p. 118.

58. Lloyd, *Man of Reason*, p. x.

59. Ibid., p. 104.

60. Holland, *Is Woman's Philosophy Possible?* p. 3.

61. Code, *What Can She Know?* p. x.

62. Warren, "Male-Gender Bias," p. 48.

63. See, e.g., Mary F. Belenky, *Women's Ways of Knowing: The Development of Self, Voice and Mind* (New York: Basic Books, 1986).

64. Sandra Harding, "Responding to Smith's Criticism," *APA Newsletter* 88, no. 3 (1989): 190.

65. Alison M. Jaggar, "How Can Philosophy Be Feminist," *APA Newsletter on Feminism* (April 1988): 7.

66. Ibid.

67. Mostly informal criticism. See also, Rosi Braidotti, "The Nostalgic Trip," *Free Inquiry* 15, no. 4 (Fall 1995): 63–64. I am hoping that this work will finally bring more of these criticisms out of the closet and into print.

68. Both Derrida and Rorty make claims about the illegitimacy and even perniciousness of classical accounts of rationality and reason.

3

The Relativism Question in Feminism

Man is the measure of all things; of the things that are, that they are; of the things that are not, that they are not.

Protagoras[1]

Given the flavor of the feminist critiques of classical epistemology discussed (and rejected) in chapter 2—their disdain for its history and their caricature of its contemporary epistemic goals—criticism has arisen centering on the problem of relativism.* In addition, given that few feminists have yet to do anything more than attempt to dismantle the 2,500 years of philosophical work hallmarking epistemology, many critics have claimed that all accounts of feminist philosophy, specifically those accounts which center around critiques of science and epistemology, embrace some commitment to relativism. In light of the logical and pragmatic problems of relativism, most philosophers, even those sympathetic

---

*Broadly defined, 'relativism' is the philosophical position which maintains, at some level or other, that 'there are no absolute truths'. A "full-blooded relativism eschews the very idea of an uninterpreted reality that is as it is independently of us or some scheme of understanding." Ted Honderich, ed., *The Oxford Companion to Philosophy* (New York: Oxford University Press, 1995), pp. 757–58.

to the political goals of feminism, find this repercussion, and therefore feminist philosophy itself, undesirable.

Though such criticism could have been viewed as "backlash," good faith attempts have been made by many feminist philosophers to show that feminist epistemologies are *not*, in the final analysis, committed to relativism.

Nonetheless, in this chapter I will argue that the main attempt to avoid the charge of relativism, given by Harding and Code, have been unsuccessful. Although both have tried to develop middle-ground positions between the absolutism of the always oppressive "supremely powerful and privileged"[2] Western white male philosophers and the "quietism of extreme relativism,"[3] neither has succeeded.

Words Are Unnecessary

It is clear that feminists should avoid relativism. First, there are the logical difficulties. Relativism, at least negatively, maintains the philosophical position that "There are no absolute truths." This claim is either incoherent or inconsistent. That is, if the claim is maintained as *absolutely* true, then it is false (for there would always be at least one absolute truth, namely the claim itself); if it is held to be only *relatively* true, then one is within her rights to hold the claim that "There are absolute truths," simultaneously, as also (relatively) true. The upshot is that the relativist, at some level, rejects the law of noncontradiction—that some claim and its opposite can both be true.

Of course feminist defenders of relativism may find this move to be nothing more than logical legerdemain. First of all, they could challenge the notion of an *absolute*—absolute truth—the desire for the immutable and indubitable—precisely what their critiques (discussed in chapters 1 and 2) have been challenging all along. Furthermore, they could retort by saying that relativism is not to be understood in only its Protagorean guise (one believer per belief), but in its richer form, via conceptual schemes. That is, "relativism is usually understood as the claim that standards, rules, principles, ideals . . . for acceptability of a belief lack validity outside some limited, suitable context."[4] In this specific case, relativized claims need to be taken within the context of women's ways of knowing, or the empowerment of women. Therefore, feminist relativists could claim that such logical prestidigitations, like the one above, hold no critical weight. Their truths are as absolute as they come, i.e., true intersubjectively.

Unfortunately, if feminist critics of science and epistemology believe that feminist philosophy is to be approached, simultaneously, as a philosophical and a political position, they will not be able to dismiss the pragmatic effects of an intersubjective absolutism so easily. That is, if intersubjective truth is the best absolute to be had, then men already have it. What has passed for absolute all along has been those truths relativized to all believers who are members of the relevant group, and 'relevant group' has been defined, at least according to the feminists discussed above, biasedly. To embrace a relativism that is really not relativistic, i.e., intersubjectively absolute (e.g., all of the "truths" of science and logic), would require falling back from every critique and comment leveled against traditional science and classical epistemology. Thus, my criticisms, and this discussion, would simply end here.

Feminist philosophical literature, however, does not, in fact, allow such an ending. The debate rages on. Despite protestations to the contrary,[5] real relativism (which must be maintained at a more interesting level than intersubjective absolutism) must, to some degree, be embraced by feminists critical of traditional science and classical epistemology.

Even in its strongest form, however, real "relativism is the basic conviction that when we turn to the examination of those concepts that philosophers have taken to be the most fundamental . . . we are forced to recognize that in the final analysis all such concepts must be understood as relative to a specific conceptual scheme, theoretical framework, paradigm, form of life, society, or culture."[6] That is, even in this guise of relativism—which embraces the idea that 'Truth is always relative to one's conceptual scheme or "social world"[7] (often determined, for example, by one's cultural heritage, race, sex, political agenda, etc.)'—feminist criticisms and ideologies lead to difficulties.

As one self-critical feminist, Claudia Murphy,[8] has pointed out:

> relativism is unacceptable because feminism is not only an epistemology but also a political ideology. Most feminists abhor the idea that one can take

isolated philosophical positions. They believe that one's philosophy is to be lived. And relativism is politically and morally repugnant. To the man who wants to treat me as an object which he owns I will not simply say "Well, that's your view." Both views can not peacefully coexist.

More specifically, relativism is unacceptable because feminists want a standpoint from which they can criticize the dominant view. . . . Feminists want to be able to argue that this view is wrong; and not just politically incorrect or emotionally upsetting but false.[9]

Murphy's point can, I think, be best represented by an example of the "need for a feminist ethic" presented by Rosemary Tong:

The ontological jolt that opened my eyes to the need for a feminist approach to ethics came unexpectedly, through discussion of Akira Kurosawa's film *Rashomon.* In this story a husband and wife traveling through the forest are attacked: The husband is killed, the wife raped. Through a series of flashbacks, the director shows us four people's different perspectives on the event. What struck me in all four versions of the story was how the woman, not the assailant, ended up being blamed or reviled for the tragedy. The bandit recounts the classic male fantasy of rape: She fought at first, but once he started she loved it. He fights her husband in hope of "winning" her as a prize. Yet when she runs away, he forgets her, because he feels no attraction to a cowardly woman. He declares to the police that she was not worth chasing. The wife claims that after the rape the bandit left her crying on the forest floor. When she looked to her husband for compassion, she found only hatred and contempt in his eyes. She begged him to kill her, to do anything but look at her with those eyes. He remained stonily silent, and she fainted. Clearly, he blamed her for the rape. The dead husband, speaking through a medium, testifies that his wife agreed to run away with the bandit after he took advantage of her. Indeed, she asked the bandit to kill her husband, as she could not go with him while her spouse lived. The rapist, disgusted by such womanish "treachery," tells her husband that he will kill or spare her, as the injured husband sees fit. The criminal is all too ready to punish the victim. The final version of the story comes from a witness, a firewood gatherer who stumbled on the scene while walking through the woods. On his account, the bandit first tried to gain the woman's love and promise of marriage but ultimately rejected her after her husband called her a "shameless whore" and refused to fight for her. After all, if rape is seen as a power struggle between men, and the husband refuses to risk death for the woman, he takes all the adventure out of it!

For me, the different stories only showed that no matter what a woman does before, during, or after a rape, in patriarchal society she will often be

blamed for her own victimization. I saw *Rashomon* as a movie about the
horror of rape and the powerlessness of women. While talking with a male
colleague, however, he mentioned to me that he used *Rashomon* in his philosophy class to demonstrate the fluid nature of truth. Just as in a court of
law different witnesses tell different stories, the director masterfully shows
us how different truths are seen with different eyes. The facts of the case
forever elude us. Objectivity is continually melting into subjectivity. What
my male friend apparently did not see, however, was the event that the observers actually *saw*: They witnessed or participated in a *rape*. Enamored
with the beauty of the myriad nature of abstract truth, he was oblivious to
the horror of the concrete event of the young woman's rape. Indeed, he told
me that it did not matter what the film was about. It could be about anything provided that it let his class discuss the differences between reality
and interpretation. In a moment of shock I realized that whereas I, as a
woman, thought the film was about rape, he, as a man, thought the film was
about truth. From then on I believed in the necessity of developing feminist approaches to ethics.[10]

The need for a feminist ethic aside, the real problem is that despite there
having been an *objectively verifiable rape*, Tong's male colleague, being a
committed relativist, had no commitment to there being this kind of fact-
of-the-matter. Since there was only "the fluid nature of truth" to be had,
what was a rape for Tong was not a rape for her male colleague.

Embracing relativism would mean that it would be both impossible
for women to resist, or for feminists to argue against, oppression by men.
One could, at best, pray for suffrage and preach to the (biologically) con-
verted.

That Voice Again

It is not odd, therefore, that the feminist epistemological corpus is strewn
with comments condemning relativism. For example: Genevieve Lloyd
wants to make it clear that simply by bringing "to the surface the implicit
maleness of our ideals of Reason is not necessarily to adopt a 'sexual relativism' about rational belief and truth."[11] Lorraine Code recognizes that
politically speaking, "feminists could not opt for an absolute relativism
that recognized no facts of the matter—no objective, external reality—but

only my, your, or our negotiated reality."[12] Helen Longino claims that her approach to feminist epistemology "is not a relativistic position."[13] Lynn Hankinson Nelson, in developing her Quinian account of feminist epistemology, argues that "relativism is unwarranted . . . that alternative epistemologies that are relativistic are inadequate—not just for reasons we would normally construe as political, but also for reasons that are clearly epistemological."[14] Elizabeth Grosz wants to make it clear that her account is not "affirming a relativism that asserts the equal value of all theories and all positions or perspectives."[15] Kathryn Pyne Addelson stresses that her feminist account of epistemology does not entail "that all is relativism and incommensurability, a whir of rhetoric signifying nothing."[16] And, finally, Sandra Harding claims that "judgmental (or epistemological) relativism is anathema to any scientific project, and feminist ones are no exception."[17]

Feminist epistemologists, rightly so, it seems, do not want to embrace relativism. Unfortunately, what feminists desire and what actually follows from their epistemic commitments are two distinct things.

Roads to Relativism

THE STRAIGHTFORWARD PATH

There are a number of ways an epistemological position can advance relativism. The most straightforward of these is to include in the position the belief that "there are no absolute truths." Another way, almost as straightforward, is to embrace the idea that "truth is always relative to one's conceptual scheme or social world (often determined, for example, by one's cultural heritage, race, sex, political agenda, etc.)." Certain feminists have committed themselves in print to both.

For instance, Lorraine Code has stated that "there is no transcendent vantage point from which, and no absolute standard by which, such judgments [e.g., epistemic competence] can be made."[18] Lynn Hankinson Nelson claims that it is "communities that construct and acquire knowledge"[19] which reflects the view that knowledge, standards of evidence, and methodologies are "of our making . . . and that these are constructed in the contexts of our various projects and practices and evolve in response to the latter and experience."[20] Linda Alcoff and Elizabeth Potter claim that what has motivated much of the work in feminist epistemology has been "skepticism about the possibility of a general or universal account of the nature and limits of knowledge, an account that ignores the social context and status of knowers . . . the impact of the social status as well as the sexed body of the knower upon the production of knowledge."[21]

The above quotations demonstrate the commitment of many feminists to the belief that "there are no absolute truths" and/or the belief that "truth is always relative to one's conceptual scheme or social world (often determined, for example, by one's cultural heritage, race, sex, political agenda, etc.)." Clearly those words are telling of the commitment by these feminists, whether they like it or not, to relativism.

MIDDLE-GROUND POSITIONS

What do the feminists want? Why is it that on the one hand they repudiate relativism and on the other they express their epistemological theories in ways that seem to embrace it? The truth is they are attempting to create a middle-ground position. Though Code is one of the proponents of a middle-ground position, ironically she claims that a "middle ground has no place for absolutes, relativist or otherwise."[22]

Despite such warnings, however, feminists sensitive to the above dilemma have attempted to develop a middle ground that, on the one hand, claims that there "is no single, transcendental standard for deciding between competing knowledge claims,"[23] and on the other, that "all knowledge attempts are socially situated."[24] (As middle-ground developers par excellence, some feminists believe that "some of these objective social locations are better than others as starting points for knowledge projects."[25])

Lorraine Code and "Mitigated" Relativism

According to Code, "The claim for relativism acknowledges the different perspectives; the claim that it needs to be mitigated indicates that there is something there, in the world, to be known and acted upon; hence, to constrain possibilities of understanding. . . . Such a relativism would assert the perspectival nature of knowledge *and* its associations with human purposes. Yet it would argue that it is possible to evaluate perspectives and purposes."[26] Although sympathetic to what she is trying to do, I see no way that such a position can be maintained. Either you believe that one can adjudicate between competing theses, at all levels of inquiry, or you do not. If you believe you can, then you are not a relativist; if you believe you cannot (because there is no thesis-independent position to make such a judgment), then you are a relativist. There is no middle ground.

Therefore, Code's attempt to "evaluate perspectives" requires what she denies: a nonperspectival evaluative stance.

Realism and Relativism

One way Code tries to defend her position is to show that "an endorsement of relativism is not tantamount to a denial of realism";[27] "that realism and relativism are by no means incompatible."[28] Although this may be true, I am at a loss how this helps her to develop her "hybrid breed of relativism."[29]

For Code, 'realism' is defined simply as the naive position that the world exists independently of us and is what it is, "a reality that is recalcitrant to inattentive or whimsical structurings."[30] Code embraces the idea that there is some fact of the matter, some "empirical-realist core that can negotiate the fixities and less stable constructs of the physical-social world."[31] This holds true whether the topic of discussion is sexism or tables and chairs.[32]

Now although it is clear that this general philosophical orientation is consistent with relativism, it is just as clear that it is consistent with skepticism (that if there is a mind-independent reality we can never know it) and absolutism (there is a mind independent of reality and we can get to know it). What determines one's epistemological position with respect to relativism is completely independent of the quasi-metaphysical position one takes toward reality. Being committed to naive realism neither hurts nor helps Code's case for a "mitigated" relativism.

The question that Code really needs to answer is not whether she believes there is a mind-independent reality, but whether or not she believes we can have knowledge of it and, if so, whether a best description exists.

Ultimately, Code must decide whether there could be such a thing as a "best" description. If she says such a description is in principle possible, whether or not we ever acquire it, then she is an absolutist; if she says that there is no way to make this kind of determination, no absolute value to be had, no way of adjudicating the goodness of any one story, then she is just another garden-variety relativist.

Subjectivity and Relativism

Another way that Code attempts to steer her middle-ground course is to show that not all versions of relativism are committed to subjectivism. She then repudiates "radical subjectivism"[33]—"a position for which knowledge claims are indistinguishable from expressions of personal opinion, taste, or bias"[34]—while maintaining a commitment to her "mitigated" relativism.

Again, this distinction is of little use in determining Code's commitment to relativism. For one thing, not all relativistic claims are committed to subjectivism, even in the way the concept is understood by Code. Under her account subjective claims are just one small subset of a larger set which contains all relativist claims. Relativist claims may vary in scope from, for example, all human beings to just me. Code has equated subjectivism with what has come to be known as Protagorean Relativism and has then claimed that although relativism embraces Protagorean Relativism, "mitigated" relativism need not. Although this may be true once again, it does not help to distinguish Code's relativism from much of what is called relativism proper.

It may be important to add that Code's understanding of subjectivism is far too narrow. There are at least some nonrelativist philosophers who maintain a commitment to subjectivism. For example, one could claim that just as there are empirically observable, externally verifiable facts of the matter there are also empirically observable facts of the matter that are not *externally verifiable* (e.g., my pain sensation right now). When talking about such "facts" (e.g., meanings[35] or seemings), it is important to recognize that simply because they are observable to only one person, the person experiencing them, this does not diminish their epistemic status in the way that relativism does. My account of my seeming may only be true for me, but this is a trivial sense of "true for me." What this really means is that it is true, but I just happen to be the only one who can access this fact of the matter.

Code is right that relativism is not committed to subjectivism and, interestingly, the opposite is true as well. She is not correct, however, that this demonstration aids her in the attempt to develop a middle ground.

The Relativism/Absolutism Dichotomy

In her most recent work[36] Code attempts to defend her "mitigated" relativism by claiming that "the relativism that my argument generates is sufficiently nuanced and sophisticated to escape the scorn—and the anxiety—that 'relativism, after all' usually occasions. To begin with, it refuses to occupy the negative side of the traditional absolutism/relativism dichotomy . . . the absolutism/relativism dichotomy needs to be displaced because it does not, as a true dichotomy must, use up all the alternatives."[37] In other words, Code claims to have developed a new form of relativism because, as she describes it, it cannot be anatomically defined in terms of the traditional concept of absolutism.

This is problematic. It may be that her definition of relativism cannot be juxtaposed to *her* definition of absolutism, but this is more a consequence of the way she has mischaracterized the latter, not the way she has finessed the former. This becomes clear when one looks at Code's description of mainstream epistemology. She claims that it has, as its main assumption, the belief "that there can be a single, monolithic philosophy that yields access to the Truth, and that all rival discourses should be dismissed or suppressed as diversions from the true path"[38] and that its absolutist inclinations have "affirmed a certainty that was never rightly [its]."[39]

There is nothing to say here except that Code has classical epistemology all wrong. As I read the corpus it is concerned with justified beliefs, but never in a way that insists on one and only one path, the infallibility of its findings, or the use of fascist politics.

The "Mitigated" Position Restated

In the final analysis, Code makes the following claims: "The position I am advocating is one for which knowledge is always *relative to* (i.e., a perspective *on*, a standpoint *in*) specifiable circumstances . . . [which, in turn are] specified *relative to* other circumstances, prejudgments, and theories."[40] In other words, she is a relativist through and through.

Sandra Harding and "Sociological" Relativism

The Old Harding

In *The Science Question in Feminism* Sandra Harding objected to critics who claimed that in her attempt to unbiasedly defend the taking of what she calls a "feminist standpoint," her arguments have led her down the path to relativism. What Harding means by "feminist standpoint theory" will be discussed below. For now it is important to note that Harding answered the objection by stating the "leap to relativism misgrasps feminist projects"[41] and tried to show that

> feminist inquirers are never saying that sexist and antisexist claims are equally plausible—that it is equally plausible to regard women's situation as primarily biological *and* as primarily social, or to regard 'the human' both as identical *and* nonidentical with 'the masculine'. The evidence for feminist vs. nonfeminist claims may be inconclusive in some cases, and many feminist claims that today appear evidentially secure will no doubt be abandoned as additional evidence is gathered and better hypotheses and concepts are constructed. Indeed, there should be no doubt that these normal conditions of research hold for many feminist claims. But agnosticism and the recognition of the hypothetical character of all scientific claims are quite different epistemological stances from relativism. Moreover, whether or not feminists take a relativistic stance, it is hard to imagine a coherent defense of cognitive relativism when one thinks of the conflicting claims.[42]

What exactly is her point? Harding may have been making one of three separate claims.

1. Agnosticism Is Not Relativism

First, if one believes that sexist and antisexist standpoints are equally plausible, then one is not necessarily committed to being a relativist. I agree, but this does not help her case; such a position is both compatible with relativism and clearly stated to be what she denies.

Agnosticism is compatible with relativism. The determination of whether one is committed to relativism is a consequence of *why* someone maintains an agnostic position. If the position is maintained because both claims are supported by the evidence equally well, this makes the position compatible with absolutism. Absolutists often maintain positions of agnosticism—a position of equal support of two (even two logically incompatible theories) pending further evidence. It may be that although one believes that not both positions are correct (which may simply be a recognition of the law of noncontradiction), at this time they are unable to rationally choose.

If, on the other hand, one claims that both sexism and antisexism are equally plausible positions, not because the evidence for both is equally pressing, but because they believe there is no objective stance from which to adjudicate the legitimacy of the two positions, then one is committed to relativism.

But given that Harding clearly refuses to embrace the relativism full-blown, and given that a serious agnosticism might land her on the side of the sexists (something which would put her at odds with her own project), it is not clear what work her retreat to agnosticism really does. Sooner or later, in the light of evidence,[43] she will have to take a stand for[44] or (given unfortunate evidence) against her standpoint, or retreat to relativism. Theoretically, of course, she can ride the agnostic fence indefinitely; but politically speaking, she will eventually have to come down on one side or the other.

2. Hypothetical Nature Is Not Relativism

It is not clear what Harding means when she says that feminists are not relativists, that they simply recognize the hypothetical character of scientific claims. Does this mean she believes scientific claims are only conjectures, postulates, or merely contingently true? Well, good, so do all traditional scientists and classical epistemologists. Does it mean one avoids relativism by denying that scientific claims are ever wrong? It depends on what one means by 'wrong'. Does 'wrong' mean really wrong, or only relatively wrong? If the former, then feminists are not, ultimately, committed to relativism; if the latter, however, then they are, whether they like it or not.

3. Relativism Is Untenable

Perhaps all Harding is saying is that the feminist position cannot be equated with relativism, because "it is hard to imagine a coherent defense of cognitive relativism."[45] But to claim that feminists could not be committed to relativism because relativism is an untenable position is merely a case of wishful thinking. It may be that feminist philosophy of science and epistemology, due to its inherent commitment to relativism, is just incapable of defense.

The New Harding

In her recent work, however, Harding no longer attempts to show that feminism is not committed to relativism. Her tack is to claim, proudly, that feminism is committed to relativism, though only to historical/sociological/cultural (HSC) relativism, not to what she has dubbed "judgmental relativism."

By distinguishing judgmental relativism—"an epistemological relativism that denies the possibility of any reasonable standards for adjudicating between competing claims"[46]—from (HSC) relativism, Harding hopes to both embrace some form of relativism and yet avoid its logical and pragmatic pitfalls.

HSC Relativism Is Not Epistemological

Unfortunately, HSC relativism, the way it is presented by Harding, is simply not interesting enough to maintain itself as a real relativism. She says: "respect for historical (or sociological or cultural) relativism is always useful in starting one's thinking. Different social groups tend to have different patterns of practice and belief and different standards for judging them; these practices, beliefs, and standards can be explained by different historical interests, values, and agendas."[47]

This "respect for" relativism, however, can do no explanatory work, for it is not an epistemological account at all; it is merely a descriptive account of individuals or societies, what is often called 'cultural relativism'. The belief that cultural relativism is true is compatible with the belief that epistemological relativism is false. Furthermore, this is not the belief with which the critics of feminism take issue. The truth (or falsity) of cultural relativism is a purely empirical matter. It is the philosophically provocative thesis—that there is no way to adjudicate between the beliefs of different individuals, cultures, etc.—in which epistemologists are interested. Unfortunately for Harding, once her position on HSC relativism becomes epistemically relativistic enough to become philosophically interesting it cannot be distinguished from what she calls "judgmental relativism" and, therefore, is susceptible to all of its problems.

Harding Is Not Really a Relativist

Perhaps Harding wants to avoid judgmental relativism because she is not a relativist at all. She does claim "that not all social values and interests have the same bad effects upon the results of research. Some have systematically generated less partial and distorted beliefs than others—or than purportedly value-free research."[48] If some are not as bad then there must be standards by which to determine which are and which are not. The belief in such standards entails a belief that epistemological relativism is false.

It seems that HSC relativism, according to Harding, "does not commit one to the further epistemological claim that there are therefore no rational or scientific grounds for making judgments between various patterns of belief and their originating social practices, values, and consequences"[49] because HSC relativism is not a form of epistemological relativism at all. In the final analysis, HSC relativism is Harding's misnomer for her feminist "standpoint epistemology." After all, HSC relativism, according to Harding, is precisely what "standpoint epistemologies call for."[50] Why she bothers to defend relativism at all, since her account does not really need it, is unclear.

Judgmental Relativism Is Not a Problem

The best answer is that Harding, though she does not want to be saddled with the problems of relativism, wants even more to avoid being slapped with the charge of dogmatic absolutism. If a "feminist standpoint" is not a form of relativism—where any standpoint is as good as any other—then it must be that some standpoints are better than others. Of course at this juncture Harding will have to say which standpoint is best and defend her decision.

Without the screen of relativism, and given the impetus for feminism—the critiques of traditional science and classical epistemology—Harding will have to defend the claim that a feminist epistemological standpoint is best. Without such a defense her position is just as biased as the supposed male-biased positions that motivated feminist standpoint theory to begin with.

This, however, she does not do, at least not directly. Instead, Harding tries to diminuate the philosophical value of the relativism issue itself by undermining its epistemic impact via its historical underpinnings. In a last-ditch effort to maintain the distinction between judgmental and HSC relativisms (while avoiding having to either face the charge of relativism or argue for her standpoint account), Harding claims that the relativism issue itself is just another male plot:

> Historically, relativism appears as a problematic intellectual possibility only for dominating groups at the point where the hegemony of their views is being challenged. Though the recognition that other cultures do, in fact, hold different beliefs, values, and standards of judgment is as old as human history, judgmental relativism emerged as an urgent intellectual issue only in nineteenth-century Europe, with the belated recognition that the apparently bizarre beliefs and behaviors of Others had a rationality and logic of their own. Judgmental relativism is not a problem originating in or justifiable in terms of the lives of marginalized groups. It did not arise in misogynous thought about women; it does not arise from the contrast feminism makes between women's lives and men's. Women do not have the problem of how to accommodate intellectually both the sexist claim that women are inferior in some way or another and the feminist claim that they are not. Here relativism arises as a problem only from the perspective of men's lives. Some men want to appear to acknowledge and accept feminist

arguments without actually giving up any of their conventional androcentric beliefs and the practices that seem to follow so reasonably from such beliefs. "It's all relative, my dear," is a convenient way to try to accomplish these two goals.[51]

One might now ask why Harding bothers discussing (judgmental) relativism at all. Perhaps she feels she has to. After all, "an implicit acceptance of pluralism, if not judgmental relativism—at least at the institutional level—appears to be the only condition under which women's voices and feminist voices, male and female, can be heard."[52] She queries: "Isn't feminism forced to embrace relativism by its condition of being just one among many countercultural voices?"[53]

In other words, Harding was unable to maintain any kind of interesting distinction between HSC relativism and judgmental relativism. In addition, she could not opt for absolutism because this would make her account as of yet unjustified and, given her attack on traditional science and classical epistemology, may be even self-refuting. Her only remaining strategy was to admit that feminist critiques of classical epistemology are committed to relativism and then appeal to the fact that feminists have no other alternative.[54]

The Latest Harding

In her most recent paper[55] Harding attempts to respond to some of the above criticisms and, finally, to defend her standpoint epistemology. Although she still maintains that "standpoint theories argue for 'starting off thought' from the lives of marginalized peoples,"[56] and that "standpoint claims that all knowledge attempts are socially situated,"[57] she nonetheless believes that "standpoint theory does not advocate—nor is it doomed to—relativism."[58]

Can one maintain this position? It depends on how one understands a belief's being "socially situated."

Let us separate three possible senses of the phrase "socially situated" as it applies to knowledge "attempts."

1. All knowledge attempts stem from human beings who are themselves located in some society or other;

2. All knowledge attempts have ramifications for society; and

3. All knowledge attempts are politically or ideologically biased; the acceptance of any belief as knowledge is a function of some prior political or ideological commitment. No independent (i.e., nonpolitical or nonideological) support for any epistemological ideal is possible.[59]

If Harding means sense 3, standpoint epistemology deviates from the tradition, but despite her protestations to the contrary it seriously embraces a full-blown commitment to relativism.

On the other hand, although senses 1 and 2 do not commit one to any interesting form of relativism, they do no work in explaining standpoint epistemology and how it differs from more classical accounts.

Standpoint Epistemology

So what is left of standpoint epistemology once the relativistic wind is taken out of its sails? Sadly, Harding does not tell us herself.

In the beginning, Harding characterized feminist standpoint as an epistemology that

> [grounds] a distinctive feminist science in a theory of gendered activity and social experience. They simultaneously privilege women or feminists (the accounts vary) epistemically and yet also claim to overcome the dichotomizing that is characteristic of Enlightenment/bourgeois world view and its science. It is useful to think of standpoint epistemologies, like the appeals to feminist empiricism, as 'successor science' projects: in significant ways, they aim to reconstruct the original goals of modern science.[60]

It had clearly stated Marxist roots and political aims.[61] But in her later work Harding deviates from these beginnings. In the aftermath of criticisms, there is, sadly, despite the fact that many feminists have claimed to have adopted Harding's feminist standpoint epistemology, no clear statement of what a standpoint epistemology is. It took a critic to actually come up with a succinct account.

I think that Cassandra L. Pinnick[62] is correct when she claims that:

Two basic claims underlie the theory. First, empiricist epistemology is based on the utopian ideal of objective inquiry that, in fact and in principle, impedes scientific progress. . . . Harding's second contention—that feminists, being a "marginalized" social group, offer a better perspective on which to base scientific inquiry.[63]

Given that I have analyzed the first claim extensively in chapter 1, I will now take a look at the second.

The big question which arises is: Is Harding correct? Does a "marginalized" perspective offer a *better* perspective on science (or any knowledge claims for that matter)?

I believe that this thesis can be challenged both as a philosophical and an empirical thesis. It can be challenged as a philosophical thesis insofar as it supports the normative belief that feminist standpoint theories—theories of knowledge which start off with thought from women's lives—are the best epistemological theories. It can also be challenged empirically, for the support for this normative belief stems from what Harding presents as empirical evidence: "starting off research from women's lives will generate illuminating critical questions that do not arise in thought that begins from dominant group lives."[64]

The Empirical Thesis

Looking at the empirical thesis first, it is clear that Harding simply does not see the factual (trees) through the feminist (forest). If she did she would realize that dominant group members *can* generate illuminating critical questions (even about their own group). The evidence for this is that they *do*, citing one of Harding's own examples: John Stuart Mill.[65] If Harding wants to claim there is knowledge accessible to women (or other oppressed people) that is not accessible to men (or those in power), she must answer every counterexample. This she has not done.

Furthermore, if she had this could mean big trouble for women and oppressed cultures. For if such people truly supplied the epistemological community with knowledge unavailable to anyone else, it would paradoxically be the moral duty of every dominant epistemologist to manage their projects while also maintaining some level of oppression. After all, if the knowledge women (as oppressed) have is so important, we must keep them oppressed to maintain the stock.[66]

So now what? Is it true that "there is enough exaggeration in *Whose Science?* to refute the claim that philosophy, science, or critical social theory done from the feminist standpoint is less distorted than mainstream thought"?[67] Do we just lay Harding to rest as a standpoint theorist without a leg to stand on?

Despite quotations to the contrary, there are bits in Harding's work that are less for the feminist standpoint than they are for some notion of equality. I say this because Harding attempts to defend the standpoint valuing of women (or oppressed peoples) by appealing to the good-making properties of democracies. She states that "democracy-advancing values have systematically generated less partial and distorted beliefs than others."[68]

In response, though, it must be noted that this assumed fact of the matter may simply be false. Many democracies have been, and continue to be, racist, elitist, sexist, antienvironmentalist, and so forth. Even countries like the United States, with explicitly democratic values and panels like the review board for the *APA Newsletter on Feminism* (with "genuine community dialogue"[69]), often act first to secure their own political agendas even at the expense of stifling dissident voices.

The Philosophical Thesis

More importantly, however, once Harding retreats to this more moderate empirical position, there is little left that is provocative let alone peculiarly feminist in the original thesis. If the goal of feminist standpoint epistemologies is to achieve an objective stance where "loyalty to femininity as well as to masculinity is to be eliminated through feminist research,"[70] I see little point in pushing her position any further.

Summary

Although Code's attempt to maintain a middle-ground position failed and, in the final analysis, her account is committed to relativism, I must say that she gave this course an honest try. I think her account, although not philosophically satisfactory, nevertheless lends sympathy to the goals of feminists with regard to the difficult epistemological positions in which they have landed themselves.

I do not believe that this is the case with Sandra Harding's account. Harding used relativism as a veil to obscure the fact that her standpoint position remains unjustified. In her attempt to assuage her critics she demonstrates precisely what is wrong with feminist epistemology: it refuses to allow for honest analysis and philosophical critique.

Many feminist roads lead to this untenable position, and those that do not lend little support to the epistemological virtues of feminism. At the very least there is severe tension between feminist epistemology and relativism, a tension that is not likely to go away. Until feminists solve this problem, until they allay the fears of relativism, every epistemologist, especially those sympathetic to the political goals of feminism, should steer clear of feminist epistemologies.

Notes

1. Protagoras, according to Samuel Enoch Stumpf, *From Socrates to Sartre: A History of Philosophy*, 4th ed. (New York: McGraw-Hill, 1988), p. 8.

2. Lorraine Code, "Taking Subjectivity into Account," in *Feminist Epistemologies*, ed. L. Alcoff and E. Potter (New York: Routledge, 1993), p. 40.

3. Lorraine Code, *What Can She Know? Feminist Theory and the Construction of Knowledge* (Ithaca, N.Y.: Cornell University Press, 1991), p. 317.

4. James Bayley, "Introduction," *Aspects of Relativism*, ed. James E. Bayley (Lanham, Md.: University Press of America, 1992), p. 2.

5. Actually the literature bears out that these critics "doth protest too much."

6. J. M. Bernstein, *Beyond Objectivism and Relativism: Science, Hermeneutics and Practice* (Philadelphia: University of Pennsylvania Press, 1983), pp. 4–5.

7. A term coined by Kathryn Pyne Addelson, "Knower/Doers and Their Moral Problems," in *Feminist Epistemologies*, ed. L. Alcoff and E. Potter, pp. 265–94.

8. Claudia Murphy, "Feminist Epistemology and the Question of Relativism," in *Aspects of Relativism*, ed. James E. Bayley.

9. Ibid., p. 135.

10. Rosemary Tong, *Feminine and Feminist Ethics* (Belmont, Calif.: Wadsworth, 1993), pp. 227–28.

11. Genevieve Lloyd, *The Man of Reason* (London: Methuen, 1984), pp. x, 109.

12. Code, *What Can She Know?* p. 319.

13. Helen E. Longino, "Subjects, Power and Knowledge: Description and Prescription in Feminist Philosophies of Science," in *Feminist Epistemologies*, ed. L. Alcoff and E. Potter, p. 113.

14. Lynn Hankinson Nelson, *Who Knows? From Quine to a Feminist Empiricism* (Philadelphia: Temple University Press, 1990), p. 40.

15. Elizabeth Grosz, "Bodies and Knowledge: Feminism and the Crisis of Reason," in *Feminist Epistemologies*, ed. L. Alcoff and E. Potter, p. 194.

16. Addelson, "Knower/Doers," p. 287.

17. Sandra Harding, "Rethinking Standpoint Epistemology: What Is Strong Objectivity?" in *Feminist Epistemologies*, ed. L. Alcoff and E. Potter, p. 61.

18. Lorraine Code, "The Impact of Feminism on Epistemology," *APA Newsletter* 88, no. 2 (1989): 28.

19. Lynn Hankinson Nelson, "Epistemological Communities," in *Feminist Epistemologies*, ed. L. Alcoff and E. Potter, p. 123.

20. Ibid., p. 141.

21. Linda Alcoff and Elizabeth Potter, "Introduction: When Feminism Intersects Epistemology," in *Feminist Epistemologies*, ed. L. Alcoff and E. Potter, p. 1.

22. Code, *What Can She Know?* p. 319.

23. Harding, "Rethinking Standpoint Epistemology," p. 61.

24. Ibid., p. 56.

25. Ibid.

26. Code, "Impact of Feminism," p. 27.

27. Ibid., p. 28.

28. Code, "Taking Subjectivity," p. 21.

29. Ibid., pp. 20–21.

30. Code, *What Can She Know?* p. 255.

31. Code, "Taking Subjectivity," p. 21.

32. Code, "Impact of Feminism," p. 28.

33. Code, *What Can She Know?* pp. 43–44.

34. Ibid., p. 3.

35. See, for example, John Searle, "Indeterminacy, Empiricism, and the First Person," *Journal of Philosophy* 84 (1987): 123–46.

36. Code, "Taking Subjectivity."

37. Ibid., pp. 39–40.

38. Code, *What Can She Know?* pp. 305–306.

39. Code, "Taking Subjectivity," p. 40.

40. Ibid.

41. Sandra Harding, *The Science Question in Feminism* (Ithaca, N.Y.: Cornell University Press, 1986), p. 138, n.7.

42. Ibid., p. 27.

43. Given the discussion of the unorthodox concept of objectivity that Harding holds in chapter 1, what could count as evidence is also problematic here.

44. It is important to point out that the relativism arises in Harding's standpoint theory precisely because she found it difficult to non-question-beggingly defend it. More will be said about this below.

45. Harding, *Science Question*, p. 27, n.7.

46. Sandra Harding, *Whose Science? Whose Knowledge? Thinking from Women's Lives* (Ithaca, N.Y.: Cornell University Press, 1991), p. 139.

47. Harding, "Rethinking Standpoint Epistemology," p. 152.

48. Harding, *Whose Science?* p. 144.

49. Ibid., p. 152.

50. Ibid., p. 142.

51. Ibid., pp. 153–54.

52. Ibid., p. 155.

53. Ibid.

54. A similar "tension" has been pointed out by Margareta Halberg, "Feminist Epistemology: An Impossible Project?" *Radical Philosophy* 53 (1989): 3–7.

55. Harding, "Rethinking Standpoint Epistemology."

56. Ibid., p. 56.

57. Ibid.

58. Ibid., p. 61.

59. This is a reformulated version of a similar criticism leveled against the charge that all educational ideals are political by Harvey Siegel, *Educating Reason* (New York: Routledge, 1988), p. 69.

60. Harding, *Science Question*, pp. 141–42.

61. This is made clear by Harding and other feminists, see, for example, Nancy C. M. Harstock, "The Feminist Standpoint: Developing the Ground for a Specifically Feminist Historical Materialism," in *Feminism and Philosophy: Essential Readings in Theory, Reinterpretation, and Application,* ed. Nancy Tuana and Rosemary Tong (Boulder, Colo.: Westview Press, 1995).

62. Cassandra L. Pinnick, "Feminist Epistemology: Implications for Philosophy of Science," *Philosophy of Science* 61 (1994): 646–57.

63. Ibid., pp. 649–50.

64. Harding, "Rethinking Standpoint Epistemology," p. 56.

65. John Stuart Mill, *The Subjection of Women* (1869).

66. This point was first brought to my attention at the Thirty-ninth Annual Conference of the Florida Philosophical Association by an undergraduate student of mine named Donald Barber.

67. Alan Soble, Review of *Whose Science? Whose Knowledge? Thinking from Women's Lives* by Sandra Harding, *International Studies in Philosophy of Science* 6, no. 2 (1992): 162.

68. Harding, "Rethinking Standpoint Epistemology," p. 71.

69. Ibid., p. 71, n.52.

70. Ibid., p. 74.

4

Feminism and Naturalism

What is so seductive about biological explanations is that they seem to
smell of material reality, even when they are equally speculative.

R. C. Lewontin[1]

Some die-hard analytic feminists challenging the "unanimity [among feminist epistemologists] about the inadequacy of contemporary analytic epistemology"[2] have asked their sisters to give classical epistemology, at least
in form, another chance. Some have suggested that: "There is an approach
to the study of knowledge that promises enormous aid and comfort to feminists attempting to expose and dismantle the oppressive intellectual ideology of a patriarchal, racist, class-stratified society, and it is an approach
that lies squarely within the analytic tradition. The theory I have in mind
is Quine's 'naturalized epistemology,' the view that the study of knowledge
should be treated as the empirical investigation of knowers."[3]

In addition these feminists have taken seriously the naturalistic
grounding of epistemology: "beginning with an assumption that we do
have knowledge, we can employ the techniques of the cognitive sciences
to help us understand how all of us—adult males and females, and children—come to have knowledge."[4]

With emphasis on the knower and a presupposition that there is knowledge, these faithful analytics have turned into trendy naturalists. Of late such work has developed into what some staunch analytic feminists have named "communal empiricism"[5]—the belief that feminist criticisms could be more effective if they took the work of Quine[6] and other contemporary naturalists more seriously.

This chapter will attempt to demonstrate the following: (1) that the metaepistemological debate between the naturalist and the nonnaturalist is not settled; (2) that both Lynn Hankinson Nelson's and Louise Antony's attempts to defend the development of a feminist epistemology (and philosophy of science) via Quinian naturalism are wrongheaded; (3) that Quine is wrong and that epistemology ought *not* be naturalized; and (4) that an actual attempt, i.e., the attempt by Jane Duran, to develop a feminist (naturalized) epistemology fails as a true epistemology, and does no real work for the feminists, e.g., help women.

The Metaepistemological Debate

KORNBLITH'S CHARACTERIZATION

I will begin with Hilary Kornblith's characterization of naturalistic epistemology. He characterizes naturalistic epistemology (as well as its relationship to classical epistemology) in terms of the respective responses of the proponents of these accounts to the following three questions:

1. How ought we to arrive at our beliefs?

2. How do we arrive at our beliefs?

3. Are the processes by which we do arrive at our beliefs the ones by which we ought to arrive at our beliefs?[7]

Kornblith claims that the nonnaturalistic epistemologist "suggests a strategy of divide and conquer"[8] while the naturalistic epistemologist does not.

The nonnaturalist, according to Kornblith, is interested in all three questions, though not all at the same time. Moreover, the nonnaturalist will consider question 1 (or some mutable alternative, for example, "How is justification related to truth?" or "Are we justified in believing that we are not Brains-in-a-vat?" the *normative* question) to be the bailiwick of philosophers, and question 2, the *descriptive* question, to be the bailiwick of empirical psychologists. Question 3, on the other hand, falls under the jurisdiction of both philosophers and psychologists and as such, an answer, according to Kornblith, requires a joint effort.

The naturalistic approach to epistemology consists for Kornblith of this: "Question 1 cannot be answered independently of question 2. Questions about how we actually arrive at our beliefs are thus relevant to questions about how we ought to arrive at our beliefs."[9] Furthermore, on this account, the degree to which an answer to question 1 is dependent on an answer to question 2 distinguishes "weak" from "strong" naturalists.

Weak naturalists claim that although scientists and philosophers are interested in two completely different questions, they will both come up with the same answer. These naturalists assume the answer to 3 is yes and therefore believe that an answer to 2 will, inevitably, be an answer to 1. That is, they believe that the belief-forming processes that we *do* have will turn out to be the belief-forming processes that we *should* have. According to Kornblith, the weak naturalist believes it is important to investigate question 1 and question 2 because "psychology and epistemology provide two different avenues for arriving at the same place."[10] Therefore, according to weak naturalists, an investigation of question 1 is as useful and important as an investigation of question 2 in our quest for a complete topographical view of the epistemological terrain.[11]

Strong naturalists, according to Kornblith, also assume that the answer to question 3 is yes. But unlike the weak naturalist, who thinks an investigation of question 1 may be useful and important, the strong naturalist refuses to acknowledge question 1 as a legitimate epistemological question. According to Kornblith, the strong naturalist claims that epistemological questions must be replaced by psychological questions because "psychological questions hold all the content there is in epistemological questions."[12] For the strong naturalist then, an investigation of question 1 is simply a waste of time.

Though clear and concise, Kornblith's characterization of the distinction between epistemological positions does not seem entirely correct.

His position suggests that the nonnaturalist is interested in all three of the above questions. But this interpretation is unacceptable for many philosophers. Epistemology for some nonnaturalistic epistemologists is an *autonomous* enterprise, one that can *and ought* be carried out without the help of psychology.

Such epistemologists are not interested in questions 2 or 3 at all. Their strategy is not one of "divide and conquer," as Kornblith claims, but rather one of refusing to acknowledge question 2 as a legitimate epistemological question, unless the answer to question 3 is an unequivocal yes. But the answer to question 3, according to the classical epistemologist is, at best, a maybe. It may be that the way we *should* is the way we *do*—and what a happy epistemological position we would be in—but the world need not be this way. It may be that we ought to live up to higher epistemic standards. Thus, unless the answer to question 3 is yes, question 2 is moot, and what is viewed as the only true epistemological question is question 1.

Concerning the weak and strong naturalistic positions, Kornblith's characterizations are also misconstrued. As stated above, Kornblith suggests that the weak naturalist presupposes that the correct answer to question 3 is yes and therefore that an investigation into question 2 is necessary if one is to get an expedient (if not complete) answer to question 1. He also suggests that the strong naturalist, like the weak naturalist, presupposes that the correct answer to question 3 is yes. (Although unlike the weak naturalist he thinks that what this entails is that there is no need to investigate question 1 at all.)

Unfortunately, this does not seem to be a fair account of either version of naturalism. Given the fact that some ways that people do in fact think are faulty or deficient (e.g., the Gambler's Fallacy*), surely the answer to question 3 need not be an unequivocal yes in order to maintain either a strong or a weak naturalistic position. Since a naturalistic account of epistemology must be compatible with psychological facts, a naturalist need not depend on an answer to question 3.

---

*The Gambler's Fallacy "consists in arguing that, because a chance event has had a certain run in the past, the probability of its occurrence in the future is significantly altered." T. Edward Damer, *Attacking Faulty Reasoning: A Practical Guide to Fallacy-Free Arguments* (Belmont, Calif.: Wadsworth, 1995), p. 189.

If one were to give a modified characterization of the contemporary debate between the naturalistic and the nonnaturalistic epistemologist, one would state the following: Nonnaturalistic epistemologists are interested only in question 1. Weak naturalistic epistemologists are interested in question 1, but think that question 1 can only be properly and expediently answered with help from the answer to question 2. Strong naturalistic epistemologists are only interested in question 2. And of those epistemologists interested in question 3, some might answer it yes, while others might answer it no.

HAACK'S CHARACTERIZATION

A more comprehensive approach to the distinction between naturalistic and nonnaturalistic epistemological positions is presented by Susan Haack. She first distinguishes the nonnaturalized project from naturalistic projects, and then proceeds to distinguish many different forms of naturalism. She calls the following epistemological position Traditional Apriorism:

> The traditional conception takes the central tasks of epistemology to be the *explication of epistemic concepts* (central among which, on the plausible assumption that justified true belief is at least a necessary condition of knowledge, is the concept of epistemic justification) and the *ratification of criteria of justification* (which, on the plausible assumption that truth is at least an essential component of the goal of inquiry, centrally involves investigating the relation between justification and truth). And the traditional approach conceives of these projects as distinctively philosophical in a strong sense; they are to be undertaken, not by any kind of empirical investigation, but a priori.[13]

Where the former project is an attempt to determine the nature of justification, the latter is an attempt to determine the nature of the connection between justification and truth, and both are attended to, at least in part, independently of any empirical evidence. Anything else, according to Haack, is a form of naturalism.

Haack distinguishes six different kinds of naturalistic positions: Revolutionary Nihilism, Revolutionary Naturalism, Scientistic Reformist Naturalism, Modest Reformist Naturalism, Normative Expansionist Naturalism, and Descriptive Expansionist Naturalism.

Revolutionary Nihilism denies the legitimacy of the above "traditional"(i.e., nonnaturalistic) project altogether, given the fact that the traditional project has been fruitless. Furthermore, this position claims that there is no need for a successor project. That is, a replacement project is neither necessary nor desirable. Using the work of Richard Rorty as a case in point, Haack claims: "Hermeneutics, his [Rorty's] alternative, is, as he puts it, more a matter of curing oneself of the urge to worry about the old epistemological questions."[14]

Revolutionary Naturalism is also a form of epistemological naturalism. But although this position denies the legitimacy of the nonnaturalistic project, it claims that it does not repudiate epistemology altogether. According to this position, the nonnaturalistic project (i.e., the explication of epistemic concepts and the ratification of criteria of justification) is misconceived and needs to be "replaced," not completely abandoned. Specifically, it needs to be replaced by the empirical study of cognitive processes.

Reformist Naturalism claims that the nonnaturalistic epistemological project is not misconceived, but only improperly approached. That is, the nonnaturalistic project must be "tackled" naturalistically. Epistemology is interested in the explication of epistemic concepts and the ratification of criteria of justification, but an a priori approach to these projects is not to be undertaken.

If the project is tackled naturalistically and from within the natural sciences, this position is called *Scientistic Reformist Naturalism*; if the project is tackled naturalistically, but from without, only partly appealing to our empirical beliefs, it is called *Modest Reformist Naturalism.*

Another form of naturalism, *Expansionist Naturalism,* claims that the classical epistemological project is legitimate but too narrowly conceived. Technological developments, specifically in neurophysiology and computer science, have shown us that much more must be included in the study of epistemology if it is to be complete.

This category is subdivided into *Descriptive Expansionist Naturalism* and *Normative Expansionist Naturalism.* Descriptive Expansionist Naturalism claims that such an expansion can be handled completely through the scientific description of the belief-forming processes themselves. Normative Expansionist Naturalism, as its name suggests, claims that in addition to these belief-forming descriptions, certain normative considerations must also be incorporated.

This way of delineating the different forms of naturalism needs amelioration, however. Although Haack correctly characterizes the nonnaturalized project and appropriately distinguishes it from all of the different forms of naturalism (in terms of the *kind* of project in which epistemologists are interested and the way in which the project is approached), the way she distinguishes the different forms of naturalism is not plausible.

First, it seems that Revolutionary Nihilism is not an epistemological position at all, let alone a naturalistic epistemological position. If no successor to the original epistemological position is "necessary or desirable," then how can this position be viewed as anything less than an account of antiepistemology (and perhaps even antiphilosophy)?

Second, Revolutionary Naturalism also is not properly a form of naturalism. Revolutionary Naturalism is more of a metaepistemological account, since its main purpose is to advocate a general naturalistic epistemological approach rather than a specific one, a notable distinction since it is the proposal to naturalize, not any specific account, which the nonnaturalist must challenge (and defeat) if she is to maintain her position.

Third, Haack seems to draw the main distinctions between naturalistic positions in a way that emphasizes the *scope,* as opposed to the *content,* of their respective accounts. When this method is applied to the other forms of naturalism, the distinction only serves to obscure their essential difference, that being the "normativeness" (or lack thereof) of their respective naturalisms.

THE DEBATE REDEFINED

I propose that the main distinction to be drawn between nonnaturalistic and naturalistic epistemology (as well as between the different forms of naturalism) is one of normativity (or lack thereof). This way a clearer and more substantive distinction is emphasized. After all, if one form of naturalism is purely descriptive it is easily and fundamentally distinguishable from others that are not.

Furthermore, the debate between the nonnaturalist and the naturalist (as well as between the various different kinds of naturalists) ultimately centers on the normative/descriptive distinction. If classical epistemology is essentially normative, then a *complete* turn to naturalism must be viewed as an abandonment of the classical project, not merely a replacement project or an alternative means to the same end.

To sum up, a concise description of the debate between nonnaturalistic and naturalistic epistemology can be given in the following way: A nonnaturalist claims that epistemological projects involve the explication of epistemic concepts and the ratification of criteria of justification. These projects must be attended to a priori. A naturalist of any stripe would, at the very least, deny that the above is the proper (i.e., the only) goal of epistemology.

To give up the search for epistemic criteria *and* to attend to the psychological search completely empirically is to be a descriptive naturalist. To maintain the search but attend to it empirically (or partially empirically) is to be a normative naturalist.

THE IMPLICATIONS OF THE DEBATE

If epistemology is fundamentally normative then nothing short of the future of philosophy rests on the outcome of this metaepistemological debate. According to the naturalist, if philosophy is to stay alive it must be reduced (to some degree or other) to science; epistemology to psychology. Again, this is because armchair philosophizing has not only not given us an answer to the classical epistemological question "What is knowledge?" it has left us stranded upon the skeptical abyss. The naturalist urges us to consider the fact that we may have simply gone down the wrong path and that the best response to our epistemological troubles is to double-back and try a completely different approach.

But things are not so bleak in the eyes of the nonnaturalistic epistemologist. Many believe progress in epistemology has been made, and those who do not, believe that there is still hope: if, as Quine claims, the "Humean predicament is the human predicament,"[15] then it is the naturalist's predicament as well. But there is no reason in principle why one could not come up with an adequate account of empirical knowledge. According to this camp, if real philosophy is to stay alive, the urge to naturalize must be resisted.

Moreover, if a sincere attempt at justification is to be undertaken, epistemology must maintain its autonomy from science as an a priori discipline committed to determining the general criteria for the justificatory status of our scientific beliefs. The nonnatural epistemologist recognizes that science can determine, at least in principle, which belief-forming processes produce a specific belief. But it is not clear that science can determine which beliefs (or processes) are themselves justified merely by empirical observation. To determine this they must first have an independent account of "justifiedness."

One who supports the trend to "go natural" may claim, at this point, that determining which beliefs (or processes) are themselves justified is precisely what science does. But this misses the point of the opposing stance. The nonnaturalist is not claiming that science is not (or ought not be) the final arbitrator for determining which of our empirical beliefs are justified, but rather science cannot make such a determination without, at some point, appealing to certain criteria of justifiedness. It is the determination of what these metascientific criteria ought to be that the nonnaturalist claims cannot be performed within the boundaries of science. Science at this point becomes the epistemology of science.

This position is held by the nonnaturalistic epistemologist primarily for two reasons. One is that there are times when the justificatory status of the beliefs or practices underlying scientific methodology, e.g., the belief that empirical evidence gives us an accurate account of the way the world is, is itself under scrutiny. To appeal to science at such a time clearly begs the question.

The other reason is that science is, at least classically, thought to be a purely descriptive enterprise. But the question about justification is, at least classically, a normative one. Given that the nonnaturalist has yet to be convinced that a normative question can be adequately answered within the confines of the purely descriptive, the naturalizing of epistemology is seen as an abandonment of the original, "real," epistemic project.

Yet the naturalist still queries: "Where else but from within science could answers to questions concerning the goodness of scientific methodology come from?" The nonnaturalist then retorts: "Answers from within commit the naturalistic fallacy, that is, they violate the distinction between 'is' and 'ought.' " Given the fact that the nonnaturalist has not yet given a straightforward answer, the debate wages on.

Naturalism and Feminism

What does all of this have to do with feminism? Given the above difficulties with feminist attempts to dismantle traditional philosophy of science (see chapter 1) and classical epistemology (see chapter 2), some
feminists have decided to stop attempting to bootstrap their theories *ex ni-
hilo* and begin building their feminist accounts on top of the framework
of the philosophical theories already available.

With this new approach to the tradition of Western philosophy, a few
brave feminists have begun to reinterpret male theories, transforming
them into theories more sympathetic with feminist political goals.[16] Two
such feminists, Louise M. Antony[17] and Lynn Hankinson Nelson,[18] will
be discussed below. I take both seriously because they attempt to feminize perhaps the single most important epistemologist of our century:
W. V. Quine.

QUINE FOR BEGINNERS

Before examining the use of Quine by Antony and Nelson, I would like
to briefly summarize Quine's position.

In 1969 Quine wrote "Epistemology Naturalized,"[19] in which he
urged contemporary epistemologists to cease attempting to create (what
he claims are) fictitious foundations for knowledge and, instead, examine
the behavioral features of the human animal which characterize knowledge. That is, he urged epistemologists to "go natural."

Since that time many epistemologists have agreed with Quine that
they should abandon the old epistemology and rethink the classical questions in the light of science, specifically psychology (or ultimately neurophysiology). As a result, many epistemologists now do their philosophical work (to some degree or other) empirically. The change in approach
is quite drastic and bucks a centuries-old tradition.

Quine takes four steps in an attempt to convince epistemologists that
they must settle for psychology. These four steps, when fleshed out with
the help of many of Quine's other writings, encompass his naturalist epistemology. The first step on Quine's agenda for conversion from classical

to naturalistic epistemology is to offer reason to doubt the fruitfulness of the (traditional) empiricistic approach to epistemology. The second step is to dislodge any suspicion that the new epistemological approach must, in principle, fail to achieve important epistemological goals. The third step is to give a positive account of the approach itself. The final step showcases the advantages of such an approach.

Step One: Discrediting Traditional Empiricism

To begin, Quine suggests one ought to abandon the classical program. By pointing out the historical fact that the classical approach has yet to succeed at the important epistemological task of grounding natural knowledge in sense experience (a task that he believes has been motivated by the "Cartesian quest for certainty"[20]), Quine suggests that the task itself needs to be abandoned. Furthermore, he continues, such an approach must, in principle, fail.

Quine points both to the attempt by David Hume to deduce the truths of science from the truths of observation, and to the attempt by Rudolf Carnap to translate the truths of science into the truths of observation and logic. Hume had to fail because, as is the case with all scientific theories, whatever hypothesis is inferred from the available evidence will always be underdetermined by all possible evidence. Since one could never have tested all of the evidence needed to actually deduce the truths of science from observation sentences, any inference made will always be merely inductive. "The most modest of generalizations about observable traits will cover more cases than its utterer can have had occasion actually to observe."[21] Or, as he states in one of his (many) quotable gems, "the Humean predicament is the human predicament."[22]

Carnap, on the other hand, also had to fail because, as Quine points out, "Carnap's constructions, if carried successfully to completion, would have enabled us to translate all sentences about the world in terms of sense data, or observation, plus logic and set theory. But the mere fact that a sentence is *couched* in terms of observation, logic, and set theory does not mean that it can be *proved* from observation sentences by logic and set theory."[23] That is, one can never translate the general truths of science from the particular truths of observation and logic. Why? Because translation is itself always indeterminate. The sentences in one language will never translate uniquely into the sentences of another.[24] "If there is one way there are many."[25]

According to Quine, then, the traditional epistemological program must fail at its main task, that of grounding our knowledge of the natural world in sense data.

Step Two: The Plausibility of a Naturalistic Account

The second step on Quine's agenda is to show that an alternative approach to epistemology will not fail at (what he takes to be) the only important epistemological task: "understand[ing] the link between observation and science."[26]

Quine, appealing to the hopelessness of the classicist ever achieving the goal of a rational reconstruction, hypothetically queries those recalcitrant to conversion. "But why all this creative reconstruction, all this make-believe? The stimulation of his sensory receptors is all the evidence anybody has to go on, ultimately, in arriving at his picture of the world. Why not just see how this construction really proceeds? Why not settle for psychology?"[27] Quine, sensitive to the fact that there are many who will resist such a conversion, then proceeds to anticipate possible objections. He assumes that classical epistemologists would resist such a conversion for one or both of the following reasons. First, such a program seems inherently circular. How can we justify our scientific theories (which tell us the way the world really is) with evidence that we get from our sensory receptors, when it is the very same science that has determined that such sensory evidence provides us with a reliable indicator of the way the world really is? It seems that our trust in science is still in need of justification. Second, "we should like to be able to *translate* science into logical and observation terms and set theory."[28]

Concerning the first reason, Quine claims that the fear of circularity is as unjustified as the hopes for a rational reconstruction on which they are based. He says that "the fear of circularity is a case of needless logical timidity,"[29] and that, "such scruples against circularity have little point once we have stopped dreaming of deducing science from observations. If we set out simply to understand the link between observation and science, we are well advised to use any available information, including that provided by the very science whose link with observation we are seeking to understand."[30] Therefore, in light of the above, epistemologists should stop dreaming about some foundation on which to ground our knowledge that is firmer than sensory evidence itself. Further, once such a hope has been abandoned, epistemologists will realize that appealing to sensory evidence in order to ground science is not only legitimate, but mandatory.

But what of the Cartesian skeptic?* How is Quine to answer the following? How do we know that our sensory perceptions are correct, that the external world is the way we perceive it to be? It seems that the fact this type of question can even be formulated offers some reason for thinking that the ground that Quine is attempting to establish is not terra firma.

Quine claims, however, that he can meet the above skeptical challenges. Such questions, though grammatical according to Quine, are not "good" questions because they stem from the belief in a "first philosophy," the hope of finding a grounding "outside" of science. According to Quine, anyone who asks such questions has obviously not yet realized that there is no such ground, not yet recognized the force of the above argument against the classical approach. Quine makes his position concerning the "badness" of these questions clear in the following quotation: "Once we have seen that in our knowledge of the external world we have nothing to go on but surface irritation, two questions obtrude themselves—a bad one and a good one. The bad one, lately dismissed, is the question of whether there really is an external world after all. The good one is this: Whence the strength of our notion that there is an external world? Whence our persistence in representing discourse as somehow about a reality, and a reality beyond the irritation?"[31] With the demise of the classical, the challenge of the radical skeptic becomes illegitimate.

This is not to say that one cannot legitimately question these scientific foundations. Quine acknowledges the fact that science can be mis-

---

*Cartesian skepticism, or "radical" skepticism, challenges, in both breadth and scope, even the most basic of our beliefs. For example, the Cartesian skeptic could ask: Could everything in front of you right now just be part of an elaborate dream? More specific for criticizing Quine: Could science be wrong, not just about this or that particular hypothesis, but what justifies or counts as evidence?

taken, but the kind of mistake that science can make is only the kind that is expected, "through the failure of predicted observations."[32]

The sense data on which those predictions are based can also be mistaken. But one is not to take such "mistakes" as disconfirming evidence against science as a whole, that is, as grounds for radical skepticism. On the contrary, Quine suggests the fallibility of the senses lends credence to the scientific endeavor. After all, we only know that something is, for example, an illusion, because it has deviated from the results predicted by science itself.

> Science is vulnerable to illusion on its own showing, what with bent sticks in water and the like, and the skeptic may be seen merely as overreacting when he repudiates science across the board. Experience might still take a turn that would justify his doubts about external objects. Our success in predicting observations might fall off sharply, and concomitantly with this we might begin to be somewhat successful in basing predictions upon dreams or reveries. At this point we might reasonably doubt our theory of nature in even fairly broad outline. But our doubts would still be immanent and of a piece with the scientific endeavor.[33]

Quine sees particular skeptical challenges, such as optical illusions, as evidence science is not susceptible to gross Cartesian skepticism, for such challenges arise from within science itself. Quine claims that if the skeptic is allowed to discredit science from within science, then the epistemologist should be permitted the very same weapon for defense. "The crucial logical point is that the epistemologist is confronting a challenge to natural science that arises from within natural science. . . . Clearly, in confronting this challenge, the epistemologist may make free use of all scientific theory."[34] As such, Quine will not sympathize with those epistemologists suffering from "needless logical timidity" when their fear applies to this specific case. The epistemologist should not avoid such an alternative approach to epistemology simply because it must make use of science in order to justify science. As is the case with his skeptical rival, the epistemologist must make the most out of the limited resources available. That resource is the stimulation of our sensory receptors, which gives rise to scientific theory and skeptical doubts alike.

Concerning the second reason that one might have for avoiding the adoption of an alternative epistemological project (i.e., the desire to achieve a translational reduction), Quine is much more sympathetic. He agrees that if we could give a translational reduction of all of the terms of science into logic and observation terms and set theory, we would have good reason for not "settling" for psychology, that is for "persisting in rational reconstruction." After all, such an achievement would legitimize theoretical science, making theoretical statements at least as secure as logic or observation terms. And psychology, Quine admits, could never supply the necessary mechanism, i.e., it could never show us how to translate sentences containing theoretical terms into sentences lacking them.

Unfortunately, no one, claims Quine, can develop such a program for translation. The underdetermination of theory and the indeterminacy of translation preclude such a project.

The evidence offered is that "science is empirically underdetermined: there is slack,"[35] even for physics. "What can be said about the hypothetical particles of physics is underdetermined by what can be said about sensible bodies, and what can be said about these is underdetermined by the stimulation of our surfaces."[36] Such empirical "slack" between observation and theory makes it possible for one to develop different (and possibly opposing) theories about the same observations. Physical theory is *in fact* underdetermined both because it is always possible that some past conflicting observation may have gone unnoticed and also because some future observation may be noticed to conflict with the theory. More important, physical theory is always underdetermined *in principle* because, for Quine, observational criteria of theoretical terms are commonly so flexible and fragmentary.

Any physical theory, then, is underdetermined, both in fact and in principle: in fact because, to put it simply, we are not omniscient; in principle because, given any physical theory, there is always another theory that is logically incompatible with that theory and yet fits all possible evidence equally well. Therefore, when the scientist is attempting to determine which of two empirically equivalent theories is the "correct" theory, she must choose a theory (a "talk" about the world) without the help of empirical evidence.

However, the talk is itself underdetermined at another level in that the sentences which make up the language have no "fact of the matter."

The second reason that Quine thinks that no one could ever develop a reductionist program (a program for translation) is that translation is, itself, indeterminate. Terms, even terms used to refer to nontheoretical scientific objects, have no meaning independent of the sentences in which they are employed, and meaning, according to Quine, is not something that is shared by terms. Meaning "is what a sentence shares with its translation,"[37] and any nonempirical connection between terms is illusory.[38]

As Quine demonstrated in *Word and Object,* there is no more reason for the field linguist to think that *gavagai* means 'rabbit' than to think that *gavagai* means 'undetached rabbit parts'. Both "translations" are equally good since both conform equally well to all the available evidence, that is to the assent-behavior of a native speaker to the word *gavagai* in the presence of an undetached bunch of rabbit parts. Given that the assent behavior elicited by the occasion sentence *Gavagai!* will be the same whether translated as 'Rabbit!' or 'Undetached rabbit parts!' there will be no way to distinguish between the two translations. They are equally correct, translationally on par.

Quine's point is even stronger. Since there is no other empirical evidence (other than the assent-behavior of the native speaker) from which to determine "correct" translation (i.e., there is "no fact of the matter"), there is no reason to think that the sentence *Gavagai!* means anything at all. And without meaning there can be no unique translation.

Given that the theory is always underdetermined by evidence, both in fact (because of time and energy) and in principle (because of the flexible and fragmentary nature of theoretical terms), and that translation is itself always indeterminate (because there is no fact of the matter and therefore no meaning), one can never translate uniquely. A complete reductive analysis seems out of the question. The antecedent of the above conditional: "If we could give a translational reduction of all the terms of science into logic and observation terms and set theory . . . ," must always be false. Hence, there is no good reason for maintaining a traditional empiricist approach.

In "Epistemology Naturalized" (as well as in other writings) Quine chooses Carnap's attempt at such a program as the case in point. Quine claims that Carnap's approach (even if complete) is unable to "offer any key to translating sentences of science into terms of observation, logic, and set theory."[39] Carnap's program allows for possible translations, but it does not offer grounds for determining which of a number of alternative translations is the "correct" one.

Quine points out that by 1936 even Carnap had given up hope of a complete program for translational equivalence. The best reduction that such a program could achieve is a reduction of a type weaker than definition. But, "reduction forms of Carnap's liberalized kind, on the other hand, do not in general give equivalences; they give implications. They explain a new term, if only partially, by specifying some sentences which are implied by sentences containing the terms, and other sentences which imply sentences containing the term."[40] Quine brings these facts to bear in order to lend more plausibility to his proposal for a new approach. Carnap's program for reduction, which historically speaking was so promising, failed. Furthermore, even Carnap relaxed his demand for definition. And once the demand for a translational equivalence is "relaxed" there does not seem to be any good reason for epistemologists to stay wedded to a program for a rational reconstruction.[41]

> To relax the demand for definition, and settle for a kind of reduction that does not eliminate, is to renounce the last remaining advantage that we supposed rational reconstruction to have over straight psychology; namely, the advantage of translational reduction. If all we hope for is a reconstruction that links science to experience in explicit ways short of translation, then it would seem more sensible to settle for psychology. Better to discover how science is in fact developed and learned than to fabricate a fictitious structure to a similar effect.[42]

According to Quine, then, there is no reason left for the classical epistemologist to be suspicious of his new approach. The fear of circularity has been shown to be misguided; the hope for translational equivalence illegitimate. Nostalgia aside, it is time to turn to psychology.

Step Three: Naturalized Epistemology

The third step on Quine's agenda is to offer a sketch of what a naturalized epistemology could be. This he describes in two ways, one positive, the other negative.

The Positive Account

His positive account is articulated most clearly in "Epistemology Naturalized" when he claims that:

> Epistemology, or something like it, simply falls into place as a chapter of psychology and hence natural science. It studies a natural phenomenon, viz., a physical human subject. This human subject is accorded a certain experimentally controlled input—certain patterns of irradiation in assorted frequencies, for instance—and in the fullness of time the subject delivers as output a description of the three-dimensional external world and its history. The relation between the meager input and the torrential output is a relation that we are prompted to study for somewhat the same reasons that always prompted epistemology; namely in order to see how evidence relates to theory, and in what ways one's theory of nature transcends any available evidence. . . .
>
> Epistemology in its new setting . . . is contained in natural science, as a chapter of psychology. . . . We are studying how the human subject of our study posits bodies and projects his physics from his data.[43]

That is, we ought no longer foolishly attempt to deduce science from sense data, or translate the truth of science into observation sentences and logic. Instead, we should simply look and see how we do, in fact, develop theory out of our sensory stimulation.

Quine then goes on to say something that, at least at first blush, seems radically different from claiming that epistemology merely becomes a chapter of empirical psychology. He says that "epistemology becomes semantics."[44]

This equating of epistemology with semantics occurs through the catalyst of the observation sentence, the most fundamental element in Quine's philosophical system. The observation sentence is, according to Quine, the linguistic element basic to both semantics and epistemology, for it determines meaning and grounds knowledge-claims.

The observation sentence determines meaning in the only way that Quine recognizes meaning: stimulus meaning. The native speaker points to some object and utters (or assents to the utterance of) a sentence. When this occurs, fully observable, empirically verifiable, completely behavioristic meaning is born. It is what we learn first. It is, therefore, anchored.

"The observation sentence, situated at the sensory periphery of the body scientific, is the minimal verifiable aggregate; it has an empirical content all its own and wears it on its sleeve."[45]

Observation sentences are special. Through the empirical evidence of native-speaker behavior they both supply the meaning of a sentence, for example, *Gavagai!* (while in the presence of an undetached bunch of rabbit parts), as well as the grounds for believing that the sentence is true. And it is through the observation sentence that epistemology becomes semantics.

> [Epistemologists] face the fact that society teaches us our physicalistic language by training us to associate various physicalistic sentences, in multifarious ways, with irritations of our sensory surfaces. . . .[46]

> For epistemology remains centered as always on evidence, and meaning remains centered as always on verification; and evidence is verification.[47]

For Quine observation sentences play a privileged role in knowledge acquisition. They are conceptually, causally, and logically prior to all other knowledge. They are conceptually prior because for both the field linguist learning a new language and the child learning her first language, it is the observation sentence that "afford[s] the only entry into language."[48] Without observation sentences there would be no other knowledge.

Observation sentences are causally prior because they are the sentences "in closest causal proximity to the sensory receptors."[49] Observation sentences articulate sense impressions in their most pristine state, without the help of superfluous background information.

Finally, observation sentences are logically prior because of their conceptual and causal proximity to sense data and our senses. Given the fact that there is nothing firmer than observation sentences, basing all truths, even the truths of science, on the truth of such sentences grounds our knowledge.

For Quine, epistemology—the study of the connection between observation and science—is a chapter of science because it is a chapter of both semantics and psychology via the observation sentence. If one wishes to study the connection between observation and science, one ought to do psychology; that is, one ought to study language and the human subject that creates and utilizes it.

The upshot is that, for Quine, "Naturalism does not repudiate epistemology, but assimilates it to empirical psychology."[50]

The Negative Account

In addition to the above positive account, naturalism is elsewhere described by Quine in the negative, as the "abandonment of the goal of a first philosophy,"[51] or the "dislodging of epistemology from its old status of first philosophy."[52]

It is not clear just what a "first philosophy" is and therefore what it is that the naturalist ought to abandon and epistemology ought to be dislodged from, but Quine does discuss this indirectly through the role of the emancipated philosopher. He discusses his account of first philosophy from the viewpoint of one who has recognized the need to reduce epistemology to psychology. With the help of Otto Neurath, Quine offers an important metaphor for his thesis of no first philosophy. Neurath has likened science to a boat which, if we are to rebuild it, we must rebuild plank by plank while staying afloat in it. The philosopher and the scientist are in the same boat.[53] So if the boat is to be improved, it must be improved a piece at a time. There is never a time when the boat, to extend the metaphor, will be dry-docked so that one could rebuild it from the ground up or abandon it altogether. The philosopher, like the scientist, is trapped on board. As Quine himself says, "My position is a naturalistic one; I see philosophy not as an a priori propaedeutic or groundwork for science, but as continuous with science. I see philosophy and science in the same boat—a boat which, to revert to Neurath's figure as I so often do, we can rebuild only at sea while staying afloat in it. There is no external vantage point, no first philosophy."[54] Epistemologists, then, when dreaming of a first philosophy are dreaming of land, a dry place from which they could, if they wanted, rebuild all of science from the ground up. But according to Quine there is no such place; if we are to improve our understanding and justify our knowledge of science, we will have to do so from within science. "It is within science and not some prior philosophy that reality is to be identified and described,"[55] and the epistemologist should "not try to justify science by some prior and firmer philosophy."[56]

Parenthetically, this is not to say that the philosopher's shipboard duties are exactly the same as the scientist's, for, claims Quine, "the philosopher's task differs from the other's [task] in detail."[57] I take this to mean that the job of the philosopher is simply more general than that of the scientist and the difference between the two is one of degree, not kind. Nor can the philosopher (or scientist for that matter) criticize the conceptual scheme as a whole, since there is no vantage point from which to achieve this task, "no such cosmic exile."[58]

Step Four: Additional Reasons for Naturalizing

The fourth step in Quine's agenda for conversion is to showcase some of the possible special features of a new approach. As Quine states, one effect of seeing epistemology in a psychological setting is that it resolves the stubborn old enigma of epistemological priority. Our retinas are irradiated in two dimensions, yet we see things as three-dimensional without conscious inference. Which is to count as observation—the unconscious two-dimensional reception or the conscious three-dimensional apprehension? In the old epistemological context the conscious form had priority, for we were out to justify our knowledge of the external world by rational reconstruction, and that demands awareness. Awareness ceased to be demanded when we gave up trying to justify our knowledge of the external world by rational reconstruction. What counts as observation now can be settled in terms of the stimulation of sensory receptors, let consciousness fall where it may.[59]

Another advantage, according to Quine, is that such an approach rubs out many traditional boundaries, specifically the boundary between science and philosophy. Such destruction, according to Quine, "could contribute to progress in philosophically interesting inquiries of a scientific nature."[60]

One such example concerns perceptual norms. Certain perceptual norms, if they could be experimentally identified, could "be taken as epistemological building blocks, the working elements of experience."[61] Moreover, the acknowledgment of certain universal perceptual traits, for example, an innate standard of perceptual similarity,[62] may find their ultimate justification in their survival value. After all, it may be that the reason we humans have a specific perceptual apparatus which gravitates toward a norm is that it best enables us to survive. Humankind's inductive speculations are reached by extrapolating along lines of perceptual similarity: experiences that begin in a similar way are expected to turn out in similar ways. Our innate standards of perceptual similarity show a gratifying tendency to run with the grain of nature. This concurrence is accountable, purely, to natural selection. Since good prediction has survival value, natural selection will have fostered perceptual similarity standards in us and in other animals that tend accordingly. Natural selection will have favored green and blue, as awareness of inductive generalization, and never grue.[63]

The example of perceptual norms is not intended by Quine to justify induction. According to him, in order to do that one must be certain that the thesis articulating the process of natural selection is correct. But the correctness of such a thesis itself depends, according to Quine, on an inductive argument. The point is that a prior commitment to science will begin with accepting the fact that induction works, and the only real question one must ask is, Why? At this point, "asking for a justification of induction is like asking for a first philosophy in support of science."[64] Neither demand can be, or need be, met.

Through the four steps outlined in "Epistemology Naturalized" (fleshed out with the help of Quine's other works), one gets a complete account of Quine's naturalized epistemology.

To summarize the above, epistemology, classically conceived, according to Quine, has been unsuccessful in its attempts to ground science in sense perception. This point is demonstrated both historically and logically, historically by the failure of Carnap, logically by showing that theories are underdetermined by evidence and that translation is indeterminate. Thus, the traditional project itself should be dropped. One should no longer attempt to provide justification for science in the classical sense. Our only recourse, according to Quine, is to assume that science is correct.

Once we assume that science is correct we realize that the important epistemological question changes. How do we (classically) justify science (derive theory from observation)? is changed to: How do we acquire our theory of the world (the connection between observation and science) and why does it work so well? We are no longer in search of a priori justifications, but a posteriori causes. To best discover such causes, then, we should study the human creature which has successfully bridged the gap. Epistemology becomes a chapter of psychology. From this "enlightened" (empiricistic) position we now see even more clearly why we should naturalize epistemology. Such an enlightened epistemology can now make free use of science and in doing so is capable of solving, actually dissolving, some very important problems. Issues concerning epistemic priority, the need for ultimate foundations, and induction are all dissolved, reduced in one fell swoop to pseudoproblems. This is what Quine means by "naturalism," and what he urges epistemologists to do when he argues that they should "settle for psychology."

ANTONY ON QUINE

In this section I will argue that Louise Antony's attempt to feminize Quine has been unsuccessful. Her desire to rewrite the Quinian canon has both misconstrued Quine and reinvented feminism in a way harmful to women.
    According to Antony,

> there is an approach to the study of knowledge that promises enormous aid and comfort to feminists attempting to expose and dismantle the oppressive intellectual ideology of a patriarchal, racist, class-stratified society, and it is an approach that lies squarely within the analytic tradition. The theory I have in mind is Quine's "naturalized epistemology"—the view that the study of knowledge should be treated as the empirical investigation of knowers.[65]

She summarizes Quine's account in terms of two "insights":

> Quine's main insight was that individual statements do not have any specific consequences for experience if taken individually—that it is only in conjunction with a variety of other claims that experiential consequences can even be derived. It follows from this that no single experience or observation can decisively refute any theoretical claim or resolve any theoretical dispute, and that all experimental tests of hypotheses are actually tests of *conjunctions* of hypotheses. The second insight—actually a corollary of the first point—was that no principled distinction can be drawn among statements on the basis of the grounds of their truth—there can be no distinction between statements made true or false by experience and

those whose truth value depends entirely on semantic or logical conventions.[66]

In other words, the two insights are given a standard interpretation, specifically from "Two Dogmas"[67]: reductionism is false (or, as it is usually understood, holism is true) and there is no analytic/synthetic distinction.

Implications of these insights are given the conventional interpretation as well. First, there is no "first philosophy,"[68] for if

> experimental tests were always tests of *groups* of statements, then if the prediction fails, logic will tell us only that *something* in the group must go, but not *what*. If logic plus data don't suffice to determine how belief is modified in the face of empirical evidence, then there must be, in addition to logic and sensory evidence, *extra-empirical* principles that partially govern theory selection. The "justification" of these principles can only be pragmatic—we are warranted in using them just to the extent that they work.[69]

Workability, therefore, offers epistemologists no choice but to accept the second implication: we must naturalize because "epistemic norms—a category that must include any principle that in fact guides theory selection—are themselves subject to empirical disconfirmation."[70]

The second implication follows, of course, from the first. Epistemology is ultimately "transformed into the empirical study of actual processes—not merely a 'rational reconstruction' of those processes—by which human cognizers achieve knowledge."[71]

Within the confines of the second "implication" Antony goes on to claim that Quine's approach teaches two valuable lessons to epistemologists, lessons she believes are compatible with feminist critiques of classical epistemology. The first is that "all theorizing *takes some knowledge for granted*"[72]—i.e., the denial of radical skepticism. The second is that we "be open to the possibility that the processes that we actually rely on to obtain information about the world are significantly different from the ones our philosophy told us had to be the right ones"[73]—i.e., the way we *should* come to knowledge may not be the way we *do* come to knowledge.

Although I agree that these are Quinian lessons, I believe neither that Quine is correct in them (a point which will be discussed in chapter 5), nor that even if he had been so, that such lessons would, as Antony claims, aid and comfort feminists. Before demonstrating the latter, I will attempt to show that much of what Antony does to Quine's account, in order to use it as a foundation for feminism, is a misconstrual of his position.

ANTONY MISCONSTRUES QUINE

To further, and I believe inappropriately, feminize Quine, Antony emphasizes three aspects of his naturalized epistemology that she believes are at the heart of feminism. The first is garden-variety Quine—the idea that one can only study knowledge, i.e., do epistemology, by "studying the knower."[74] What could a naturalized account of epistemology prescribe if not this? If "epistemology in its new setting . . . is contained in natural science, as a chapter of psychology,"[75] then what is the main lesson if not to study, to some degree or other, the knower?

I agree with Antony that this is a Quinian lesson. I also concur that it is one embraced by feminists. Criticisms of disembodied knowledge are at the heart of a number of feminist critiques of epistemology—Whose knowledge? Which knowers?[76] Men? Women?

The second lesson, however, is not so clearly Quinian. Antony claims that, according to Quine, epistemologists must give up "neutrality as an epistemic ideal."[77] Antony attacks "objectivity as neutrality"[78] because she believes that "the best empirical theories of knowledge and mind do not sanction pure neutrality as a sound epistemic policy."[79] And although it may be that Quine's account is consistent with the prescription that "[w]e must treat the goodness or badness of particular biases as an empirical question,"[80] he definitely does not mean to say there is neither an objective fact of the matter, nor that science—a science which attempts to achieve objectivity—is not the correct route. Quine believes scientific beliefs are the jewels in our crown. As he claims:

> The most notable norm of naturalized epistemology actually coincides with that of traditional epistemology. It is simply the watchword of empiricism: *nihil in mente quod non prius in sensu.* This is a prime specimen of naturalized epistemology, for it is a finding of natural science itself, however fallible, that our information about the world comes only through impacts on

our sensory receptors. And still the point is normative, warning us against telepaths and soothsayers.[81]

Quine may be an "enlightened"[82] empiricist, but he is still a scientific realist.

Antony's account is consistent with Quine's in that they both prescribe an empirical study of the knower in order to develop an epistemology; but when the theories are fleshed out the two theorists part ways. According to Quine, knowers only work the way they work—where "[e]volution and natural selection will doubtlessly figure into [the] account"[83]—and this "human subject of our study"[84] only works one way. There is, therefore, only one science, not, as Antony suggests, a "biased" bunch of sciences.

Quine may believe in an ontological relativity—that if there is one translation, there are many[85]—but this is not a dismissal of neutrality qua scientific objectivity. It may be there are empirically equivalent accounts of 'rabbits', 'undetached rabbit parts', or 'rabbit stages', but the underlying physical phenomena which will be impinging on our retinas will be what it is and our retinas will be what they are. In the first place, for Quine all scientific theorizing is ultimately stimulated by the fundamental subatomic plenum that makes up the universe. And this plenum is a "stubborn fact."[86] In the second, our bodies, being part of this plenum, will be keyed in properly; our fundamental perceptual equipment is, after all, "innate."[87]

Both the observer and the stuff observed is what it is. Therefore, "science, thanks to its links with observation, retains some title to a correspondence theory of truth."[88] It does not, as Antony seems to believe, proceed haphazardly or in a biased way from "some location or other."[89] Instead of a "biased" bunch of sciences, there is for Quine but one.

As Quine so eloquently states, "the truth of physical theory and the reality of microphysical particles, gross bodies, numbers, sets, are not impugned by what I have said of proxy functions and of wildly deviant but empirically equivalent theory formulation. Those remarks had to do *not* with what there is and what is true about the world, *but only with the evidence for what there is and what is true about the world.*"[90] Anything less than this kind of objectivist interpretation of Quine's account trivializes his commitment to naturalism.

ANTONY REREAD

The better way, then, of interpreting Antony's account of Quinian naturalism seems clear: that we must realize that human knowledge requires bias, otherwise it would not be *human* knowledge. Therefore, if we are out simply to see "how this construction really proceeds,"[91] we have no choice but to acknowledge that it will proceed with bias, i.e., *humanly*.

Nevertheless, since we are all human—women and men, black and white, rich and poor—there is, de facto, no provocative, i.e., perceptual or conceptual, bias to acknowledge. In the end the point is moot.

Antony has only two possible responses to this. Either dismiss the idea that Quine, like the feminists, does not "sanction pure neutrality as sound epistemic policy;"[92] or assume that women are, in fact, fundamentally different kinds of cognizers than men, i.e., that there is no such thing as a transsexual species of theory construction; that there is the male version and the female version, and that their fundamental neurophysiological distinctions can account for real bias.

Naturally, the first move would be out of the question for Antony because it would sever the connection between Quine and the feminists. The whole essence of the feminist movement toward developing its own epistemological "voice"[93] hinges on the supposed male adherence to scientific objectivity. That is, it is often claimed that the desire for neutrality qua objectivity is really a veil of partiality and sexism.[94] For Antony to allow Quine the luxury of maintaining a commitment to neutrality would simply be admitting that he is *not* a feminist.

The second choice is nearly as undesirable. If Antony has to buy into the notion of essentialism[95]—that women are, by their very nature, different from men—in order to save her thesis that Quine is a feminist, she will be risking the important practical result feminist epistemologies were designed to facilitate, i.e., the empowerment of women.

If there really are two kinds of thinkers from which two different (possibly incompatible) epistemologies could be developed, then if there were competition there would be no way to adjudicate *objectively*. In such instances, as Quine says, "we can fight."[96] This is not, I believe, a route women ought take. The risk would be too high, especially with the sex/gender that is assumed, by most feminists, to be power hungry and militant.

To complicate things, Antony rides the fence with respect to essentialism and its implications. On the one hand she condemns anyone who claims to be purporting anything about "all human beings"[97] without seriously testing *all* human beings (not literally 'all' but all kinds). On the other hand, she admonishes anyone who is sexist or racist on the ground that they categorize human beings into natural kinds, for example, as male or female, black or white.

Antony's problem is not so much with essentialism per se, but with the misuse of it—that is, when we misconceive a "social kind"[98] as a natural kind. Racism is used as an example.

According to Antony, the (I am assuming she believes) false belief that "blacks are 'innately' less intelligent than whites"[99] follows not from essentialism per se, but from seeing race, which is a social kind, incorrectly, as a natural kind.

But what if race really is a natural kind? And what if the empirical findings reveal the same result? Would they be racist or true?[100] More importantly for this discussion, is sex more properly a social or natural kind? And is 'woman' (or 'man') a designation of natural sex or socialized gender?

Of course, I really do not believe there is a problem here. While criteria for determining race may be mere "convention,"[101] I am hard pressed to see that this is the case for sex. Even when there is a dispute about the actual number of sexes, the determining criteria are purely biological, not sociological. Fausto-Sterling, for example, claims there are definitive biological distinctions between males and females, true hermaphrodites, and pseudo-hermaphrodites—where external genitalia do not match chromosomes.[102]

Furthermore, while 'woman' may, by some stretch of our complicated societal norms, designate merely a gender,[103] I think we can acknowledge without doing any serious investigation that it also clearly designates a sex. Reproductive characteristics are not mere social constructs. If this were the case societies—which are made up of individuals—would have preceded the (presocietal) individuals themselves.

Putting aside the question of whether or not 'woman' is a natural kind or whether Antony is truly committed to essentialism, the point is that an essentialist account of epistemology would most likely be harmful to women. Because of this Antony will have to work a lot harder if she wants feminism—with its distaste for scientific objectivity—to be at peace with Quinian naturalism.

ONE MORE TRY

The third aspect of a naturalized epistemology that is, according to Antony, both consistent with Quine and essentially feminist, is the recognition that "biases are good when and to the extent that they facilitate the gathering of knowledge—that is, when they lead us to the truth. Biases are bad when they lead us away from the truth."[104]

Like the second, this is a misconstrual of Quine. First, to reiterate the earlier point, Quine does not believe that everything, especially science, is biased. Second, even if he did, he would not believe that any one (biased) account could be "better" than any other. On what grounds could such a claim be made or defended? Since science itself is the final arbiter of truth, there could never be, according to Quine, a way of adjudicating the "best science" contest. Antony it seems is reinventing what she claims (and most scholars agree) Quine specifically rejects: a "first philosophy"[105] from which to determine the goodness of science itself. And the truth of science, according to Quine, is something that must be granted.[106]

Finally, it is simply not clear what about this thesis would be of particular interest to feminism even if Quine did adhere to it. If feminists are really interested in achieving garden-variety truth, why insist on criticizing traditional accounts of science (and the philosophy of science) which are attempting to achieve the very same results?

In her bid for compatibility, Antony, via the above three aspects of Quine's naturalized epistemology, ends up distorting both feminism and Quinian naturalism. In her desire to offer feminists some firm analytic foundations, she has misconstrued Quine's objectivist commitment to science as a whole—his "unregenerated realism, the robust state of mind of the natural scientist who has never felt any qualms beyond the negotiable uncertainties internal to science."[107] Even more remarkably, in her attempt to stay faithful to the spirit of Quinian naturalism she has conjured up a most *unfeminist* feminism.

NELSON ON QUINE

Lynn Hankinson Nelson offers a much more elaborate and sophisticated account of Quine's naturalism. But, like Antony, in her attempt to rework Quine for feminists, Nelson stretches Quine's account in ways inconsistent with his program as a whole.

For one thing, she attempts to justify the very project of developing a feminist epistemology as something which follows from Quine's call to naturalize. Nelson claims that

> Quine's general vision of a 'naturalized epistemology' [acts] as a reminder that it is not inexplicable that changes in our social and political theorizing should call for changes in our epistemology—provided, of course, that we are willing to recognize such beliefs and theories in the network of our going theories—a recognition made compelling by feminist science criticism.[108]

In light of Quine's naturalism, however, even as understood by Nelson, this seems odd. For one thing, Quine does not see epistemology as something separate from science. Concerning epistemology and science there is, according to Quine, "reciprocal containment."[109] This is something that Nelson herself recognizes when she states that "Quine maintains that a theory about how we go about theorizing, and epistemology, is firmly *within* science."[110] So even by her own lights, it makes no sense to talk about a change in our epistemology. If epistemology is within science, and vice versa, then what we really need to talk about is a change in our science.

Still, Quine would not have been keen on Nelson's proposal. As stated above (in the section on Antony), his unregenerate realism allows only the questioning of specific hypotheses within science, not the questioning of science as a whole. The latter endeavor would require that there be some type of extrascientific investigation. To talk of changing science would require a first philosophy outside of science, an endeavor Quine clearly rejects.[111]

No amount of empirical evidence (the only evidence there is for scientists or Quine) could, for Quine, get us to give up our belief that it is empirical evidence that gives us science. As stated above with respect to Antony, we must "grant the truth of natural science,"[112] at least most of it.

Furthermore, although Quine certainly allows that bits of science can change, it is not clear that they can be changed by our social and/or political theorizing as suggested by Nelson. Such theorizing, for Quine, would only be as good as the science on which it is based. Any theory, including those developed by feminists (see chapter 1), that attempts to undermine the very nature of science, specifically through the abandonment of the concept of 'objectivity', could not even be entertained. Again, for Quine, since there is no way to criticize science from without, the only way would be from within (as emphasized by Quine through the frequent use of Neurath's boat model),[113] and "from within" is not the route plotted by most social/political criticisms of science.

Certainly, it is not the approach used by those feminists who claim to be critics of science. As demonstrated in chapter 1, feminist criticisms of science strike deep at the heart of science, at its fundamental methodological principles.

Unfortunately for these feminists, the Quinian lesson, once heeded, is permanent: Once epistemology is naturalized, it can never be "ized" as anything else, let alone femininely.

This problem will be discussed more fully below. For now it is sufficient to warn feminists that when the collection of scientific evidence becomes the only game in town, there is no amount of theorizing that will ever undermine the data itself. Women, like every other aspect of the material universe, will be at the mercy of empiricism.

In the final analysis, it does not seem to be the case that the spirit of Quine's naturalism can be stretched to fit Nelson's commitment that social and political factors weigh in the determining of science.

Nor is it clear that Quine's commitment to community assent with respect to the verification of language can be expanded to embrace what is at the heart of Nelson's project: the belief that "it is communities [not individuals] that construct and acquire knowledge."[114]

Briefly, Carol Gilligan is, once again, responsible for setting the trend that the notion of 'community', especially when juxtaposed with 'individual', is one of the main desiderata of feminist theorizing. Since then much of the feminist literature has claimed that the desire to maintain individuality is male and, therefore, epistemically and morally inferior to the womanly desire to see oneself in community.[115] Nelson, swept up by the feminist tide, decides to take this notion of community seriously and attempts to rework Quinian naturalism in a way that is consistent with its agenda.

> On one level, the focus on communities is in keeping with a long-standing feminist insight into the collective nature of the feminist political experience and feminist knowing, an insight that is clearly reflected in standpoint epistemologies, but also in the claims made by some feminists who have opted for a feminist empiricism. What I am suggesting is that the shift in focus to communities precludes the conclusion that feminist empiricism subverts empiricism. The shift I am advocating does not subvert empiricism, but it does fundamentally alter it.[116]

Nelson attempts alteration from two different angles: to offer an outline of Quine which is in keeping with standard interpretations and to argue that Quine did not go far enough. With respect to the first, she claims that Quine's proposal is that "epistemology should be 'naturalized' and, specifically, that it be pursued in empirical psychology."[117] (I, of course, have no problem with this interpretation.)

She then proceeds to announce that with

> the shift to holism, the collapse of the analytic/synthetic distinction, and the view that physical-object ontology is our conceptual first . . . Quine argues that the dream of an epistemology as 'first science' must be given up and epistemology recognized as a part of science. . . . Quine suggests that our epistemological questions be pursued in neuroscience. . . . Epistemology and philosophy (and, Quine maintains, philosophy of science is philosophy enough) are recognized and pursued as part of empirical science.[118]

Again, I have no problems. The acceptance of holism and the rejection of a "first philosophy" is standard Quinian fare. But after this brief overview I am forced to take exception to Nelson's interpretation of Quine. She says that Quine may be involved in a project "of correlating specific beliefs to specific neurophysiological states and correlating these states (or specific behaviors) to specific stimuli,"[119] or,

> he may envision the task of naturalized epistemology as arriving at a general explanation of how beliefs, understood to be neurophysiological states, are caused by stimuli, and seeing what the "slippage" is between the

"meager input"[120] accorded the species as evidence for its theories, and the "torrential output"[121] the species produces—but without concern to explain any specific belief.[122]

Since Quine's corpus often discusses the "stimulation of [one's] sensory receptors"[123] or the "surface irritations"[124] on one's retinas, it would seem that the first of the above two choices would be the obvious one. Unfortunately, though, Nelson is more sympathetic to the latter.[125]

Taking seriously Quine's challenge to explain *how* we are to "understand the link between observation and science,"[126] Nelson attempts to build a human bridge between the two:

> what we are concerned to do in constructing an epistemology is to offer causal explanations for how theories, beliefs, and claims have been arrived at; explanations that are in keeping with what we experience. Because, for example, we have been successful at theorizing, an adequate epistemology will need to be able to explain why and how, and this is why I have insisted that epistemologies that do not (or cannot) provide an account of how theories are constrained by evidence are inadequate.[127]

She claims that one of the factors beyond the meager input, which more adequately explains the torrential output, is that we think as a species and not as individuals. "It would appear to be the rest of us, the communities within which the individual comes to be capable of having beliefs at all, the communities that actually construct theories and arrive at standards of evidence, that fill in the gap for the species."[128]

For Nelson, then, a naturalized epistemology (which at this point in her book she proceeds to develop without regard for Quine[129]) "will need to include more than neuroscience. Its primary focus will be on human social groups."[130] She readily admits at this point that

> we will need to go beyond Quine's focus on language communities—a focus that along with his exclusion of politics and values is relevant to science, is probably responsible for his assumption of a "homogeneous we."
>
> We will need to look at the practices and experiences within the relevant subcommunities and our largest community to explain the differences separating subcommunities, and to evaluate these differences. . . . We will need to include the work that feminists have done evaluating social and political theories to reconsider the assumption that political beliefs

and theories, and values, are not subject to empirical control, that there is
no way to judge between them.[131]

Without help from Quine (and maybe even in direct repudiation of his
program), Nelson claims that "it is clear that a naturalized epistemology
will have to encompass more than empirical psychology, and that it will
need to focus, centrally, on communities rather than individuals."[132]

It is not necessary, therefore, to point out the distinction between Nelson and Quine, unlike with Antony above; for this is something she readily admits. Instead, I would like to challenge Nelson to explain why she
depends on Quine at all.

It seems that if one is committed to Quine's version of naturalism,
then one cannot focus on communities. The legitimacy of Quine's naturalism—both in terms of the discrediting of traditional epistemology and
establishing the plausibility of a naturalized account—even as understood by Nelson, is fundamentally dependent on the goodness of his arguments concerning language. And his arguments concerning language—
the learning of language, the indeterminacy of translation, and the
underdetermination of theory by evidence—are all grounded in the observation sentence.

As stated above, for Quine, observation sentences play a privileged
role in knowledge acquisition. They are foundational. Therefore, once the
focus of knowledge is switched from the individual to the community, in
keeping with Nelson's desire to feminize, the observation sentence no
longer plays its foundational role and, therefore, *Quine's* naturalism
ceases to be grounded.

Despite Nelson's desires to the contrary, one cannot shift the focus of
knowledge from the individual to the community without undermining the
"foundational" character of the observation sentence. Once the observation sentence—the heart of Quine's naturalism—is reworked, it is not
clear what is left that is Quinian. This fact in and of itself is not a problem. However, if Nelson deviates too far from Quine, it becomes unclear
why she depends on his theories to begin with. Either her feminist empiricism needs Quine or it does not. If it does, then it should fall for it all,
hook, line, and sinker.

Quine as Feminist

Despite my objections to Antony's attempt to show that Quine denies the neutrality of science and Nelson's attempt to show that Quine ought to entertain communities, as opposed to individuals, as knowers, there is much of Quine (correctly pointed out by both Antony and Nelson) that seems to be, at least at first blush, consistent with feminist epistemic ideals. Unfortunately, Quine's system cannot be broken up into small bits to be used when convenient to justify an analytic feminism. Quine's system, as a whole, is greater than the sum of its parts.[133]

In addition, there are two other problems that need to be addressed with respect to any attempt to apply Quinian naturalism to epistemology, specifically a feminist epistemology. First, one has to show that classical epistemology—both in terms of its method (a priori) and content (epistemic certainty)—ought to be abandoned. Second, once abandonment has occurred, anything that takes its place should be attended to purely scientifically. At this time, two questions now present themselves: Is Quine right, that epistemology be naturalized? and, more directly relevant to our discussion here, Does Quine's naturalism aid what is at the heart of feminism, i.e., the empowerment of women? (For my answer to the former see chapter 5. If one chooses to skip my analysis of Quine or if one has already settled on her own analysis of Quine, or both, proceed to chapter 6 for an answer to the latter.)

Notes

1. R. C. Lewotin, "Women Versus the Biologists," *New York Times Review of Books*, April 7, 1994, pp. 31–35.

2. Louise M. Antony, "Quine as Feminist: The Radical Import of Naturalized Epistemology," in *A Mind of One's Own*, ed. Louise M. Antony and Charlotte Witt (Boulder, Colo.: Westview Press, 1993), p. 187.

3. Ibid.

4. Jane Duran, *Toward a Feminist Epistemology* (Savage, Md.: Rowman and Littlefield, 1991), p. 8.

5. Carol Caraway, Review of *Who Knows? From Quine to a Feminist Empiricism* by Lynn Hankinson Nelson, *Teaching Philosophy* 14, no. 2 (June 1991): 221.

6. See Lynn Hankinson Nelson, *Who Knows? From Quine to a Feminist Empiricism* (Philadelphia: Temple University Press, 1990), and Antony, "Quine as Feminist."

7. H. Kornblith, "Introduction: What Is Naturalistic Epistemology?" in *Naturalizing Epistemology*, ed. H. Kornblith (Cambridge, Mass.: MIT Press, 1985), p. 1.

8. Ibid.

9. Ibid., p. 3.

10. Ibid., p. 6.

11. There is an implied rejection of the "fact/value" distinction here. This will be discussed further below.

12. Kornblith, "Introduction," p. 6.

13. Susan Haack, "Recent Obituaries of Epistemology," *American Philosophical Quarterly* 27, no. 3 (1990): 200.

14. Ibid., p. 203.

15. W. V. Quine, "Epistemology Naturalized," in *Ontological Relativity and Other Essays* (New York: Columbia University Press, 1969), p. 72.

16. See Antony and Witt, *A Mind of One's Own.*

17. Antony, "Quine as Feminist."

18. Nelson, *Who Knows?*

19. Quine, "Epistemology Naturalized."

20. Ibid., p. 74.

21. Ibid.

22. Ibid., p. 72.

23. Ibid., p. 74.

24. For more on Quine's indeterminacy thesis, see chapter 5.

25. Quine, "Epistemology Naturalized," p. 75.

26. Ibid., p. 76.

27. Ibid., p. 75.

28. Ibid., p. 76.

29. Quine, *The Roots of Reference* (LaSalle, Ill.: Open Court Press, 1973), p. 2.

30. Quine, "Epistemology Naturalized," p. 76.

31. W. V. Quine, "Posits and Reality," in *The Ways of Paradox and Other Essays* (Cambridge, Mass.: Harvard University Press, 1966), p. 217.

32. W. V. Quine, *Theories and Things* (Cambridge, Mass.: Harvard University Press, 1981), p. 22.

33. Ibid.

34. Quine, *Roots of Reference*, p. 2.

35. W. V. Quine, "The Scope and Language of Science," in *The Ways of Paradox and Other Essays*, p. 241.

36. Ibid.

37. W. V. Quine, *Word and Object* (Cambridge, Mass.: Harvard University Press, 1960), p. 32.

38. For more on Quine's theory of meaning, see chapter 5.

39. Quine, "Epistemology Naturalized," p. 77.

40. Ibid.

41. More is said about the Quine/Carnap debate in chapter 5.

42. Quine, "Epistemology Naturalized," p. 78.

43. Ibid., pp. 82–83.

44. Ibid., p. 90.

45. Ibid., p. 89.

46. Quine, "Scope and Language," p. 240.

47. Quine, "Epistemology Naturalized," p. 89.

48. Ibid.

49. Ibid., p. 85.

50. W. V. Quine, "Five Milestones of Empiricism," in *Theories and Things,*
p. 2.

51. Ibid.

52. Quine, "Epistemology Naturalized," p. 87.

53. Quine, *Word and Object,* p. 3.

54. W. V. Quine, "Natural Kinds," in *Ontological Relativity and Other Essays*
(New York: Columbia University Press, 1969), pp. 126–27.

55. Quine, *Theories and Things,* p. 21.

56. Quine, *Roots of Reference,* p. 34.

57. Quine, *Word and Object,* p. 275.

58. Ibid.

59. Quine, "Epistemology Naturalized," pp. 84–85.

60. Ibid., p. 90.

61. Ibid.

62. Quine, "Natural Kinds," p. 123.

63. Quine, *Roots of Reference,* pp. 19–20. 'Grue' is the color and object if it
is green now, but will, at some time in the near future turn blue, a property which
would make it hard to identify objects, and which is claimed to not be "projectable."
See Nelson Goodman, *Fact, Fiction and Forecast,* 4th ed. (Cambridge, Mass.: Harvard University Press, 1983).

64. Quine, *Roots of Reference,* p. 20.

65. Antony, "Quine as Feminist," p. 187.

66. Ibid., p. 201.

67. W. V. Quine, "Two Dogmas of Empiricism," in *From a Logical Point of
View* (New York: Harper and Row, 1963).

68. Quine, "Epistemology Naturalized," p. 87.

69. Antony, "Quine as Feminist," p. 201.

70. Ibid., p. 210.

71. Ibid., p. 202.

72. Ibid.

73. Ibid.

74. Ibid., p. 210.

75. Quine, "Epistemology Naturalized," p. 83.

76. See, for example, Jane Duran, *Toward a Feminist Epistemology*, and, of course, Sandra Harding, *Whose Science? Whose Knowledge? Thinking from Women's Lives* (Ithaca, N.Y.: Cornell University Press, 1991).

77. Antony, "Quine as Feminist," p. 215.

78. Ibid., p. 210.

79. Ibid.

80. Ibid., p. 215.

81. W. V. Quine, *Pursuit of Truth* (Cambridge, Mass.: Harvard University Press, 1990), p. 17.

82. See Roger Gibson, *Enlightened Empiricism* (Tampa, Fla.: University Press of Florida, 1988).

83. Quine, "Five Milestones of Empiricism," p. 72.

84. Quine, "Epistemology Naturalized," p. 83.

85. Ibid., p. 75.

86. Quine, "Moral Values," in *Theories and Things*, p. 63.

87. Ibid., p. 56.

88. Ibid., p. 63.

89. Antony, "Quine as Feminist," p. 215.

90. Quine, "Relativism and Absolutism," *The Monist* 67 (1984): 295.

91. Quine, "Epistemology Naturalized," p. 75.

92. Antony, "Quine as Feminist," p. 210.

93. This is taken from Carol Gilligan, *In a Different Voice* (Cambridge, Mass.: Harvard University Press, 1982).

94. See, for example, Evelyn Fox Keller, *Reflections on Science and Gender* (New Haven, Conn.: Yale University Press, 1985).

95. Much of my thinking on the connection between essentialism and feminism has been aided by R. Natasha Mohr, a student of mine who is now studying for her Ph.D. in philosophy at the University of Nebraska.

96. Quine, "Moral Values," p. 65.

97. Antony, "Quine as Feminist," p. 216.

98. Ibid., p. 217.

99. Ibid.

100. See, for example, J. Phillippe Rushton, *Race, Evolution and Behavior* (New Brunswick, N.J.: Rutgers University Transaction Press, 1994).

101. Antony, "Quine as Feminist," p. 217.

102. See, for example, Anne Fausto-Sterling, "The Five Sexes: Why Male and Female Are Not Enough," *Science* (March/April 1993): 20–25.

103. Whatever 'gender' means, see p. 25 n. 4.

104. Antony, "Quine as Feminist," p. 215.

105. Quine, "Natural Kinds," p. 127.

106. Quine, *Roots of Reference*, p. 3.

107. Quine, "Five Milestones of Empiricism," p. 72.

108. Nelson, *Who Knows?* p. 299.

109. Quine, "Epistemology Naturalized," p. 83. See also, Quine, *Roots of Reference*, p. 2; Quine, *Word and Object*, p. 3; and Quine, "Natural Kinds," pp. 126–27.

110. Nelson, *Who Knows?* p. 23.

111. For example, Quine, "Epistemology Naturalized," p. 87; Quine, *Word and Object*, pp. 3, 275; Quine, "Natural Kinds," pp. 126–27; W. V. Quine, "Things and Their Place in Theories," in *Theories and Things*, p. 21; Quine, *Roots of Reference*, p. 34.

112. Quine, *Roots of Reference*, p. 3.

113. For example: Quine, "Natural Kinds," pp. 126–27; W. V. Quine, "The Nature of Natural Knowledge," in *Mind and Language*, ed. S. Guttenplau (Oxford: Clarendon Press, 1975), p. 68; Quine, "Five Milestones of Empiricism," p. 72.

114. Lynn Hankinson Nelson, "Epistemological Communities," in *Feminist Epistemologies*, ed. L. Alcoff and E. Potter (New York: Routledge, 1993), p. 123.

115. See, for example: Jean Grimshaw, *Philosophy and Feminist Thinking* (Minneapolis: University of Minnesota Press, 1986), pp. 149, 163–64; Nancy J. Holland, *Is Woman's Philosophy Possible?* (Savage, Md.: Rowman and Littlefield, 1990), p. 172; Lorraine Code, *What Can She Know? Feminist Theory and the Construction of Knowledge* (Ithaca, N.Y.: Cornell University Press, 1991), pp. 79, 123, 275; Lorraine Code, "Taking Subjectivity into Account," in *Feminist Epistemologies*, ed. L. Alcoff and E. Potter, p. 26; Harding, *Whose Science?* p. 58; Rosemary Tong, *Feminine and Feminist Ethics* (Belmont, Calif.: Wadsworth, 1993), p. 182; Linda Alcoff and Elizabeth Potter, "Introduction: When Feminism Intersects Epistemology," in *Feminist Epistemologies*, ed. L. Alcoff and E. Potter, pp. 8–9; Helen E. Longino, "Subjects, Power and Knowledge: Description and Prescription in Feminist Philosophies of Science," in *Feminist Epistemologies*, ed. L. Alcoff and E. Potter, p. 105; Elizabeth Potter, "Gender and Epistemic Negotiation," in *Feminist Epistemologies*, ed. L. Alcoff and E. Potter, pp. 161–65; Kathryn Pyne Addelson, "Knower/Doers and Their Moral Problems," in *Feminist Epistemologies*, ed. L. Alcoff and E. Potter, p. 273.

116. Nelson, *Who Knows?* p. 297.

117. Ibid., p. 34.

118. Ibid., p. 95.

119. Ibid., p. 282.

120. Quine, "Epistemology Naturalized," p. 82.

121. Ibid.

122. Nelson, *Who Knows?* p. 283.

123. Quine, "Epistemology Naturalized," p. 75.

124. Quine, "Posits and Reality," p. 228.

125. Nelson, *Who Knows?* p. 284.

126. Quine, "Epistemology Naturalized," p. 76.

127. Nelson, *Who Knows?* p. 292.

128. Ibid., p. 285.

129. This is not a problem in and of itself, but then one has to wonder why bother with Quine at all.

130. Nelson, *Who Knows?* p. 287.

131. Ibid., pp. 296–97.

132. Ibid., p. 293.

133. This is the main reason I have included, albeit at a basic level, an account of Quine as a whole in chapter 5.

5

Is Quine Right?

Socrates: But if true belief and knowledge were the same thing, the best of jurymen could never have a correct belief without knowledge. It now appears that must be different things.

Theaetetus: Yes Socrates, I have heard someone make the distinction. I had forgotten, but now it comes back to me. He said that true belief with the addition of an account was outside its range. Where no account could be given of a thing, it was not 'knowable'.

Plato[1]

Before examining the question, Should epistemology be naturalized? it is important to point out that Quine's entire program for naturalizing is suspect. His argument in favor of naturalism is the following:

(1) Traditionalism (what I call 'classicalism') or Naturalism,

(2) Not Traditionalism (classicalism),
therefore,

(3) Naturalism.

The argument is clearly valid; but is it sound?

Premise Two

Quine claims that premise (2) is true and, therefore, that one ought to abandon traditional epistemology. He makes this claim for two reasons: (1) Scientific theory is underdetermined by its evidence (and therefore, as Hume pointed out, we can never deduce the truths of nature from the truths of sense experience); and more importantly, (2) every sentence in the theoretical language (i.e, sentences about the truths of nature) will always, at best, translate into sentences in the object language (i.e., sentences about the truths of observation and logic) indeterminately. Therefore, as the failure of Carnap demonstrated, we can never translate the truths of nature into the truths of sense experience.

What needs to be determined, then, is whether Quine is correct concerning the above: Is Quine right that theory is always underdetermined and that sentences about the truths of nature only indeterminately (i.e., nonuniquely) translate into sentences about the truths of observation and logic? Furthermore, even if he is correct about these two facts, does this entail that traditional epistemology ought to be abandoned?

THE DOCTRINE OF THE UNDERDETERMINATION OF THEORY

Briefly, Quine is asserting that our theories about the world always "transcend" our sensuous experiencing of the world itself. Furthermore, it is possible that we could develop two different, competing theories about the same empirical observations. Therefore, we could never know, in principle, which, if any, is the uniquely correct theory.

Quine exposes this fact about physical theory because he thinks that once the epistemologist makes this fallibilist realization, she will loosen her hold on traditional expectations. He has suggested that the motivation behind the desire to adhere blindly to classical epistemology is the false belief that this program can aid the epistemologist in her search for certainty. Once the Holy Grail of certainty has been proven unattainable, though, the epistemologist is free to abandon her quest. The doctrine of underdetermination is meant to expose the quest for certainty as fruitless. So two questions need to be answered. First, is it true that theory is always underdetermined by its evidence? If so, is this reason to abandon traditional epistemology? Quine makes three separate claims which together comprise the doctrine of underdetermination: (1) Theory is underdetermined by past observations because it is always possible that some future observation will disconfirm it. (2) Theory is underdetermined by past and future observations because it is always possible that a disconfirming instance was overlooked. (3) Theory is underdetermined by all possible observation because it is possible that two logically incompatible theories can be empirically equivalent. Only the last of these claims (being an "in principle" claim) has any philosophical bearing on the case against certainty. This (strong) claim states that all theory is, in principle, underdetermined by all possible evidence. If this were true, it would clearly count as justification for abandoning any hope for certainty. For if we could never deduce the truths of science from the truths of observation, the best that we could hope for is to, by way of induction, develop theory from observation. But, in so doing we see that some other, incompatible theory can be induced from the same evidence. Therefore, we would never know which, if any, is the uniquely correct theory. Fallibilism would be an essential component of epistemology; and if classical epistemology is incompatible with fallibilism, then it must be abandoned.

But traditional epistemology need not be incompatible with fallibilism. Classical epistemology can, in both approach and content, remain compatible with fallibilist constraints. Therefore, even if underdetermination (in its strongest sense) were true, one need not abandon all classical epistemological programs. Interestingly, though, the (strong) doctrine of underdetermination is not true, at least not in any nontrivial sense.

In his article "On Empirically Equivalent Systems of the World," Quine investigates two problems with the (strong) doctrine of underdetermination. First, it seemed to him false that for every physical theory there is, even in principle, another physical theory that is empirically equivalent to, and yet logically inconsistent with, it. The problem is with the notion of logical inconsistency, for to say that two theories are logically inconsistent is to say that "there is no reconstrual of predicates that would render the two logically equivalent."[2] But as Quine recognizes, given a drastic enough reconstrual of predicates, this need not necessarily be the case.

Second, even if it were impossible, in principle, to reconstruct the predicates in two supposedly inconsistent theories to render them equivalent, this fact could never be determined. The metatheory which claims that 'it is impossible to render two supposedly inconsistent theories equivalent', if true, could never be 'known' to be such. The metatheory will itself be underdetermined by all possible evidence. And if this is the case, then some other, incompatible theory can be induced from the same evidence. We would then never know which, if any, is the uniquely correct metatheory. If Quine is right that 'theory is (strongly) underdetermined', we could never know it. In the light of the above, Quine concluded that "in its full generality, the thesis of underdetermination thus interpreted is surely untenable."[3] But this admission did not force Quine to give up on the doctrine completely. Instead he reformulated the doctrine in terms of (1) and (2) above, i.e., as an in-fact claim about physical theories. As he himself states, "the thesis needs to be read as a thesis about the world."[4]

Unfortunately, once the status of the doctrine is reduced to one of "in fact" as opposed to "in principle," it seems to lose all philosophical import. Under this formulation the doctrine, though true, at best states that some theories are in fact underdetermined by some evidence. But this empirical point, even if true, offers no support for Quine's claim that the classical epistemological project is misguided. Furthermore, even if the doctrine is philosophically important (that is, it leads us to think of the possibility of two empirically equivalent yet logically incompatible theories), one is hard-pressed to see how this "conception" lends any credence to the dismissal of classical epistemology. On the contrary, the possibility of two empirically equivalent yet logically incompatible theories concerning the same observations seems to support, not undermine, the belief that the search for extrascientific criteria is not misguided. (And determining what these considerations should be, the desiderata for such considerations, is exactly what classical epistemology attempts to determine.)

Thus, there is no reason to think that the doctrine of underdetermination, as a philosophical thesis, is both true and philosophically serious. More importantly for this discussion, it is not clear that even if it were true it would force the dismissal of classical epistemology.

The Thesis of the Indeterminacy of Translation

Quine's thesis of the indeterminacy of translation states that manuals for translating one language into another can be set up in divergent ways, all compatible with the totality of speech dispositions, yet incompatible with one another.[5] Furthermore, "there is no answer to the (pseudo) question of which translation is the uniquely correct one."[6] This is because two different (conflicting) manuals of translation "can both do justice to all dispositions to behavior."[7] According to Quine, "the only facts of nature that bear on the correctness of translations are speech dispositions."[8] Therefore, translation from one manual to another, one language to another, will always be indeterminate. That is, we will never be sure we have the "correct" translation, because there is no such thing as the "correct" translation. Given that the only facts that bear on determining "correctness" are speech dispositions (of native speakers), and given that two incompatible translations can both fit these facts equally well, it follows that there is no "correct" translation: both are equally "correct."

The importance of this thesis is that if true, it shows that Carnap's attempt at rational reconstruction was doomed to failure. His attempt to translate all of the truths of science into observation terms, logic, and set theory not only failed in fact, but any such program must fail in principle.

But why is a rational reconstruction so important? According to Quine, it is a desired goal of classical epistemologists because such a construction would legitimize theoretical concepts (specifically those necessary for science) to the same degree as their logical and observational primitives. If we were able to develop a program for reducing the former to the latter, it would "establish the essential innocence of physical concepts, by showing them to be theoretically dispensable."[9] In other words, sentences containing theoretical terms would be as epistemically secure, as indubitable, as their observational or logical counterparts.

Rational reconstruction will inevitably fail because a program for reduction presupposes the possibility of "strictly deriving the science of the external world from sensory evidence."[10] But as Hume demonstrated years before, physical theory is always underdetermined by its evidence. So since linguistics itself is simply a part of behavioral science (and hence ultimately a part of some physical theory), any account of such a reduction will suffer the same underdetermination.

A program for rational reconstruction must also fail because translation, when it does occur, is indeterminate. Any construction of physicalist discourse in terms of sense experience, logic, and set theory would have been seen as satisfactory if it made the physicalist discourse come out right. If there is one way there are many, but any would be a great achievement.[11] Therefore, even if a semantic account of the reduction can be given, "how could we have told whether it was the right one?"[12] More to the point, there would be no determination of the "right one" to make.

Furthermore, the problem of indeterminacy is not to be viewed as a problem derived from the contingent factors of a given situation. It is not merely a matter of not having enough information. The problem is that, for Quine, there is no other information to be had; there are no mental facts of the matter. Therefore, the determination of the "correct" translation or the "real" belief is misguided and should be abandoned. Once abandoned, there is no reason to continue to create manuals for translation. We might as well "just see how this construction really proceeds."[13] We might as well "settle for psychology."[14]

Is Translation Indeterminate?

Quine suggests that the indeterminacy of translation thesis is supported in three separate ways. First, it is supported by the recognition "that there can be logically incompatible and empirically equivalent physical theories A and B."[15] That is, the theory is supported by the fact that we recognize that at least portions of physical theory are underdetermined, that there is "empirical slack." As Quine says, "If I can get people to see this empirical slack as affecting not just highly theoretical physics but fairly common-sense talk of bodies, then I can get them to concede indeterminacy of translation of fairly common-sense talk of bodies."[16]

Second, Quine sees indeterminacy as supported by the fact that "the thesis is a consequence of my behaviorism"[17] (an approach which he claims is "mandatory"[18]). And third, it is supported by the inscrutability of reference, for it is suggested that some "arguments for indeterminacy of translation can be based on the inscrutability of terms."[19]

Empirical Slack

According to Quine, the fact that scientific hypotheses are underdetermined by their evidence, that there is empirical slack, lends support to the indeterminacy thesis. Furthermore, semantic theories are also underdetermined. Therefore, when attempting to translate the sentences (specifically theoretical sentences) of one language into the sentences of another, "the same old empirical slack, the old indeterminacy between physical theories, recurs in second intention."[20] In other words, although semantic theories are not underdetermined by evidence per se, they are dependent on certain empirical theories that are themselves underdetermined. When the field linguist attempts a "radical translation" from some radically foreign language (a language with which no one from the linguist's community is even remotely familiar) into her own language, she begins with observation sentences. An example of an observation sentence is: 'Lo Rabbit!' The linguist begins with sentences like this because they "hinge pretty strictly on the concurrent, publicly observable situation,"[21] presumably, in this case, on the presence of a rabbit.

Because of this close connection between the use of the sentence and the ability empirically to verify its correct usage, observation sentences are the linguist's "entering wedge"[22] into the native language. "He [the linguist] tentatively associates a native's utterance with the observed concurrent situation, hoping that it might be simply an observation sentence linked to that situation. To check this he takes the initiative, when the situation recurs, and volunteers the sentence himself for the native's assent or dissent."[23] With the help of some conjecture (presupposing, for example, that head nodding represents assent behavior) the linguist can test his theory that *Gavagai!* "translates" into 'Lo Rabbit!' Therefore, by watching the assent behavior of the foreigner while she is queried, *Gavagai?* in the presence of a particular stimulus-creator (a rabbit), the linguist is able to "translate" the observation sentence of one language into an observation sentence of another. *Gavagai!* "translates" to 'Lo Rabbit!' because the foreigner assents to *Gavagai!* under the same stimulus conditions (again presumably in the presence of a rabbit) in which the linguist would assent to 'Lo Rabbit!' With only minor conjecture then, the linguist is able to translate one language into another in the only way that she can, "by an inductive equating of stimulus meaning."[24]

But "unlike observation sentences, most utterances resist correlation with concurrent stimulations that the linguist can share."[25] So how is the linguist to continue to develop her manual for translation? She does so by trial and error. The linguist will start with those sentences which contain observation sentences. By treating the observation sentences as words, and by attempting to pair off these more complex sentences with complex sentences that contain these "words" in her own language, she will be able to come up with a tentative translation. Such tentative translations are what Quine calls "analytical hypotheses."[26]

Unfortunately there is a problem surrounding the development of analytical hypotheses: as is the case with hypotheses in physics, they suffer from underdetermination. It will always be the case that given one analytical hypothesis, there could exist another analytical hypothesis that fits all possible evidence equally well and yet is inconsistent with the first.

Analytical hypotheses will, eventually, have to be assessed. Concerning the translation of theoretical statements (of which the native language will inevitably be, at least partly, composed), the linguist would need to depend heavily on analytical hypotheses. As is the case in the linguist's own language, such translations bring with them a great deal of "baggage." (For example, you will need to know a great deal about our ordinary concept of matter in order to understand what is meant by "electron.") Therefore, according to Quine, theoretical statements are a case in point of how and when translation is indeterminate.

For Quine, then, at least one reason for indeterminacy of translation is that it follows from the doctrine of underdetermination. From the fact that physical theory is underdetermined by its evidence, and the fact that linguistics is a part of behavioral science and hence ultimately of some physical theory, it follows (though trivially) that translation is underdetermined, i.e., indeterminate.

Two problems come to mind with this argument. First, as discussed above, Quine, correctly, abandoned the (strong) account of the doctrine of underdetermination. He no longer agrees that all physical theories are underdetermined by all possible evidence. For although there can be empirically equivalent theories, they are not necessarily incompatible. Unfortunately, without the strong account of the doctrine of underdetermination, indeterminacy no longer follows trivially.

The second difficulty with the argument is that Quine is presupposing that linguistics is a part of (or at least reducible to) physics. The truth of this presupposition depends on what is meant by "linguistics." If Quine means the science of language in terms of syntax, etymology, phonetics, and how we learn language, then he is probably correct. But Quine means more than this; in particular, he means to include semantics, the "meaning" of words. But if this is the case, then the truth of his claim is not so clear. It is not so obvious that a theory about the meanings of sentences is a part of (or reducible to) some physical theory.

Quine, of course, does not recognize a distinction between semantics and linguistics; but to presuppose an equivalence would clearly beg the question. In order to complete the task of defending the thesis of the indeterminacy of translation, Quine will have to show that a distinction between semantics and linguistics is a distinction without a difference. He will have to demonstrate that the only meaning, in fact, is stimulus meaning.

Furthermore, Quine claims that the thesis of the indeterminacy of translation is not simply a semantic "case" which falls under the doctrine of underdetermination, for concerning the former "there is simply no fact of the matter."[27]

Thus, concerning translation there is an "additional" indeterminacy. Even if the doctrine of underdetermination were false, or even if we simply settle for one overall theory of the world as opposed to another, there would still exist an indeterminacy to translation. The bottom line is that this indeterminacy (which goes "beyond" any indeterminacy in physical theory, i.e., underdetermination) stems from our inability to get clear on the traditional semantic account of sameness of meaning. (This will be discussed in detail below in connection with Quine's arguments for holism.) At this point it must be noted that the fact (if true) that there is empirical slack does not, by itself, demonstrate the truth of the indeterminacy thesis.

Behaviorism

In his article "Indeterminacy of Translation Again," Quine reviews his arguments from *Word and Object* in which he claims to have demonstrated that the only meaning that sentences have is stimulus meaning, that "there is nothing in linguistic meaning beyond what is gleaned from overt behavior in observable circumstances."[28] The thesis of the indeterminacy of translation is, according to Quine, a consequence of this. Quine's behavioristic conception of language can be summed up in the following:

> Each of us learns his language by observing other people's verbal behavior and having his own faltering verbal behavior observed and reinforced or corrected by others. We depend strictly on overt behavior in observable situations. As long as our command of our language fits all external checkpoints, where our utterance or our reaction to someone's utterance can be appraised in the light of some shared situation, so long all is well. Our mental life between checkpoints is indifferent to our rating as a master of the language.[29]

In other words, meaning is just stimulus meaning; there is nothing else. Full stop.

The process for translation, then, from source to target is the following. First, translate all those sentences which are closely linked to publicly observable situations, i.e., observation sentences. Second, test the translation via the native's assent to the use of the "Jungle" observation sentence at the appropriate time (i.e., given the recurrence of the original publicly observable situation). (This step requires a substep, namely, the conjecturing by the linguist that a specific sign is the sign for assent in Jungle society.) Third, translate all "complex" nonobservation sentences. (This step also requires substeps. First, "dissect" these sentences. Second, treat as words those segments that contain observation sentences. Third, create analytical hypotheses: with the help of English, attempt to "pair up" those complex sentences in Jungle that contain "words" with those complex sentences in English that contain those same "words.")

To set constraints on the above three steps (which are steeped in conjecture), the linguist may bring the following: Continuity, Empathy, and Simplicity. "Continuity is helpful; successive utterances may be expected to have some bearing on one another."[30] Empathy, the psychological attitude resulting from the linguist putting herself in the native's shoes, "is what sustains our radical translator all along the way."[31] 'Simplicity' is, simply, simplicity.

Concerning both observation and nonobservation sentences, it is the translator's psychological conjectures about what the native believes that allow her to proceed. After all, it is possible that the native is "believing" undetached rabbit parts or rabbit stages as opposed to rabbit when he exclaims *Gavagai!* in the presence of a rabbit. But according to Quine, the translator "will favor" the interpretation of *Gavagai!* consonant with the former belief. Why? Because by presupposing that the former belief was in fact the one that the native held, the translator would be forced to assign too many falsehoods (either to herself or) to the native. Therefore the translator (believing that no one could believe so many falsehoods) will have no other choice. Thus, the principle of charity* is born.

At this time the constraint of simplicity comes into play. For the linguist "will not cultivate these values [beliefs that stand to reason or are consonant with the native's observed way of life] at the cost of unduly complicating the structure to be imparted to the native's grammar and semantics."[32] Again, the linguist compares herself to the native. In assuming that the native has a brain similar to her own, she concludes that the native must have a language like her own, that is, one that is manageable, useable, i.e., simple.

Therefore, because the translator "puts herself in the native's shoes," she is not totally without guidelines for interpretation. By recognizing the biological need for simplicity, the translator is forced to find a balance between a translation that affords the native language as many true beliefs as possible without unduly complicating its structure. The upshot of all of this is that when the native's behavior seems to be one of assent when the linguist queries *Gavagai?* in the presence of a rabbit, the linguist performing radical translation has no choice but to translate the sentence *Gavagai!* into the sentence 'Lo Rabbit!'

According to Quine, the thought experiment above depicts the difficulties inherent in radical translation, specifically, that there is no "fact of the matter" to translation. The Gavagai example "exposes the poverty of ultimate data for the identification of meanings."[33] That is, according

---

*The principle of charity holds that "(other things being equal) one's interpretation of another speaker's words should minimize the ascription of false beliefs to that speaker." Ted Honderich, ed., *The Oxford Companion to Philosophy* (New York: Oxford University Press, 1995), p. 130.

to Quine, the above (hypothetical) "case study" demonstrates that there is no nonbehavioristic "data" available for translation, i.e., no meanings.

And if there is no nonbehavioristic data, and the behavioristic data that is available is not sufficient to ensure a unique translation, the linguist must depend entirely on conjecture concerning the behavior of the native speaker (e.g., determining whether behavior X is an assent behavior), conjecture concerning the way the world is, conjecture concerning the structure of human languages in general, and, most importantly, conjecture concerning the connection between all of the above. The translator must use this tiresome and cumbersome method of trial and error "not because meanings of sentences are elusive or inscrutable . . . [but] . . . because there is nothing to them, beyond what these fumbling procedures can come up with."[34] Meaning simply is stimulus meaning.

But if meaning is just stimulus meaning, then there is an indeterminacy inherent in translation. "Indeterminacy means not that there is no acceptable translation, but that there are many."[35]

Contrary to this, John Searle, in his article "Indeterminacy, Empiricism, and the First Person," has argued that public facts are not the only facts about meaning. Between the publicly observable situation (the stimulus) and the verbalization of some sentence (the response) there is something else that constitutes meaning. And understanding this "something else" is what semantics is really all about. Meaning cannot simply be reduced to referring.

As Searle points out, this nonpublicly observable aspect of meaning becomes apparent when one examines meaning in the first-person case, in which Quine's thesis of the necessarily public character of semantic evidence fails to capture what meaning is all about. When I say, for example, 'Lo Rabbit!' in the presence of a rabbit, I mean to be talking about (referring to) a rabbit and not a rabbit stage or undetached rabbit parts. But as Searle has pointed out,

> if Quine were right, then I may not mean what I think I mean. But this is absurd. If the argument [above] is valid, then it must have the result that there isn't any difference for me between meaning rabbit or rabbit stage, and that has the further result that there isn't any difference for me between referring to a rabbit and referring to a rabbit stage, and there isn't any difference for me between something's being a rabbit and its being a rabbit

stage. And all of this is a consequence of the behaviorist assumption that there isn't any meaning beyond behaviorist meaning. Once we concede that as far as behaviorist 'stimulus meaning' is concerned, 'There's a rabbit' and 'There's a rabbit stage' are "stimulus synonymous," then the rest follows because on the behaviorist hypothesis there isn't any other kind of objectively real meaning or synonymy.[36]

In other words, if the indeterminacy inherent in all translation is really a function of a sentence's lack of any objective meaning independent of "stimulus meaning," then I would not be able to mean anything in particular (because I could mean anything at all) even to myself by any of my expressions. But of course I know what I mean. Therefore, reductio ad absurdum, there must be an objective meaning independent of "stimulus meaning."

If this consequence of linguistic behaviorism does not itself serve to demonstrate the absurd consequences of the indeterminacy thesis, a consequence that Quine himself noticed, Searle points to the thesis's self-refuting nature. Searle reminds the reader that the reason the translator is able to

> understand the "Gavagai" example at all is precisely because meaning is something more than "stimulus meaning." If the indeterminacy thesis were really true, we would not even be able to understand its formulation; for when we were told there was no "fact of the matter" about the correctness of the translation between rabbit and rabbit stage, we would not have been able to hear any (objectively real) difference between the two English expressions to start with.[37]

In light of the above arguments, it is clear that the indeterminacy-of-translation thesis follows directly from linguistic behaviorism. If linguistic behaviorism were true, then the thesis of the indeterminacy of translation would be true. Unfortunately there is much wrong with linguistic behaviorism. To be specific, the "semantic" thesis, the essence of which states that the only meaning that sentences have is "stimulus meaning," leads eventually to the absurd consequence that I (let alone anyone else) may not know what I mean by any of my locutions. Furthermore, if linguistic behaviorism were true, the indeterminacy thesis itself would be incomprehensible. Therefore, linguistic behaviorism, *as a theory of meaning*, ought to be abandoned.

However, it does not follow from the above discrediting of Quine's linguistic behaviorism that the indeterminacy thesis is false, only that Quine has yet to demonstrate that it is true.

Also, it must be mentioned that Quine is attempting to account for the connection between our language and the extralinguistic objects to which it refers without reference to the (traditional) concept of meaning. Quine, believing that meanings are "obscure intermediary entities"[38] that ought to be abandoned, attempts to develop a theory of reference based entirely on empirical investigations into our actual linguistic behavior (specifically children learning their first language and adults learning a new language). To then claim that his theory of reference does not do everything we wanted a theory of meaning to do seems like a misplaced objection. This fact, Quine would claim, is due to the nature of language itself and not to his behavioristic account of it.

Although I am sympathetic to this move, it is important to realize that simply stating a disbelief in meaning, claiming that a theory of reference ought to be developed independently of a theory of meaning, does not make it a virtuous enterprise. Even bringing the failures of past attempts to offer an account of meaning (via, for example, intentions) does not seal the fate of classical semantics.

Inscrutability

When Quine suggests that the thesis of indeterminacy can be given assistance from whatever arguments can be based on the inscrutability of terms, it is not clear just what connection between the two he thinks exists. He calls it "pressing from below."[39]

The doctrine of the inscrutability of terms, usually called the inscrutability of reference, claims that although the stimulus meaning for a specific term, for example, *Gavagai*, correlates with the stimulus meaning for another specific term, for example, 'Rabbit', there is insufficient reason for believing that just because 'Rabbit' refers to rabbits that *Gavagai* necessarily refers to rabbits as well. After all, *Gavagai* may not refer at all, or if it does, then it may refer to rabbit stages or undetached rabbit parts.

As is the case with the arguments from underdetermination and behaviorism, the argument from inscrutability, which is used to support indeterminacy, is, at bottom, grounded in the following: There is no meaning (for terms, sentences) other than stimulus meaning. All semantic facts, if there are any, must be publicly observable. If there is no distinction to be made on the basis of publicly observable evidence, then there is no distinction. But as demonstrated above, this does not seem to be the case. There seems to be good empirical (though not necessarily publicly observable) evidence that there is more to meaning than what meets the eye (or ear, etc.), namely, that *I know what I mean by the terms and sentences I use.* There does not seem to be any reason to believe that translation is inherently indeterminate. Furthermore, there is some reason, namely, the case of the first person, for believing that it fundamentally is not. By way of the inscrutability thesis, then, the truth of the indeterminacy thesis remains inadequately demonstrated.

What Does All of This Prove?

If it could be shown that translation was indeterminate, then Quine would have had good reason for doubting that any program, like Carnap's, of rational reconstruction could have succeeded. But as demonstrated above (via the arguments concerning empirical slack, behaviorism, and inscrutability), indeterminacy has not been shown.

Interestingly, Quine does not even need to discuss the thesis of indeterminacy in order to demonstrate the inevitable failure of Carnapian programs of rational reconstruction. What he needs to show, and what he attempts to demonstrate elsewhere, is that if holism is true, then there is no way such a program could succeed. A program of rational reconstruction is a program of reduction, and reductionism presupposes that each statement, taken in isolation from its fellows, can admit of confirmation and disconfirmation. If this is not true, that is, if holism is true, then any program of rational reconstruction is doomed to failure. In addition to the above, it has been claimed that the most important single statement in Quine's writings is one that articulates the holism thesis: a statement about the world does not (usually) have a separable fund of empirical consequences that it can call its own. An analysis of this thesis will be given below.

Is Holism True?

In light of the failure of the arguments for underdetermination and indeterminacy, it can be stated that Quine has not provided good reason for
thinking that a program of rational reconstruction is doomed to failure
and, therefore, that we ought to abandon classical epistemology. But as we
have seen, Quine has also proposed the doctrine of holism to support his
urging to give up the Carnapian attempt to translate each sentence (taken
separately) of science into an observation sentence, i.e., a sentence composed of observation terms, logic, and set theory.

To repeat, the holism thesis claims that sentences of a theory are not
separately vulnerable to adverse observations because it is only jointly as
a theory that such sentences imply their observable consequences. In
other words, the individual sentences of a theory do not usually—observation sentences are exceptions—have unique ranges of confirming and
inferring observations associated with them. Thus, we can adhere to any
one of the sentences of the theory in the face of adverse observations by
revising truth values of other sentences in the theory.

It is this doctrine, then, that serves to "usher out" classical epistemology, whether empiricist or rationalist. "Holism serves to usher out empiricistic classical philosophy by showing both that the truths of nature
can neither be deduced from nor rationally constructed from such a basis
[a posteriori, synthetic, nonscientific truths and norms revealed by ex-
perience], and, further, that there simply are no analytic truths of the sort
envisioned by these empiricists."[40]

Holism serves to usher out rationalist classical philosophy in like
manner. Classical rationalists contend that reason reveals to them certain
a priori, synthetic, nonscientific truths and norms (e.g., Descartes's *cog-
ito* and its "mark" of clarity and distinctness) sufficient for deducing all
other truths. Quine's argument against rationalism consists first in denying the a priori character of any such alleged truths and norms, and second, in denying that even if there were such truth and norms, they would
be sufficient for deducing all other truths.

The holism doctrine is supported, according to Roger Gibson,[41] by
three separate arguments: (1) The scientific practices argument, (2) the
language learning argument, and (3) the reductio argument. (An analysis

of this last argument incorporates two other important arguments, namely, the argument against the maintaining of an analytic/synthetic distinction, and the argument against reductionism.)

The Scientific Practices Argument

What is the scientific practices argument and how is it used to defend holism? "The scientific practices argument is simply the claim that, as a matter of fact, a scientist involved in testing some hypothesis, H, must assume the truth of a set of auxiliary assumptions, A, and the hypothesis can always be saved by making drastic enough adjustments in A."[42] In other words, since it is just an empirical fact that scientists must assume the truth of auxiliary assumptions when testing some hypothesis, then holism is true.

Quine, following the discovery of Pierre Duhem, may be correct in claiming that some kind of auxiliary assumptions are always required in the testing of scientific hypotheses, but it does not follow from this that the thesis of holism is, at least in any nontrivial sense, true. For even if Duhem is right, that given any refutation of an experiment by a recalcitrant observation: $(H \& A) \to O$, $\sim O$, therefore $\sim(H \& A)$ that observation merely refutes either the hypothesis or the auxiliary hypotheses, not necessarily the hypothesis alone, this fact does not demonstrate that Quine's holism thesis is, in any interesting sense, true.

This thesis (the Duhem thesis) when combined with Quine's belief in verificationism (that the meaning of a sentence is identical with the empirical evidence for its truth) entails Quinian holism: that the sentences of a theory cannot, separately, be shown to be true or false. Only jointly, as a part of a theory, do sentences face the tribunal of experience in which "any statement can be held to be true come what may."[43]

But Quine cannot use the practice of actual scientists as evidence for the thesis of holism. First, it trivializes the thesis. As Adolf Grünbaum has pointed out:

> It can be made evident at once that unless Quine restricts in very specific ways what he understands by "drastic enough adjustments elsewhere in the (theoretical) system" the D-thesis [holism] is a thoroughly unenlightening

truism. For if someone were to put forward the false empirical hypothesis H that "Ordinary buttermilk is highly toxic to humans," this hypothesis could be saved from refutation in the face of the observed wholesomeness of ordinary buttermilk by making the following "drastic enough" adjustment in our system: changing the rules of English usage so that the intention of the term "ordinary buttermilk" is that of the term "arsenic" in its customary usage. [44]

As Grünbaum correctly asserts, "a necessary condition for the nontriviality of Duhem's thesis is that the theoretical language be semantically stable in the relevant respects."[45]

Unfortunately for Quine, this point cannot be easily digested. For if it is assumed that theoretical language is semantically stable, then there seems to be no reason for believing that every hypothesis can be saved. Using the above example of buttermilk, it becomes obvious that in the face of the observed wholesomeness of buttermilk, if we assume that "buttermilk" means buttermilk, "toxic" means toxic, etc., we would be forced to abandon the hypothesis that buttermilk is toxic.

Furthermore, in actual scientific practice, language, even theoretical language, is, for the most part, quite stable. Certain terms may be up for discussion, but for the most part the community of scientists accepts the language (even the theoretical language) to be semantically sturdy. (If this were not the case it would be a miracle if they could get anything done at all!) Second, Quine cannot use the above fact about the actual practices of scientists as evidence for his holism thesis. For one thing, such a move would be a non sequitur; for another it is simply false. "The argument is a non sequitur because there is no logical guarantee at all of the existence of the required kind of revised set A' of [nontrivial] auxiliary assumptions such that (H & [nontrivial] A') → O' for any one component hypothesis H and any O'."[46]

If the Quine/Duhem thesis is rewritten to take the objection of triviality into account, then it must take seriously the fact that the hypothesis in question is being examined within a certain accepted domain of knowledge. As such, there is no general program for disconfirmation, no "law" (H & A) → O, but only particular cases of disconfirmation within a particular domain (H & [nontrivial] A') → O'.

As such, simply demonstrating that the falsity of the hypothesis H is not deductively inferable from the lack of observational success ~O, does not, at least immediately, lead to the truth of the holism thesis. It must first be demonstrated that ~O is logically incompatible with O', and that A is really A' (that is, that A' is some nontrivial auxiliary hypothesis).

If it is the case that the holism thesis is, at best, a trivial thesis, then its truth must be established separately for each and every refutation. And without such particular confirmations, a belief in the truth of the holism thesis "is an unempirical dogma or article of faith."[47]

How does this affect Quine? According to Gibson, "like water off a duck's back."[48] Referring to an old piece of correspondence between Quine and Grünbaum where Quine admits that "the thesis, as I have used it *is* probably trivial,"[49] Gibson simply responds by saying that "Quine's primary interest in the D-thesis lay in its service in the cause of ushering out traditional epistemology, and not in the D-thesis itself as, say, a substantive claim about scientific theories."[50] This is a mere dismissal.

In a later work Quine himself dismisses Grünbaum's criticism without much ado.

> It is difficult to see how anyone can question holism, in the sense now before us. Grünbaum has indeed argued against holism, but in a stronger sense than is here entertained. He construes holism as claiming that when a prediction fails, we can always save the hypothesis by so revising the backlog of accepted theory that it, plus the threatened hypothesis, will imply the *failure* of the prediction. I am making no such presumption. Inactivating the false implications is all that is at stake. Explaining the unexpected counter-observation is quite another step of scientific progress, which may or may not be made in the fullness of time.
>
> Holism in this moderate sense is an obvious but vital correction of the naive conception of scientific sentences as endowed each with its own separable empirical content.[51]

The Language Learning Argument

The language learning argument claims that "the bulk of scientific, or referential, language is learned via irreducible leaps of analogy (viz., analogical synthesis)."[52] These "leaps" clearly allow an indeterminacy in meaning and reference, and the filling in of this indeterminacy along with its "empirical slack" requires a larger fund of knowledge. This is why, according to Quine, holism "occurs." The learning of language is not separable from a much larger fund of language in which it occurs, and which is in turn dependent on some ontology. For Quine, then, evidence for the truth of holism comes from the realization that one cannot learn language without the help of analogical synthesis (i.e., analogies).

This claim about the way that language is in fact learned is clearly an empirical claim. But what empirical evidence does Quine offer for this claim? And does such a theory, even if correct, answer semantic questions about meaning?

How Is Language Learned?

According to Quine, who is ultimately an empiricist, language learning, like all learning, begins with perception of the world. But for Quine this perception need not be made with the conscious awareness of the perceiver; it may be more fundamental, more physical, like the unconscious stimulation of nerve endings. He calls this kind of passive perception of the world reception.[53]

Through repeated stimulus to nerve endings and repeated conditioning, human beings are able to "recognize" receptual and perceptual similarities respectively. This ability to "recognize" similarities in perceptions (both conscious and unconscious) is something that Quine argues must, at least for certain perceptions, be innate. For this is the only way to explain how children can learn languages at all, and why certain accounts of perceptual similarity are universal throughout any language community. This fact would also help to explain why there are similar perceptual commitments in all human beings, for evolution would have ensured their survival. Therefore, although standards of perceptual similarity can be altered through experience, this phenomenon is the exception, not the norm. Learning in general, for Quine, is a matter of developing habits of perceptual and receptual similarity. These habits are developed first with the help of innate mechanisms and later through conditioning. Those perceptions and receptions that produce pleasure will be recognized and repetition will be attempted. Simply stated, "to learn is to learn to have fun."[54]

Learning language is a particular case of learning. It, too, is devel-

oped through conditioning. The child is first taught by ostension (observation sentences) and later by a combination of ostension with the help
of analogical synthesis (the rest of language). In either case, it is through
the act of conditioning that the child actually learns language. When the
child says the right thing, under the right circumstances (right as being
determined by the expert, i.e., an adult language speaker), she is re-
warded. What all of these facts about the learning of language mean for
Quine is that language is a purely social, public phenomenon. "The
structure resulting from these two general methods of language learning,
the language acquired, consists of a socially conditioned, continuously
evolving network for dispositions to respond verbally in various types of
stimulus situations."[55] The child, for example, when confronted with an
apple, hears her father say "Apple!" Then, when she repeats this sound
she is praised, positively reinforcing the socially established connection
between the stimulus apple with the response "Apple!"

What Does This Empirical Thesis Entail?

Not being a behavioral psychologist and not having studied psychology,
specifically child psychology, more specifically that aspect of child psychology which deals with language learning, I will not discuss its empirical adequacy. But what I believe becomes apparent from the above discussion is that only empirical evidence will vindicate Quine's thesis
about language learning.

More importantly for this discussion, I think that it is obvious that regardless of whether Quine's empirical claim about how children might
learn language is correct or not (specifically the part about analogical hypotheses), this has nothing to do with the doctrine of holism. The doctrine
of holism, at least at first blush, seems to be a philosophical (or at least
metascientific) claim about scientific theories, not a scientific theory itself.
As such, the language learning argument cannot support the holism thesis.

The Reductio Argument

The reductio argument runs as follows:

If every sentence of a theory had its own unique set of confirming and infirming experiential conditions, then we ought to be able to arrive at an acceptable theory of the confirmation of individual sentences, and we ought
to be able to draw an absolute analytic-synthetic distinction. However, we
have not been able to do either of these two things. Therefore, not every
sentence of a theory has its own unique sets of confirming and infirming experiential conditions (i.e., therefore holism). Conversely, if holism is true,
then epistemological reductionism is impossible and the quest for an absolute analytic-synthetic distinction is folly.[56]

Let H stand for the holism thesis; let C stand for the claim that one is able
to arrive at an acceptable theory of the confirmation of individual sentences (what is thought of by Quine as Carnap's goal for translation, also
called the program of rational reconstruction), and let A stand for the
claim that one is able to draw an absolute analytic-synthetic distinction.

Schematically, the two "reductio arguments" (A and B below) which
Gibson offers in defense of the holism thesis are:

(A) (1) If ~H, then (C and A)
    (2) ~C or ~A
therefore,
    (3) H.
And, conversely,
(B) (1) If H, then (~C and ~A)
    (2) H
therefore,
    (3) ~C and ~A.

Clearly the arguments above are valid, but are they sound? I will examine each in turn.

Argument (A) can be viewed as claiming the following: If either we
cannot come up with an acceptable theory of confirmation of individual
sentences (~C) or if we are unable to draw an absolute analytic-synthetic
distinction (~A), then holism is true (H). Therefore, Quine need only
demonstrate that ~C is true or that ~A is true in order to demonstrate that
H is true. He need not do both.

Is ~C True?

Why does Quine think that one cannot arrive at an acceptable theory of the confirmation (or disconfirmation) of individual sentences, that is, that ~C is true? Because, at bottom, Carnap failed in his attempts to develop a program of rational reconstruction.

Carnap's plan was to give significance to all statements (not terms), not merely statements about sense data, by way of a radical reductionism. "Carnap believed that one could give other significant statements (statements about physical objects) the epistemological weight that sense-data language had by translating all of the sentences of the former one by one into sentences of the latter. Unfortunately his program for translation was never completed. The construction of even the simplest statements about the physical world was left in a sketchy state."[57] Furthermore, "his [Carnap's] treatment of physical objects fell short of reduction not merely through sketchiness, but in principle."[58]

Why was such a program in principle doomed to failure? First, according to Quine, it was doomed because a complete account of translation was never developed. Second, and I think more important, it was doomed because of the ambiguity of the meaning of certain "connectives" (specifically "is at") found in the statements which needed to be translated.

The first reason is, of course, not philosophically satisfying. Just because Carnap did not develop such a program does not mean one cannot, in the future, be developed. The second reason is more substantial and is related to Quine's views concerning the ambiguity of meaning in general and will be discussed below. What is really at issue, however, is a third reason.

The third reason for accepting that ~C is true, that is, for rejecting what he calls the dogma of reductionism, is, simply, that holism is true.

Clearly, if Quine is to defend holism he must either defend his rejection of reductionism via his arguments against the analytic-synthetic distinction (arguments which are intimately connected to this discussion of the ambiguities in meaning), or by arguing against the analytic-synthetic distinction alone (that is, by showing that ~A is true). He must show why he accepts ~A, that is, why he rejects the analytic/synthetic distinction.

Is ~A True?

Why does Quine think that ~A is true, that is, that there is no ana-lytic/synthetic distinction? Why does he believe that the "fundamental cleavage between truths which are analytic, or grounded in meanings in-dependently of matters of fact, and truths which are synthetic, or grounded in fact,"[59] is a mere dogma of empiricism? The short answer is simply that the notion of analyticity stands in need of clarification. The long answer is another story altogether.

Quine begins his crusade against this cleavage with a discussion of analyticity itself. He looks to Hume's and Leibniz's distinctions between relations of ideas and matters of fact, and truths that could not possibly be false and truths that could possibly be false, respectively. He then moves to a discussion of Kant, who actually posited the "analytic/syn-thetic" distinction per se. According to Kant (à la Quine), "a statement is analytic when it is true by virtue of meanings and independent of fact."[60]

"Meaning" is then examined, and Quine shows that it, too, is am-biguous. He traces the notion of meaning to the Aristotelian notion of essence and then back to its contemporary state, divorced from essence. "Thus from the point of view of the doctrine of meaning it makes no sense to say of the actual individual, who is at once a man and a biped, that his rationality is essential and his two-leggedness accidental or vice versa. Things had essences for Aristotle, but only linguistic forms have meanings. Meaning is what essence becomes when it is divorced from the object of reference and wedded to the word."[61] But according to Quine, once meaning and its object of reference are sharply distinguished, the concept of meaning itself can be abandoned. And if all that is left is lan-guage (no objects), then the concept of meaning can be replaced by the concepts of synonymy (of words) and analyticity (of statements).

But again Quine queries: What is it really for a statement to be ana-lytically (as opposed to synthetically) true? He recognizes that philoso-phers usually talk about two classes of analytical statements: logical truths, where a true statement remains true under all interpretations of its components (e.g., No unmarried man is married), and synonymous truths, where a true statement can be turned into a logical truth by substitution of a synonym (e.g., No bachelor is married). Quine has no argument with the first class of analytic statements, logical truths. But he is disturbed by the second class, synonymous truths, because such a description depends "on a notion of 'synonymy' which is in no less need of clarification than analyticity itself."[62]

Therefore, if we are to defend a notion of analyticity, we must become clear as to what we mean by "synonymy." A natural suggestion would be to try to explain the notion of synonymy in terms of the notion of "by definition." After all, it seems that unmarried man is by definition synonymous with bachelor. But if we try to explain 'synonymy' in terms of 'definition', we find that we have made little headway because the notion of definition "hinges on prior relations of synonymy"[63] and not the other way around.

Another natural suggestion "is that the synonymy of two linguistic forms consists simply in their interchangeability in all contexts without change of truth value . . . salve veritate."[64] And although this concept is less vague (since it appeals only to a prior conception of a linguistic "form"), it does not render the desired results. "Under these conditions, 'bachelor' need not be synonymous with 'unmarried man'. Truths which become false under substitution of 'bachelor' and 'unmarried man' are easily constructed with the help of 'bachelor of arts' or 'bachelor buttons'; also with the help of quotation, thus: 'Bachelor' has less than ten letters."[65]

Furthermore, even if this account of interchangeability salve veritate were without the above difficulties, Quine claims that it is not clear that such an account offers a "strong enough condition for synonymy, or whether, on the contrary, some heteronymous expressions might be thus interchangeable."[66] For the notion of synonymy must be strong enough to account not merely for interchangeability, that is, extensional agreement relativized to a language, but for turning truths into logical truths, what Quine calls cognitive synonymy.

Synonymy, according to Quine, is supposed to be something more than just the accidental matter of fact (e.g., the fact that humans and only humans are creatures that have both kidneys and hearts) that two statements ("creature with kidney" and "creature with heart") share the same extension. In other words, the statements created through the interchanging of terms cannot just be true (accidentally); they must be true by definition, or analytically, to be considered synonymous. Now we are back at where we started.

"Analyticity at first seems most naturally definable by appeal to a realm of meanings. On refinement, the appeal to meanings gave way to an appeal to synonymy or definition. But definition turned out to be a will-o'-the-wisp, and synonymy turned out to be best understood only by dint of a prior appeal to analyticity itself. So we are back at the problem of analyticity."[67] For Quine, then, the case is clear: the notion of analyticity is not (clear). "And, without a clear notion of the concept of analytic itself, there does not seem to be any reason to maintain the analytic/synthetic distinction. But, for all its a priori reasonableness, a boundary between analytic and synthetic statements simply has not been drawn. That there is such a distinction to be drawn at all is an unempirical dogma of empiricists, a metaphysical article of faith."[68]

Has Quine offered good reason for thinking that the analytic/synthetic distinction ought to be abandoned? It depends. If he is claiming that the distinction ought to be abandoned because there are no analytic truths (the "strong" claim), then I think that, if he is right about this, then he does have good reason for dismissing the distinction as bogus. (But I think he is wrong.) If, on the other hand, he thinks that the distinction ought to be abandoned simply because the notion of analyticity (or synonymy) is in need of clarification (the "weak" claim), then even if he is right (and I think that he is), this alone does not support the abandonment of the distinction.

Concerning the "weak" claim, although it is clear that Quine has demonstrated this, it is trivial. Most difficult concepts, even some that Quine himself is fond of, are in need of further explication. Two points need to be made here. First, if Quine is to be consistent and if he insists on a complete reductive analysis for the term "analytic," he should insist on a complete reductive analysis for all terms. Second, there is no reason to insist on such rigor. Quine may be right in pointing out that such clarity of definition is not to be found (concerning the notion of "analytic" or any other term), but he is incorrect in thinking that anything as drastic as the elimination of such a term from our scientific vocabulary needs to take place. Concerning the "strong" claim I am much less sympathetic. Quine has not demonstrated that there are no analytic truths.

However, it seems intuitive that some statements are true by definition, and that, for example, 'No bachelors are married' is one such truth. This statement is true not because of any empirical facts about the world, but simply because of the meanings of the terms themselves. Quine would, of course, respond by saying that terms have no meanings, only sentences have meaning, and only stimulus meaning. But such a response, at this stage in the argument, holds little weight. Part of what is at issue here is whether terms (or sentences) have meanings at all, specifically meanings that can be fixed to more than one term. To make such an assumption clearly begs the question.

Quine, presupposing his naturalistic behavioristic conception of language, has confused developing an adequate test for determining analyticity with understanding the notion of analyticity. Given that Quine would only consider an operational test (or definition) as adequate, then he may be correct in claiming that we have no adequate test for determining analyticity. But it does not follow from this that we do not understand the notion. We do, and one obvious example that we do is the fact that we can understand Quine's objections.

Furthermore, even if Quine had demonstrated that there are no truths that are true "come what may," this does not demonstrate that there are no analytic truths.

This point can be clarified by noticing that there is no contradiction in claiming that a statement is analytic and yet claiming that it is open to empirical disconfirmation (separately or as part of a whole). Despite what is traditionally believed, one can, at least in principle, acquire (empirical) evidence against analytic truths.[69] And if this is the case, then the class of analytic truths and the class of truths that are true "come what may" are not extensionally equivalent. Therefore, Quine's demonstrating that there are no truths that are true "come what may" does not demonstrate that there are no analytic truths.

But more to the point for this discussion is the fact that the notion of analyticity does not speak to the doctrine of holism at all. Even if Quine had demonstrated the truth of the strong thesis, and therefore the illegitimacy of the analytic-synthetic distinction, this would not speak at all, let alone determine the truth of, the doctrine of holism. The two are entirely distinct doctrines.

The doctrine of analyticity expresses the semantic fact that some sentences are necessarily true. The holism doctrine makes an epistemic point that no statement, taken in isolation of its fellows, can admit of confirmation. These doctrines are not, at least logically, incompatible. It may be that the same truth is both analytic and yet confirmable only in concert with other truths. So demonstrating that there are no analytic truths does not, in and of itself, demonstrate that holism is true.

Quine, in not taking seriously the distinction between what something is and the test for its verification, has misconstrued his arguments against analyticity (actually against the concept of "sameness of meaning") as arguments in support of holism. Of course, Quine does not recognize such a distinction. What something is completely accounted for by its verification criteria. There is nothing to the truth of any sentence independent of its confirmation criteria. In the final analysis, Quinian holism follows from his naturalistic, behavioristic (N-B) concept of language.

Again, though, the truth of the N-B thesis has yet to be determined, and, ultimately, precisely what is at issue. To presuppose its truth in order to defend the rejection of the analytic/synthetic distinction is to beg the question.

Furthermore, holism may yet be vindicated, for there is still one more charge that the proponents of the analytic/synthetic distinction must face. Analytic truths are, according to Quine, a subset of a larger set of truths, namely, those truths which are knowable a priori. And the a priori/a posteriori distinction is itself, according to Quine, bogus. Unfortunately, the only reason offered by Gibson for Quine's rejecting the more general a priori/a posteriori distinction is that holism is true. Analytic (and other kinds of a priori) statements were said to be just those that a theorist could hold true in the face of all experiences. But if holism is true, then "it is misleading to speak of the empirical content of an individual statement—especially if it is a statement at all remote from the experiential periphery of the field."[70] While the debate concerning the legitimacy of the holism doctrine itself is at issue, such a move is clearly question-begging. Furthermore, Quine is presupposing that the class of all a priori truths entails the class of all analytic truths, and therefore, that the toppling of the former will simultaneously topple the latter. This presupposition, however, does not seem to be correct. That is, the entailment does not seem to hold up (either way). One could, at least in principle, come to know a contingent truth independent of any empirical evidence, i.e., by reflection alone, and yet this is, in fact, contingent, i.e., not analytic. One could, at least in principle, come to know an analytic truth via empirical evidence alone. Therefore, even if Quine had evidence in favor of the demise of the a priori/a posteriori distinction, it would not entail the demise of the analytic/synthetic distinction. (The connection between the two aside, I do not think that Quine is correct in leveling the same criticisms mutatis mutandi against the a priori/a posteriori distinction as against the analytic/synthetic distinction. For one thing, the a priori/a posteriori distinction does not suffer from the same ambiguity as the analytic/synthetic distinction. At least there is not the same ambiguity if the distinction is articulated in terms of the knower and not the truth that is being known. There certainly does seem to be something different from coming to know a truth with the help of empirical evidence as opposed to coming to know through reflection alone.)

Of course, this is not the understanding of the distinction that Quine was rejecting. Quine was rejecting the distinction as a distinction of the truth itself in that he believed that it fell prey to the same arguments as the analytic/synthetic distinction. But Quine aside, there is no reason why the concept of the a priori should not be maintained in the manner above.

In the final analysis, neither the scientific-practices argument, the language-learning argument, nor the reductio argument satisfactorily support the holism thesis.

In addition to Quine's failure to demonstrate empirically the soundness of this argument, it must be mentioned that it would seem that Quine's only recourse is to admit either that he has no reason for believing that the holism thesis is true or that he is appealing to some other (nonempirical) kind of reason. Either horn of this dilemma would be unacceptable for Quine. It seems that Quine is caught between the two. The first horn would be unacceptable, for even Quine recognizes that one must offer some kind of reason for one's claims. He certainly does not want to be accused of simply replacing one dogma for another. The second horn would be unacceptable because then Quine would be admitting that there is something "from without" that can be appealed to, i.e., that there is a first philosophy. And if there is a first philosophy, then the turn to naturalism has little appeal.

Most importantly for this discussion, even if holism is true (despite *all* Quine's failure to demonstrate this), it would not follow that classical epistemology ought to be abandoned.

For, even granting the truth of holism, it is not true that *all* classical epistemology must fail, but that *only one specific brand of classical epistemology must fail: Carnapian empiricism.* But unless Carnapian empiricism exhausts the possibilities of classical epistemology, classical epistemologists can rest easy.

The doctrine of underdetermination was intended by Quine to demonstrate that one must accept fallibilism. Assuming, as Quine did, that fallibilism is incompatible with classical epistemology, an acceptance of fallibilism meant a rejection of the classical account. But Quine has misrepresented the classical account, for it can be made compatible with fallibilism, and he has not been successful in showing that either indeterminacy or holism are true. That is, he has not demonstrated that translation is inherently indeterminate, and therefore we have little reason for doubting that a program of rational reconstruction could ever succeed. In addition, neither the scientific-practices argument, the language-learning argument, nor the reductio argument offer sufficient support (separately or collectively) for holism. Therefore, Quine has not offered sufficient reason for thinking that holism is true.

Furthermore, even if holism is true (which I think it is), this fact does not tell against classical accounts. The fact that statements (individually) are not (generally) confirmable (or disconfirmable) would be a problem only for a very specific kind of traditionalism: Carnapian empiricism.

In the final analysis, Quine's rejection of classical epistemology is, at best, premature, and, at worst, wrongheaded.

Premise One

Again, Quine's argument in favor of naturalism is the following:

(1) Traditionalism (classicalism) or Naturalism,
(2) Not Traditionalism (classicalism),
therefore,
(3) Naturalism.

Above I have shown that Quine has not offered sufficient reason to accept premise (2) as true. That is, Quine has not been successful in demonstrating that classical epistemology ought to be abandoned. But even if he had, it would not follow, at least immediately, that naturalism ought to be adopted in its stead. In order to make such a move, Quine would have to establish the fact that classical epistemology and naturalistic accounts are contradictory. He has not done this. Moreover, the rejection of classical epistemology does not seem to entail the acceptance of naturalism. Skepticism (if not some other "middle ground" position) is a real alternative to the adoption of naturalism in the wake of the (supposed) demise of the classical. Quine recognizes that the move to naturalism is not something that can be handled simply by logic. Therefore, he attempts to strengthen his case by both dismissing skepticism and by offering independent reasons for accepting naturalism.

In order to complete this analysis, then, I will attempt to show that Quine has been unsuccessful in both endeavors. He has neither given us good reason for dismissing skepticism, nor offered sufficient reason for adopting naturalism.

Furthermore, I will attempt to offer some reasons why naturalism cannot replace a more classical account as an adequate epistemology because such a move would create certain metaproblems: (1) Naturalism, as a philosophical position, is self-refuting. (2) Naturalism is not an epistemology.

AN ACCOUNT OF NATURALISM

According to Roger Gibson:[71]

> (1) . . . naturalism: the recognition that it is within science itself, and not in some prior philosophy, that reality is to be identified and described.[72]

> (2) . . . naturalism: abandonment of the goal of a first philosophy prior to natural science.[73]

Quine defines 'naturalism' in the following ways:

> (1) . . . naturalism: abandonment of the goal of a first philosophy. It sees natural science as an inquiry into reality, fallible and corrigible but not answerable to any super-scientific tribunal, and not in need of any justification beyond observation and the hypothetico-deductive method.[74]

(2) ... naturalism, ... [a] readiness to see philosophy as natural science trained upon itself and permitted free use of scientific findings.[75]

(3) ... my position is a naturalistic one; I see philosophy not as an a priori propaedeutic or groundwork for science, but as continuous with science. I see philosophy and science as in the same boat —a boat which, to revert to Neurath's figure as I so often do, we can rebuild only at sea while staying afloat in it. There is no external vantage point, no first philosophy.[76]

Quine claims that his naturalism has two sources, both negative.

One of them is despair of being able to define theoretical terms generally in terms of phenomena, even by contextual definition. A holistic or system-centered attitude should suffice to induce this despair. The other negative source of naturalism is unregenerate realism, the robust state of mind of the natural scientist who has never felt any qualms beyond the negotiable uncertainties internal to science.[77]

Since holism has been examined as a justification for the relinquishing of the classical approach (above) and it has been determined to be, at best, an inconclusive reason for the abandonment of classical epistemology, I will now concentrate on the second part of the claim—that unregenerate realism justifies one's turning to naturalism.

Scientism

According to Gibson, Quine offers two defenses of unregenerate realism. First, in defense, he offers the fact that unregenerate realism can meet the challenge of skepticism. Second, Quine (according to Gibson) claims that unregenerate realism needs no further justification, nothing further, that is, than its ability to conform to science itself (i.e., the hypothetico-deductive method).

Quine's response to the question of how the new epistemologist can legitimately use the findings of science to justify science has, I believe, two parts. "First, he argues that skepticism about science presupposes science. Second, he argues that science needs no justification beyond measuring up to the demands of the hypothetico-deductive method."[78] What will be examined now are the above justifications for unregenerate realism (and therefore, the turn to naturalism.)

Must All Skeptical Doubts Arise from Within Science?

In light of the above "demise" of the old empiricism, Quine suggests that the new "enlightened" empiricist take the prospect of a naturalistic epistemology seriously. Unfortunately, it may seem, at least at first blush, that such a naturalistic account is circular, given that any defense of scientific theory is grounded, ultimately, on science itself. But this fact does not discourage Quine from his proposal to naturalize. Quite the contrary; he attempts to demonstrate that the epistemologist has no other recourse, and that this circularity is epistemologically benign.

Quine argues for this position by pointing out that the opponent of science is also dependent on the findings of science. By pointing to traditional skeptical challenges (motivated by illusion such as, for example, the straight stick that looks bent when submerged in water), Quine attempts to show that skepticism is ultimately committed to science. Skepticism, claims Quine, arises in the following way. First, there is an experience of a physical occurrence. Second, this purported physical occurrence turns out to be a mere chimera. But, claims Quine, the only way that such an illusion can be recognized as an illusion, i.e., as illusory, is if there is a third step, namely, recognizing that the illusion is an illusion of an X. Therefore, according to Gibson, Quine has demonstrated that the recognition of illusion can only occur "relative to a prior acceptance of genuine bodies with which to contrast them [illusions]."[79] But such acceptance requires a former notion of genuine body. This notion of body is given by (low-level) science. Therefore, in the final analysis, skepticism is grounded in science. Given that it is sensory evidence of this sort (e.g., illusion) that enables the epistemologist to question the legitimacy of science, it turns out that ultimately it is science that is "thus needed as a springboard for skepticism."[80] The skeptical challenge, then, presupposes the self-same science that it is designed to criticize.

Instead of faulting the skeptic for using science as a self-refuting weapon against science, Quine makes an interesting move. First, he views the weapon as something that, to make the fight fair, he, too, is free to use. He claims that it is legitimate for the skeptic to use science to defeat science only if it is legitimate for the naturalist to use science to justify science. And second, he points out that skeptical questions are, ultimately, scientific questions. I am not accusing the skeptic of begging the question; he is quite within his rights in assuming science in order to refute science; this, if carried out, would be a straightforward argument by reductio ad absurdum. I am only making the point that skeptical doubts are scientific doubts.[81]

Quine has killed two birds with one stone. He has opened the door for his own free use of science in order to justify science. After all, if the skeptic can use science as a weapon for an attack upon science, it is only fair that the naturalist be allowed the same weapon for defense. He has offered evidence that there is no "first philosophy," no way to stand outside science, either to criticize or defend it. Even skeptical questions, according to Quine, are ultimately scientific questions.

This line of defense does not seem to be legitimate, for it trivializes skepticism, which is not merely a fleeting state of doubt that springs up on the occasion of illusion. As a matter of fact, skeptical doubts need not arise in the presence of any empirical evidence at all. These doubts can arise a priori. Cartesian skepticism—about the correctness of all of our perceptual evidence—is a case in point. Descartes (and many others), from the comfort of an armchair, questioned the correctness of his perceptions without the aid of an actual illusion. That is, he seriously questioned the existence of genuine objects when, in his search for knowledge, he supposed "that the sky, the air, the earth, colors, figures, sounds, and all external things, are nothing better than the illusions of dreams."[82] Descartes was questioning the certitude of empirical knowledge in toto, not the certitude of one perception relative to another. Therefore, at least at first blush, it does not seem to be the case that (all) skeptical doubt arises from within science.

Quine Is Not Free to Utilize Science

But even if it is the case that skeptical doubt must arise from within science, Quine is not free to utilize science when attempting to answer these doubts. To do so would be to argue in a circle.

It may be true that science itself teaches that there is no clairvoyance and that the only information that can reach our sensory surfaces from external objects must be limited to two-dimensional optical projections and various impacts of air waves on the eardrums and some gaseous reactions in the nasal passages and a few kindred odds and ends.[83]

But this is not enough to meet the challenge of the skeptic. Even if the skeptic must be committed to science (in the sense of relying on at least some of her perceptions), this fact alone would not, as Quine thinks, lessen the viciousness of his circular reasoning. If Quine is to take the skeptic seriously, he must face the challenge to science from outside the scope of science itself.

As Barry Stroud has pointed out, "even if 'skeptical doubts are scientific doubts' in the sense that the skeptical challenge arises because we originally accept many things as true about the physical world, it does not follow that we can make free use of what we accept as physical science in an attempt to meet that [skeptical] challenge."[84] Why? Because,

> even if viewed as a scientific doubt the skeptical force of the doubt remains intact. Suppose we have asked how any knowledge at all of the physical world is possible; and suppose that we have asked it because of what we take at the outset to be true about the physical world—in particular about the processes of perception. If we then arrived by reductio at the general skeptical conclusion which Quine thinks is at least coherent, we would find all our alleged knowledge of the physical world suspect; on either horn of the dilemma [whether or not science is true] none of it could be seen as knowledge. At that point in our investigation surely no scientific "knowledge" could then be unproblematically introduced to meet the skeptical challenge. We would have reached a tentative conclusion that nothing we believe about the physical world amounts to knowledge, so it would then be to no avail to appeal to some of those very beliefs about the physical world in the hope of showing how they all amount to knowledge after all. We would find ourselves precluded from using as independently reliable any part of what we had previously accepted as physical science; whatever we chose would be as open to question as everything else.[85]

It seems that as long as Quine allows that the skeptical question is legitimate, whether or not that question is viewed from within or without science, its skeptical force remains.

Unregenerate Realism

Insofar as Quine uses this appeal to the scientific origin of skeptical questions (i.e., "unregenerate realism") to justify science, and that appeal fails to noncircularly meet the challenge of the skeptic, naturalism remains unjustified.

But Quine does not rely solely upon unregenerate realism for his positive account of naturalism. According to Gibson, "the defender of science will have made his case if he can show that his science measures up to observation and the hypothetico-deductive [H-D] method."[86] Science, for Quine, needs no extrascientific justification. Unfortunately, this attempt to justify naturalism also fails because this kind of "justification" (conforming to the H-D method) is only as good as the H-D method itself, and the H-D method has not been independently justified. Furthermore, part of what is at issue here is the justificatory status of the H-D method itself. To argue in favor of the method simply by citing the method is, of course, to argue in a circle.

Quine could respond by claiming that the H-D method is self-justifying, or, more correctly, that there is no way to justify science except from within science itself. Given that there is no first philosophy from which we can stand "outside" science in order to judge science, there is no alternative but to justify science in the only way that we can, that is from within science, by presupposing the legitimacy of science and the H-D method. But this move does not work, first because this line of reasoning begs the question. The discussion of the H-D method arose within the context of Gibson's arguments attempting to defend Quine's positive thesis of naturalism. Part of this defense requires that the claim that the negative account of naturalism—i.e., that there is no first philosophy—be true. But while the debate between the naturalist and the nonnaturalist is being waged, to assume that there is no first philosophy clearly begs the question.

Quine may respond to this latter objection by claiming that asking for a justification of the H-D method is like asking for a justification of induction. This, according to Quine, would be a wasted effort. As he states, "the Humean predicament is the human predicament."[87] My response here is simply to recognize that there is a serious problem of induction, but to claim that the solving of this problem is something that must be tackled. Quine's brushing off of the problem is inadequate.

Science Must Be Extrascientifically Justified

In light of the above, then, it seems that some extrascientific justification of unregenerate realism or the H-D method is the only way to support naturalism without question-begging. Of course, for Quine to do so would be self-refuting.

There Is No "First Philosophy"

But what of naturalism as a negative thesis? Is Quine justified in claiming that there is "no first philosophy"? First, we have to get clear on what Quine means by the expression "no first philosophy."[88] In Quine's works this expression has taken on the following forms: (1) There is no "science" "prior to natural science";[89] (2) There is "no infallible, incorrigible inquiry into reality";[90] (3) There is no need for a "super-scientific tribunal"[91] or "an a priori propaedeutic or groundwork for science";[92] and (4) We must see philosophy simply as "natural science trained upon itself."[93] I will examine each of the above to see if Quine is justified in claiming that there is "no first philosophy."

Concerning the last formulation first, I think that the answer is quite simply and obviously no. Even if Quine is correct in claiming that much of what has been called philosophy (e.g., philosophy of language, philosophy of science and epistemology) should be "seen" as some aspect of natural science "trained upon itself," he would be hard-pressed to show that much else of what has been called philosophy (e.g., ethics, aesthetics, and metaphysics) should be viewed in this way. Unless much more work is done, the scope of Quine's claim must be narrowed if it is to be taken seriously.

But narrowing the scope of Quine's claim does not, in this case, lessen its force. Simply claiming that epistemology must go the way of empirical psychology, as has been demonstrated, is certainly serious enough to deserve attention.

What of the second interpretation of the "no first philosophy" thesis? Is Quine correct in stating that there is no infallible, incorrigible inquiry into reality? Yes, but, in stating this it should not be assumed that naturalism is the only alternative.

Concerning the notion of infallibility, it has already been stated that one can consistently maintain a form of classical epistemology that embraces fallibilism. One could, for example, claim that a belief's being justified does not entail that the belief be true (or vice versa). The two are separate (though connected) notions. To claim that the classical epistemologist must view his beliefs about science as infallible is to misconstrue the classical position. Therefore, Quine could be correct that there is no infallible inquiry into the nature of reality and yet be incorrect in claiming that there is "no first philosophy."

Concerning the notion of incorrigibility, it is not clear why Quine objects to this. Incorrigibility like indubitability, as stated above, is a hallmark of "mental" beliefs, not scientific ones. It is beliefs about one's own mental states, not factual claims about the external world, that, at least classically, have been said to have the property of incorrigibility; that is, one cannot be wrong about one's own mental states. But the debate between the classical and naturalistic epistemologist is not (ordinarily) about the mental. It is a debate about the status of our extramental scientific beliefs. Furthermore, Descartes aside, few traditional philosophers ever attempted to defend the position that beliefs about the external world were incorrigible. Although Quine may be correct that there is no incorrigible way to inquire into reality, this point does not bear at all on the debate between the classical and naturalistic epistemologist.

Parenthetically, in addition to the above, even if classical accounts do entail the goal of establishing infallible and/or incorrigible (scientific) beliefs, Quine's demonstrating that such a goal cannot be reached does not, in and of itself, entail naturalism. Skepticism is at least as plausible a default position. Therefore, even if Quine had properly characterized the goals of the classical position, and even if he had adequately demonstrated that such goals could not be reached, he has not demonstrated that one should turn to science. At best he has shown that the abandonment of a "first philosophy" entails disjunction skepticism or some otherism (not necessarily naturalism).

This last point, then, speaks directly to the first formulation. If there really is no "science" prior to natural science, then maybe we will have to settle for the fact that science is itself not justified. Again, it does not follow directly from the fact that there is no "first philosophy" that science is self-justified.

This brings us to the third of the above interpretations of the phrase "no first philosophy": that there is no need for a superscientific tribunal, no need for an a priori propaedeutic or groundwork for science. Concerning this interpretation Quine is simply mistaken.

There is a need for a superscientific, extrascientific, metascientific, or whathaveyouscientific tribunal, and the need is (among other places) precisely where Quine denies there is any: determining the adequacy (justificatory status) of specific scientific claims, arguments, and methodologies. There are a host of questions about science, such as, Ought we take empirical evidence seriously, or Does science give us the best view of the world? These seem to be legitimate questions.[94]

Of course, one could deny that the above questions are "legitimate" questions or, more simply, extend the scope of science to incorporate all of the above. Both of these moves are indefensible, however.

The latter move is indefensible because it considerably weakens the claim that there is "no first philosophy." To say that everything is science simply by stipulating that everything is science makes the thesis true but trivial because the classical questions are still legitimate; they are just called "scientific."

On the other hand, attempting to claim that such questions are illegitimate would require a prior argument demonstrating that there is, in fact, "no first philosophy." But this is precisely the sort of argument that Quine claims cannot be given. It seems, then, that Quine cannot fairly or consistently rule such questions out of court. To sum up, Quine has not demonstrated, on any appropriate characterization of the traditional position, that there is "no first philosophy." Quine has not demonstrated that his negative grounds for naturalism are secure.

Given that Quine has not succeeded in showing that his grounds for naturalism, positive or negative, are secure, his arguments in favor of naturalism are themselves ungrounded. Even if one were justified in abandoning the classical project (which I have shown is not the case), one would not be justified in adopting naturalism in its stead.

METAPROBLEMS

In addition to these problems I think that naturalism suffers from problems at a "meta" level that are even more serious. Any attempt to argue in favor of a naturalized epistemology, and therefore all of Quine's arguments in favor of a naturalized epistemology, are self-refuting. Even more importantly, naturalized epistemology does not seem to be, properly, epistemology. These issues will be discussed below.

One Cannot Argue for Quinian Naturalism

In attempting to analyze Quine's writings, I am constantly bothered by the feeling that Quine is not arguing for his position, at least not in the traditional sense. Instead he is simply making a suggestion: Why not naturalize?

Perhaps Quine, like a salesman who really believes that his product is better than his competitor's, is simply out to "sell" his product. By first offering examples of how the competitor's product failed at a specific task and then suggesting that the consumer should adopt his product in its place, Quine hopes simply to persuade his opponent that his position is better.

My feelings aside, though, I believe that it is only proper to assume that Quine, being one of the greatest contemporary philosophers (scientists?), not as far as I know one of the greatest salesmen, must have good reasons for urging the abandonment of the classical program in favor of a naturalistic one.

And what reasons has Quine offered? It seems, at least at first blush, that he is offering a classical, even a priori argument in favor of naturalism! But if this is the case then there is at least one area of philosophy that must remain nonempirical, namely, the examination of the metaphilosophical debate between the Quinian naturalist and the classical epistemologist

Should Epistemology Be Naturalized?

The most serious objection to such an account is that it cannot, in principle, fulfill one important function of epistemology: The development of a general account of the criteria for determining the justificatory status of our beliefs. As Gibson correctly points out, there are some philosophers who view Quine's proposal to naturalize epistemology as too radical to be considered epistemology. They believe that epistemology simply cannot be naturalized; such an attempt would be tantamount to abandoning epistemology altogether. They believe this because they regard psychology as a descriptive discipline and epistemology to be a normative one. Thus psychology cannot do the job of epistemology: the job of providing an analysis of justified true belief.[95]

Even if Quine's arguments for naturalism were sound, naturalism would not be considered a satisfactory account by some epistemologists because it would not be merely an alternative approach to the achieving of epistemological goals. To some epistemologists, the naturalizing of epistemology would mean the abandonment of epistemology (and maybe even philosophy) altogether.

The debate focuses on two interrelated questions: (1) What counts as the proper epistemological task? and (2) What counts as a proper approach to that task?

The "old" epistemological question was something like the following: 'How is knowledge possible?' or 'What are the criteria of justification?' The "old" epistemological answer was something that was normative in nature and discoverable by some means that were ultimately beyond experience, i.e., knowable through reason alone, knowable a priori. Epistemology, according to this program, could only be accomplished through an a priori "investigation" into the necessary and sufficient criteria for determining what we ought to believe. No amount of experience could ever tell us what, in the manner of Kant, must necessarily be so and not otherwise. Epistemology then, in order to do justice to its own endeavors, cannot be naturalized.

But the kind of classical question stated above is not the kind of epistemological problem that Quine is trying to solve. Quine, like Rorty, denounces the notion of justification itself. He claims that what we really need to answer (the only thing that we can answer) is a question like the following: "Given only the evidence of our senses, how do we arrive at our theory of the world?"[96]

What seems at first to be clearly two different questions, Quine argues, are ultimately the same question, though viewed in two different ways. According to Quine, there "is no gratuitous change of subject matter, but an enlightened persistence rather in the original epistemological problem."[97] This change of questions must occur, he thinks, because the old question is illegitimate: it stems from a tradition that presupposes "truth is correspondence, that knowledge is incorrigible, and the existence of the external world needs to be demonstrated."[98] The upshot of all of this is that the classical question is not answered because it is illegitimate.

With the classical question out of the way, the epistemologist, according to Quine, is free to substitute another, naturalistic question in its place.

Furthermore, he soothes, the classical epistemologist should not feel as if epistemology is being abandoned altogether because of this change of view. Underlying both the classical and the enlightened questions is one goal: the attempt to understand the connection between what we perceive through our senses and the scientific theory that we develop. According to Quine: "If we are out simply to understand the link between observation and science, we are well advised to use any available information, including that provided by the very same science whose link with observation we are seeking to understand."[99] And what does that very same science tell us? It tells us, according to Quine, that "the stimulation of his sensory receptors is all the evidence anybody has to go on, ultimately, in arriving at his picture of the world."[100]

One can still ask whether the above claim is, itself, a scientific claim. It seems not to be; rather, it seems to be a metascientific claim about science, specifically about what counts as evidence.

Although Quine claims that with this change of question came a necessary change of answer, this does not seem to be the case. Quine claims that with the change in question, no longer was an a priori investigation into the nature of knowledge necessary, or even possible, and that an adequate epistemology must be developed completely naturalistically. All we really need to do is study our (human) psychologies. But if the above metaquestion concerning the nature of the claim is legitimate, then there is, still, a need for an a priori investigation into the nature of knowledge, albeit, at a different level.

QUINE HAS NOT BEEN SUCCESSFUL

Quine's original argument is the following:

> Traditionalism (classicalism) or Naturalism,
> Not Traditionalism (classicalism),
> therefore,
> Naturalism.

This argument is clearly valid, but it is not sound. As demonstrated above, Quine has not provided good reason for abandoning classical epistemology. The reasons offered—underdetermination, indeterminacy, and holism—are not sufficient for warranting a complete dismissal of classical epistemology. Furthermore, even if the abandonment of the classical program were warranted, Quine would have to supply independent justification for accepting a naturalistic program. Such justification (I have argued here) is not adequate. Quine has not been able to meet the skeptical challenges to epistemology, and the fact that science can meet scientific challenges, while not trivial, does not suffice to support naturalism.

Metaepistemological considerations also demonstrate difficulties for a naturalized epistemology. First, any naturalistic account tends to be self-refuting. Second, and more importantly, purely naturalistic accounts of epistemology cannot, in principle, be epistemologies. Given the fact that epistemology is radically normative, naturalistic considerations, taken alone, cannot satisfactorily accomplish epistemological tasks.

In view of the fact that Quine has not offered good reasons for either abandoning classical epistemology or for adopting naturalism, it becomes clear that a yes answer to the question, 'Is Quine right?' is without support. Quine has not shown us that we should naturalize epistemology.

Notes

1. Plato, *Theaetetus* (201).
2. Roger F. Gibson, *Enlightened Empiricism* (Tampa, Fla.: University Press of Florida, 1988), p. 118.
3. W. V. Quine, "On Empirically Equivalent Systems of the World," *Erkenntnis* 9 (1975): 323.
4. Ibid., p. 324.
5. W. V. Quine, *Word and Object* (Cambridge, Mass.: Harvard University Press, 1960), p. 27.
6. Gibson, *Enlightened Empiricism*, p. 102.
7. W. V. Quine, "Things and Their Place in Theories," in *Theories and Things* (Cambridge, Mass.: Harvard University Press, 1981), p. 23.
8. W. V. Quine, "Reply to Hilary Putnam," in *The Philosophy of W. V. Quine*, ed. Edwin Hahn and Paul Arthur Schilpp (LaSalle, Ill.: Open Court Press, 1986), p. 429.

9. W. V. Quine, "Epistemology Naturalized," in *Ontological Relativity and Other Essays* (New York: Columbia University Press, 1969), p. 76.

10. Ibid., p. 75.

11. Ibid.

12. Ibid.

13. Quine, "Epistemology Naturalized," p. 75.

14. Ibid.

15. W. V. Quine, "On the Reasons for the Indeterminacy of Translations," *Journal of Philosophy* 67 (1970): 181.

16. Ibid., p. 183.

17. W. V. Quine, "Indeterminacy of Translation Again," *Journal of Philosophy* 84 (1987): 5.

18. Ibid.

19. Quine, "On the Reasons," p. 183.

20. Ibid., p. 179.

21. Quine, "Indeterminacy of Translation," p. 6.

22. Ibid.

23. Ibid.

24. Quine, "On the Reasons," p. 179.

25. Quine, "Indeterminacy of Translation," p. 6.

26. Ibid., p. 7.

27. Quine, "Indeterminacy of Translation," p. 10.

28. Ibid., p. 5.

29. Ibid.

30. Ibid., p. 7.

31. Ibid., p. 8.

32. Ibid., p. 7.

33. Ibid.

34. Ibid., p. 8.

35. Ibid., p. 9.

36. John Searle, "Indeterminacy, Empiricism, and the First Person," *Journal of Philosophy* 84 (1987): 130–31.

37. Ibid., p. 131.

38. W. V. Quine, "Two Dogmas of Empiricism," in *From a Logical Point of View* (New York: Harper and Row, 1953), p. 22.

39. Quine, "On the Reasons," p. 183.

40. Gibson, *Enlightened Empiricism*, p. 26.

41. Gibson's first book, *The Philosophy of W. V. Quine*, was actually prefaced by Quine with his complete approval. His second book, *Enlightened Empiricism*, was not so prefaced, but he is considered to be, nonetheless, one of the few people who Quine believes really understands his account.

42. Roger F. Gibson, "Quine on Naturalism and Epistemology," *Erkenntnis* 27 (1987): 68.

43. Quine, "Two Dogmas," p. 43.
44. Adolf Grünbaum, "The Falsifiability of Theories: Total or Partial? A Contemporary Evaluation of the Duhem-Quine Thesis," *Synthese* 14 (1962): 20.
45. Ibid.
46. Ibid., p. 19.
47. Ibid.
48. Gibson, *Enlightened Empiricism,* p. 35.
49. W. V. Quine, "Letters to Professor Grünbaum," in *Can Theories Be Refuted? Essays on the Duhem-Quine Thesis,* ed. S. Harding (Dordrecht, Holland: D. Reidel Publishing Co., 1976), p. 131.
50. Gibson, *Enlightened Empiricism,* pp. 35–36.
51. W. V. Quine, *Pursuit of Truth* (Cambridge, Mass.: Harvard University Press, 1990), p. 16.
52. Gibson, "Quine on Naturalism," p. 66.
53. W. V. Quine, *The Roots of Reference* (LaSalle, Ill.: Open Court Press, 1973), pp. 1–4.
54. Ibid., p. 28.
55. Roger F. Gibson, *The Philosophy of W. V. Quine* (Tampa, Fla.: University Press of Florida, 1982), p. 41.
56. Gibson, "Quine on Naturalism," pp. 66–67. See also Gibson, *Enlightened Empiricism,* pp. 37–42, for an explanation of the reductio argument.
57. Quine, "Two Dogmas," p. 36.
58. Ibid.
59. Ibid., p. 26.
60. Ibid.
61. Ibid., p. 27.
62. Ibid.
63. Ibid., p. 30.
64. Ibid.
65. Ibid.
66. Ibid.
67. Ibid., p. 32.
68. Ibid., p. 34.
69. See Edwin Erwin, "The Confirmation Machine," in *Boston Studies in the Philosophy of Science,* vol. 7, ed. Roger C. Buck and Robert S. Cohen (Dordrecht, Holland: Reidel Publishing Co., 1971).
70. Quine, "Two Dogmas," p. 43, quoted in Gibson, *Enlightened Empiricism,* p. 28.
71. Gibson, "Quine on Naturalism," p. 57; Gibson, *Enlightened Empiricism,* pp. 23–24.
72. Quine, "Things and Their Place," p. 21.
73. W. V. Quine, "Five Milestones of Empiricism," in *Theories and Things,* p. 67.
74. Ibid., p. 72.

75. W. V. Quine, "Russell's Ontological Development," in *Theories and Things*, p. 85.

76. Quine, "Ontological Relativity," in *Ontological Relativity and Other Essays*, pp. 126–27.

77. Quine, "Five Milestones of Empiricism," p. 72.

78. Gibson, *Enlightened Empiricism*, p. 29.

79. Ibid., pp. 29–30.

80. Quine, "Nature of Natural Knowledge," p. 68.

81. Ibid.

82. Descartes, *Meditations on First Philosophy*, p. 22.

83. Quine, *Roots of Reference*, p. 2.

84. Barry Stroud, "The Significance of Naturalized Epistemology," in *Naturalizing Epistemology*, ed. Hilary Kornblith (Cambridge, Mass.: MIT Press, 1979), p. 85.

85. Ibid., pp. 84–85.

86. Gibson, *Enlightened Empiricism*, p. 59.

87. Quine, "Epistemology Naturalized," p. 72.

88. Quine, "Ontological Relativity," p. 127.

89. Quine, "Five Milestones of Empiricism," p. 72.

90. Ibid.

91. Ibid.

92. Quine, "Ontological Relativity," p. 126.

93. Quine, "Russell's Ontological Development," p. 85.

94. Harvey Siegel, "Empirical Psychology, Naturalized Epistemology and First Philosophy," *Philosophy of Science* 51 (1984): 674.

95. Gibson, "Quine on Naturalism," p. 75.

96. Quine, *Word and Object*, p. 1.

97 Quine, *Roots of Reference*, p. 3.

98. Gibson, *Enlightened Empiricism*, p. 83.

99. Quine, "Epistemology Naturalized," p. 76.

100. Ibid., p. 75.

6

Feminism and Naturalism, Part 2

And suppose that men are naturally dominant because of the miraculous testosterone. . . . Why should feminists be reluctant to admit it, or anti-feminists think that it clinches their case? Even if men are naturally inclined to dominance it does not follow that they ought to be allowed to run everything.

J. R. Richards[1]

To return more directly to the focus of this book, the important question really is: will going natural—that is, reducing (to some level or other) normative theories of justification to descriptive neurophysiological accounts of our collective mental processes—be particularly feminist, i.e., vindicate women as "knowers"?

Hardly. Gender-neutrality is not ensured by a naturalized epistemology any more than androcentrism is endemic to classical normative accounts (see chapter 2). It is not clear that naturalized accounts would be feminist in the only way that matters, i.e., good for women.

In the first place, naturalism, at least in its most general articulation, has been a nemesis of women. 'Naturalism' is a concept "commonly used in patriarchal discourses to justify women's social subordination and their secondary positions relative to men in patriarchal society."[2] There is no easier justification for discrimination than an appeal to the ways things are, naturally.

Of course, this is not the sense of 'naturalism' that is discussed by Quine. But even the Quinian version of naturalism does not make things any more palatable for the feminists. Quine's naturalized account of epistemology is nothing more than science studying science by assimilating epistemology "to empirical psychology."[3] And science itself is on shaky ground with respect to feminism. "A naturalized epistemology, and given the demise of foundationalism there can be no other kind," according to Nelson, "will explain how we have gone about constructing theories. If our theories prove successful—if they help us to make sense of and to predict experiences—then, if an epistemology provides a correct account of how we know, that epistemology provides the 'how' of successful theorizing."[4]

In his now famous 1969 plea Quine queries the rationalists and empiricists who are on the "wild-goose chase in search of some privileged class of unconditionally accepted, nonscientific truths":[5]

> But why all this creative reconstruction, all this make-believe? The stimulation of his sensory receptors is all the evidence anybody has to go on, ultimately in arriving at his picture of the world. Why not just see how this construction really proceeds? Why not settle for psychology?[6]

He adds that any

> scruples against circularity have little point once we have stopped dreaming of deducing science from observations. If we are out simply to understand the link between observation and science, we are well advised to use any available information, including that provided by the very science whose link with observation we are seeking to understand.[7]

According to Quine, "the fear of circularity is a case of needless timidity."[8] In the final analysis, science is all there is.

And what does our now scientific epistemologist discover about this epistemology/science?

> [He] comes out with an account that has a good deal to do with the learning of language and with the neurology of perceptions. . . . Evolution and

natural selection will doubtlessly figure in this account, and he will feel free to apply physics if he sees a way.

The naturalistic philosopher begins his reasoning within the inherited world theory as a going concern. He tentatively believes all of it.[9]

This account, at least in light of recent criticism of science (and the philosophy of science), is a far cry from feminism.

For one thing the appeal to evolution and natural selection has, at least historically, often been used not to help but to harm women. From the myths about vaginally centered orgasm (which make women feel as if penises, and therefore men, are a necessary part of their sex life) to the definition of women's work (centering around the home and care of children, not the higher paying and often more intellectually rewarding work in the public sector) to the sexual neediness of men (having been used as a way of avoiding the seriousness of rape and other forms of assault on women), the biological evidence via the standard accounts of evolution and natural selection have had substantial political ramifications for women. Almost all feminist theorists make some comments about the man-the-hunter model of human evolution and its antecedent unjustified political ramification.[10] But "the strongest of the feminist arguments about justice for women have *nothing whatever* to do with the extent to which men and women are alike or different by nature."[11]

With respect to those feminists following at Quine's heels, they should, at the very least, keep a skeptical eye on his slavish devotion to science en toto, to "the robust state of mind of the natural scientist who has never felt any qualms beyond the negotiable uncertainties internal to science."[12]

Finally, all feminists must remember that the original criticisms of traditional science (and philosophy of science) are chronologically and logically prior to all other criticism. Without solid science criticism, the critiques of classical epistemology are on shaky ground.

This can be demonstrated by reexamining the brief history of feminist criticism. Back in chapter 2, Carol Gilligan's *In a Different Voice* was discussed as having motivated what I have called first-generation feminism. Gilligan's goal was "to expand the understanding of human development by using the group left out in the construction of theory [i.e., girls and/or women] to call attention to what is missing in its account."[13] Thus, she opened the door for the first wave of feminist science critiques leveled against science by working scientists.[14] This form of science criticism was later dubbed by Harding "feminist empiricism"—the critique of science that "argues that sexism and androcentrism are social biases correctable by stricter adherence to existing methodological norms of scientific inquiry."[15]

The second generation of critiques was started by Harding herself. No longer were feminists content to play by the old boys' rules, simply asking that they take their own criteria more seriously as well as acknowledge the work of women in their field. Now it was time to criticize the method(s) of science itself, more specifically, the concept of 'objectivity', and the distinction between 'fact' and 'value' became the main foci of feminist criticism. Objectivity and value-neutrality were ostensibly exposed as a male-biased myth that could be unveiled only from a "feminist standpoint." "Briefly, this proposal argues that men's dominating position in social life results in partial and perverse understandings, whereas women's subjugated position provides the possibility of more complete and less perverse understandings."[16]

Second-generation feminism was clearly the most philosophically provocative. It started with an all-out assault on critical analysis, perhaps even "the abandonment of philosophy altogether,"[17] via criticisms of everything philosophical, from logic[18] to ethics.[19]

Though feminist epistemologists now stand at a more reasonable place, the above outline shows that they cannot accept both Quinian naturalism and the feminist historical/logical beginnings to ground their own epistemological programs. A school of thought that gives science carte blanche is not compatible with one that must remain skeptical of science at some, if not all, levels of inquiry.

Finally, naturalized accounts of epistemology are problematic in their own right. First, in its heart of hearts epistemology is a normative enterprise. This is something even Quine accepts.[20] If the attempt to determine the justificatory status of our beliefs is completely abandoned, and we simply settle for the descriptive enterprise of discovering the psychological/neurophysiological mechanisms behind belief acquisition itself, we have ceased to do epistemology.

Even Nelson remarks that justification takes on a different role:

"When epistemology is recognized to be a part of science and not ante-cedent to it, it is not playing a justificatory role—at least not as that role is commonly construed."[21] As Jaegwon Kim says, "If justification drops out of epistemology, knowledge itself drops out of epistemology."[22]

What kind of knowledge did we desire anyway? As philosophers we want to answer some very difficult and fundamental questions, e.g., Theaetetus-like questions concerning the difference between true belief (with or without an account) and knowledge; or Cartesian questions con-cerning the radical skeptic; or, most pressing to the contemporary epis-temologist, questions challenging induction, the nature of evidence, and the privileged epistemic position of science itself. Appealing to science in any of these cases seems an act of desperation, an attempt to end the play via the *deux ex machina*.

In conclusion, the feminist proponents of naturalized epistemology have not demonstrated either that classical epistemic criteria are funda-mentally androcentric, nor have they succeeded in showing that a natu-ralized account is necessarily more feminist than its nonnatural com-petitors. I therefore suggest that feminists don their classical garb with pride and resist the temptation to go natural.

Is Any Naturalism Good for Women?

DURAN: NATURALISM AND FEMINISM

Jane Duran prefaces her book *Toward a Feminist Epistemology* with the following comment: "The unsophisticated question that presents itself quite naturally to the philosopher examining work in feminist theory of knowledge is *what precisely is it that is to count as a theory of knowledge here [within the context of feminism] in any interesting sense?*"[23] The short answer is what Duran calls feminist epistemics, a theory of justifi-cation which she claims is "simultaneously naturalized and gynocen-tric."[24] The long answer will be fleshed out as follows.

The Development of Duran's Account

Duran's project revolves around an attempt to wed what has been loosely called "feminist epistemology" with more classical theories of knowledge. The offspring of such a bond, Duran's "feminist epistemic," is billed as an account which brings out the best of both feminist and nonfeminist epistemology, while leaving the worst behind.

From feminism will be gained the respect for the Gilligan empirical lesson that women, taken as whole, are more interested in "contextualization, communicative awareness, and bodily awareness"[25] than their male counterparts. For while the latter is concerned with universal, categorical imperatives and the role of the individual, the former is more concerned with existential, hypothetical imperatives and the role of relationships. What will be lost, it is intended, will be the sloppy and metaphorical nature of much of the work in feminist theory involving epistemology.

From classical epistemology will be gained, according to Duran, the "virtue"[26] of "precision and, to some extent, rigor of work."[27] Abandoned will be the characteristics that, she claims, are most androcentric, namely, an epistemology that has any one or more of the following elements: a "large skeptical component . . . [caused by the desire] to create a foundation or incorrigible basis for knowledge,"[28] i.e., the desire to "obtain epistemic certainty";[29] an articulation that is exclusively "normative and idealized";[30] placing an "emphasis on reason, pure and speculative, divorced from the influence of the passions and bodily functions."[31] By combining the best of both, avoiding the sloppiness of feminist theory and the androcentrism inherent in classical epistemology, Duran attempts to create an analytic/feminist epistemology.

Duran's Naturalism

Duran's project is to "integrate feminist theory and naturalized epistemology"[32] to show that "naturalized epistemology meshes with and can become a part of feminist theory."[33]

Naturalism and Feminism Presuppose that We Have Knowledge

Duran's motivation for focusing on naturalized epistemology is twofold. First, according to Duran, naturalized accounts of epistemology have something fundamental in common with feminist accounts, specifically, the assumption that "we can and do have knowledge . . . that those we deem to be knowers actually do possess knowledge."[34] Like the Gilliganites of old, who assumed that women, despite how they arrived at their moral beliefs or what moral beliefs they arrived at, are good moral agents, naturalists assume that humans, despite how they arrived at their epistemic beliefs or what epistemic beliefs they arrived at, are good epistemic agents.

Duran's fundamental metaepistemological belief, then, is that women can and do (in general) have knowledge and it is the epistemologist's job to see how it is acquired, i.e., by what neurophysiological mechanisms. The fundamentally naturalistic "rib" developed by male epistemologists is now being used to create feminist epistemics. As in the case with both naturalisms, the classical, fundamentally normative, epistemic endeavor—i.e., the attempt to develop, a priori, the general criteria for determining the justificatory status of our beliefs—is simply abandoned.[35] In its place is something completely descriptive: an examination of "the actual modes of cognizing and coming-to-knowledge."[36]

It is important to note that many feminist theorists would not want to develop anything from men's theories, and therefore would not want to superimpose naturalism on to feminist accounts of epistemology. These more radical (philosophical) feminists would disavow Duran's work out of hand, simply on the grounds that it attempts even to make sense of, let alone incorporate, male methods and concepts.

Naturalism Focuses on the Body

The second reason Duran turns to naturalized accounts is that she believes that such epistemologies, by their very nature, are less sexist because of their focus on the body, specifically the brain. "Awareness-of-body," Duran claims, is a key element of feminism.

Now it is not clear what it means for a theory of knowledge to have commitments to awareness-of-body in the context of most feminist writing, and Duran points this out. For her, though, there is no poetry and no "weak metaphor,"[37] something often claimed about much of what is written under the rubric of feminist philosophy. A justified belief, for Duran, is one that is produced given certain stimuli and specific neural processes.

Feminist Epistemics

In light of the above motivations Duran creates "A Feminist Epistemic"[38]—an "analytic framework that integrates feminist theory and naturalized epistemology";[39] an epistemological account that maintains what is good about men's epistemology, i.e., its rigor, while taking seriously the concerns of women, i.e., it relies heavily on the notions of "contextualization and communication."[40] The result is the following theory of "justification": A belief is justified if it coheres with all the other beliefs in one's system. One's system, in turn, is justified only if it coheres with the social norms and practices of the surrounding community, i.e., the utterances are processed in the brains of all its members in such a way that communication among all of its members can take place. She offers the following as a formalized account:

> A statement p is justified from the naturalized cohering standpoint if:
> (i) the statement is in a justifying network or set of statements, J, for cognizer s at t;
> (ii) if it appears that the set J is underdetermined, conflicting justifying sets or networks are discarded on contextual grounds, the grounds including:
> (a) that the set J that is picked out is most fully in accord with social norms and practices, such practices reducing to:
> (1) specification of each justifier for statement-to-be-justified p results from a process of epistemic intent on the part of the challenger manifesting itself in a string of utterances, which when heard by the epistemic agent result in a neurophysiological passage of the utterance into symbolically encoded information correlated with certain semantic interpretations if the utterance falls into the category of information that the agent has processed before the utterances must be recognized by the epistemic agent as intended to produce a state of doubt;

(2) epistemic agent in a state of doubt responds to challenger with verbal output (processed along the specific lines);

(3) challenger recognizes the output as justifiers and such recognition is manifested in output of acquiescence (or further challenge);

and (b) that social communication itself is the norm by which (a) is judged.[41]

Given that Duran offers us little in terms of nonjargonized explanation of her "naturalized gynocentric model,"[42] and no concrete examples, I believe the best way to approach the above account is simply in terms of straightforward coherentism. That is, beliefs are justified if they cohere to all of *our* other beliefs. What makes this particular account (once its bare bones are exposed) feminist is unclear, but it must have something to do with how "our" is fleshed out.

Criticisms

What for Quine in the sixties was a way of avoiding the futility of "creative reconstruction"[43] is for Duran in the nineties a way of avoiding sexism. One ought to "go natural" because naturalized accounts of epistemology are "less androcentric than the tradition of pure epistemology."[44] What was once the Humean predicament (the age-old problem of justifying our beliefs) and therefore, according to Quine, the human predicament, is now, according to Duran, more precisely the woman's predicament—and the solution, it seems, is coherentism discoverable through cognitive science.

But will this treatment work? Will going natural—that is, reducing normative theories of justification to descriptive neurophysiological accounts of our mental processes that result in a community's ability to communicate—vindicate women as "knowers"? Furthermore, is the turn to naturalism really necessary? Is classical epistemology inherently sexist? In what follows I will show that: (1) Duran's articulation of classical epistemology, specifically its desire for certainty, is a caricature; (2) there is no real evidence that once classical epistemology is properly characterized, via its commitment to the normative, that its nature is fundamentally androcentric; and (3) that even if classical epistemology is fundamentally sexist, a naturalized account would not be any less so.

Classical Epistemology Caricatured

Duran claims that one of the essential attributes of classical epistemology is its desire to create a "foundational or incorrigible basis for knowledge"[45] or the desire to "obtain epistemic certainty."[46] This is an exaggeration.

First of all, 'foundationalism' and 'incorrigibility' are two entirely different concepts. 'Incorrigibility', by which I mean 'beyond correction', is, as stated earlier, a hallmark of "mental" beliefs, not scientific beliefs. It is beliefs about one's own mental states, not factual claims about the external world, which may have the property of incorrigibility. One cannot be wrong, for instance, that she is having a pain-sensation-nowly. However, most foundationalist accounts of epistemology are not interested in this kind of belief; instead, they are interested in offering epistemic foundations to our scientific beliefs which may not be infallible. 'Incorrigibility' is, therefore, not really an issue for most contemporary foundationalist epistemologists.[47]

The second point is that foundationalism is not committed to absolute certainty. Foundationalism is compatible with fallibilism since foundations need only be justified, and not be certain.

Even if Duran has offered reasons for rejecting her account of foundationalism on the grounds that its desire for certainty and indubitability indicate its sexism, she is arguing against a straw account. Few, if any, contemporary foundationalist epistemologists[48] currently maintain such commitments, and the burden of proof is on her to indicate which account, precisely, she is rejecting.

Is Foundationalism Androcentric?

Duran is correct, however, that foundationalists are committed to some notion of the normative. After all, there has to be something special about certain beliefs—they have to be more true, more justified, more firmly grounded, or more something—for them to be "foundational." Now the question is, Is the concept of 'normativity' essentially androcentric?

The Historical Fallacy, Again

For Duran that which is most objectionable is the fact that *normative* epistemologies avoid alluding "to the manner in which cognizers actually function."[49] Of course, this is just to make the analytic claim that normative accounts, not being descriptive, are not naturalized accounts. Nevertheless, it is still not clear just what it is about the concept of normativity that is sexist. One possible (sympathetic) reading tells us that what is sexist is the fact that classical epistemologies, having been written by men and having been used by men to oppress women, often appealed to the normative. The norms, actually endorsed historically, were, in fact, consistently and intentionally associated with men's, not women's, "ways of knowing." Therefore, normative accounts may be branded androcentric simply by association.

Of course, arguing from the history of philosophy, at best, determines only the fact that men have been sexist, not that the concepts they employ are inherently so. It seems a category mistake to call principles of knowledge acquisition, as opposed to the person upholding those specific principles, sexist.

The Hermeneutic Fallacy, Again

This, though, is not her only line of attack. Duran goes on to claim that any classical (normative) epistemology is "androcentric precisely because it has cut context off from the knower . . . [by accepting] the divorce of in-the-bodiness from knowing."[50]

Although I agree that much of the philosophical literature emphasizes mind over body, thinking over feeling, I am at a loss to see how such a program is essentially androcentric. Is it because the dichotomy itself, or the act of dichotomizing, is sexist? In addition, there are many examples in the Western philosophical corpus of men who celebrate body, including Plato and Nietzsche. Even entire schools of thought, for example, existentialism and phenomenology, attempt to balance their epistemic commitments between mind and body.

Even if one grants Duran the fact that the history of Western philosophy and psychoanalysis is littered with sexism, and given that these same texts are filled with dichotomies—e.g., mind/body—the connection between the two seems tenuous.

Duran, however, in line with most feminists, claims that the attempt to dichotomize mind/body, thinking/feeling is the philosophical "articulation of the aggression that the male child employs to separate himself from the mother. . . . [T]he male child pulls away from the female nurturing figure by separating himself psychologically from the figure and by devaluing females and female-oriented activities."[51] Aside from the fact that most of psychoanalysis is on shaky evidential ground at best, my question is: When did 'body' become a female (as opposed to a male) concept and when did 'feeling' become a strictly female-oriented activity?

One can appeal to the vast history of Western philosophy where texts can be read with an androcentric slant. According to Duran, "Not only did Plato and other thinkers emphasize a mode of knowing that was divorced from the body because the senses were prone to err, but the entire mode of being-in-the-body experienced by males is such that it lends itself to a greater separation of the realm of the mental from the realm of the physical."[52] Again, granted that there was an attempt by Plato, Descartes, and many others to escape their corporealness, why must I, as a woman, associate myself with body? To read the text this way is to presuppose precisely that which is at issue: that women must associate themselves with body and that women's ways of knowing must include feeling.

Is Duran's Naturalism Less Sexist?

The above criticisms, however, do not get to the heart of the problem with Duran's account: that a naturalized account of epistemology would be feminist in the only important way, i.e., good for women.

As already noted, at least in its most general articulation, 'naturalism' has been the enemy of women. It is one of the terms that is "commonly used in patriarchal discourses to justify women's social subordination and their secondary positions relative to men in patriarchal society."[53] There is no easier justification for discrimination than an appeal to the ways things are, naturally.

Within Duran's specific account of naturalized epistemology, the situation is even more problematic. If one's beliefs are justified only insofar as they are arrived at by certain processes and the justifying set to which they belong is only as good as it jibes "with social norms and practices,"[54] then given certain empirical evidence about those processes or certain societies and their norms, women's beliefs could be easily ruled unjustified.

This becomes obvious if one imagines a society primarily composed of men, or one in which men are in all positions of power. In such a society it is possible that men arrive at their beliefs in ways entirely different from those of women or that men's language is inaccessible to most women (or if not inaccessible in fact, viewed as such by most men). Oddly enough, this is precisely the society in which many radical (philosophical) feminists claim we live. And in such a society it would be permissible, actually obligatory, to discriminate against women (see them as subordinate), on the grounds that they are incapable of justified beliefs.

The fact that women can have no justified beliefs, moreover, would not be an accidental characteristic, something that education and nurturing could eliminate. The beliefs would be unjustified by their very nature; the truth of the claim—"women are irrational"—would be analytic.

Of course, Duran could envision a world in which women make up the power structure of the community and determine its language, social norms, and what counts as an appropriate mental process. Although this would make for an environment in which women's beliefs would be justified, such a world neither does nor must exist. Naturalism, at best, does not entail feminism. At worst, the naturalizing of epistemology may be used to help justify discrimination[55] and therefore undermine the very reason for developing a feminist epistemic.

Duran's Naturalized Epistemology Is Not

In addition, one could object to Duran's account on the grounds that it cannot, in principle, fulfill one important epistemic function: the development of a general account of the (a priori) criteria for determining the justificatory status of our beliefs. It cannot answer the original epistemic question: What makes a belief good or, at least, better than some other belief?

Simply defining 'justified' as 'obtained by a certain mental process' only stalls the question at another level of inquiry; it does not answer it.

For one could recognize precisely what neurophysiological processes one does, in fact, use and still wonder about which ones *ought* to be used. The truly epistemological question remains open.

Furthermore, it seems that Duran (and other reliabilists*) are committed, albeit at another level of inquiry, to the same classical concept of justification they seek to eliminate. After all, naturalists will not choose just any brain process, e.g., one that ensures false or inconsistent beliefs. Naturalists want to choose processes that are good. But by what metacriteria will "goodness" be determined? And is not the search for these criteria precisely what the classical epistemologist claims must be conducted a priori? This, I have argued elsewhere,[56] is true of all naturalisms. Duran's is no exception.

Summary

Duran has not demonstrated either that classical epistemology is fundamentally androcentric, or that a naturalized account is necessarily feminist. Given this, along with the fact that naturalized accounts of epistemology cannot fulfill their function, we should dismiss naturalism and reinstate the classical/normative/nonnatural epistemological project as the only truly epistemic project and the only project that is apolitical, unbiased, objective, and, ultimately, good for everyone, even women.

NATURALISM, OF ANY STRIPE, IS NOT GOOD FOR WOMEN

What is most important to point out, however, is that naturalism, Quinian or post-Quinian, is not good for women, because at bottom it must be committed to some form of essentialism. If one is not a feminist, this essentialism can be represented sex/gender-neutrally and would, therefore, be politically benign. Whether male or female, as humans, we are together.

Remember, at the heart of epistemological naturalism is the belief that science, ultimately, will be the final arbiter in deciding the "justi-

---

*Reliabilism is an account of epistemic justification which claims that a belief is justified if it has been obtained via a reliable mechanism—a cognitive activity which produces more true than false beliefs. See Alvin Goldman, *Epistemology and Cognition* (Cambridge, Mass.: Harvard University Press, 1986).

fiedness" of our beliefs. For the naturalist denies the possibility of radical skepticism and assumes that we have knowledge—empirical knowledge, that is, for that is all the knowledge there is to be had. Such an assumption forces the epistemologist to concentrate on the beliefs *we* do have, rather than on the beliefs *we* should.

But what kind of 'we' is this? Again, without political boundaries 'we' can be seen as sex/gender-neutral. But feminism, as determined above by feminists themselves, is, finally and fundamentally, political, with the very specific goal of empowering women. As such it cannot, at least not fully, embrace the gender-neutral 'we'. It must make a distinction between men and women.

Furthermore, the difference between men and women cannot be something inconsequential or contingent. It must be essential; women must be fundamentally and inherently different.

Here I will examine the "difference argument" and its reliance on essentialism, the assertion that women are not just different, but inherently different. Lorraine Code, for example, describes the belief in such difference as the "belief in an essence, an inherent, natural, eternal female nature that manifests itself in such characteristics as gentleness, goodness, nurturance, and sensitivity."[57]

Whether that difference, that essential female quality, is the result of nature or nurture, essentialism states that it cannot be overcome. If we are different as a result of nature, then giving women the same cognitive tools as men will not benefit women, since women naturally cannot use the same tools men use. If our difference results from nurture, then giving women the same tools as men is an impossibility due to cultural and social constraints. Women and men will always be taught to think differently and be treated differently, hence they will develop differently.

Two things follow from the above. First, women *may* not be able to play with the men's toys/tools. Second, given the first, women ought to develop their own.

Given that the attempt to do the latter, develop women's epistemic tools, has proved problematic (the point of chapters 1, 2, and 3) either because those consistent with feminist theory are worthless in helping women, and those that have been used to help women are, in fact, the same ones men have always used, the choice is to adopt the former.

Unfortunately, an adoption of the former could lead very quickly to sexism. Clearly, naturalism—even an account developed by a woman with the express goal of helping other women—is no friend of feminism.

Notes

1. Janet Radcliffe Richards, *The Skeptical Feminist* (Harmondsworth, UK: Pelican, 1982), p. 44.

2. Elizabeth Grosz, "Conclusion: A Note on Essentialism and Difference," in *Feminist Knowledge: Critique and Construct*, ed. S. Gunew (New York: Routledge, 1990), p. 333.

3. W. V. Quine, "Five Milestones of Empiricism," in *Theories and Things* (Cambridge, Mass.: Harvard University Press, 1981), p. 72.

4. Lynn Hankinson Nelson, *Who Knows? From Quine to a Feminist Empiricism* (Philadelphia: Temple University Press, 1990), p. 291.

5. Roger F. Gibson, *Enlightened Empiricism* (Tampa, Fla.: University of South Florida, 1988), p. 25.

6. W. V. Quine, "Epistemology Naturalized," in *Ontological Relativity and Other Essays* (New York: Columbia University Press, 1969), p. 75.

7. Ibid., p. 76.

8. W. V. Quine, *The Roots of Reference* (LaSalle, Ill.: Open Court Press, 1973), p. 2.

9. Quine, "Five Milestones of Empiricism," p. 72.

10. See, e.g., Lynda Birke, *Women, Feminism and Biology: The Feminist Challenge* (New York: Methuen Press, 1986).

11. Richards, *The Skeptical Feminist*, p. 43.

12. Quine, "Five Milestones of Empiricism," p. 72.

13. Carol Gilligan, *In a Different Voice* (Cambridge, Mass.: Harvard University Press, 1982).

14. See, e.g., Evelyn Fox Keller, *Reflections on Science and Gender* (New Haven, Conn.: Yale University Press, 1985), and Ruth Bleier, *Science and Gender: A Critique of Biology and Its Theories on Women* (New York: Pergamon Press, 1984).

15. Sandra Harding, *The Science Question in Feminism* (Ithaca, N.Y.: Cornell University Press, 1986), p. 24.

16. Ibid., p. 26.

17. Alison M. Jaggar, "How Can Philosophy Be Feminist?" *APA Newsletter on Feminism* (April 1988): 7.

18. See, e.g., Ruth Ginzberg, "Feminism, Rationality and Logic," *APA Newsletter* 88, no. 2 (1989): 34–39, and Andrea Nye, *Words of Power: A Feminist Reading of the History of Logic* (New York: Routledge, 1990).

19. See, e.g., Nel Noddings, *Caring: A Feminist Approach to Ethics and Moral Education* (Berkeley: University of California Press, 1986).

20. W. V. Quine, *Pursuit of Truth* (Cambridge, Mass.: Harvard University Press, 1990), pp. 19–21.

21. Nelson, *Who Knows?* p. 291.

22. Jaegwon Kim, "What Is Naturalized Epistemology?" *Philosophical Perspectives* 2 (1988): 381–405.

23. Jane Duran, *Toward a Feminist Epistemology* (Savage, Md.: Rowman and Littlefield, 1991), p. xi.

24. Ibid., p. 124.

25. Ibid., p. 114.

26. Ibid., p. 108.

27. Ibid., p. 126.

28. Ibid., p. 80.

29. Ibid., p. 25.

30. Ibid., p. 106.

31. Ibid., pp. 7–8.

32. Ibid., p. 114.

33. Ibid., p. 106.

34. Ibid., p. 4.

35. I realize that some naturalisms claim to be "normative," see, for example, Susan Haack's work. I think that such middle-ground projects are problematic. See, e.g., E. R. Klein, "Is 'Normative Naturalism' an Oxymoron? A Response to Mc-Cauley," *Philosophical Psychology* 5, no. 3 (1992): 307–308.

36. Duran, *Toward a Feminist Epistemology*, p. 112.

37. Ibid., p. 114.

38. Ibid., p. 116.

39. Ibid.

40. Ibid.

41. Ibid., pp. 103–32.

42. Ibid., p. 127.

43. Quine, "Epistemology Naturalized," p. 75.

44. Duran, *Toward a Feminist Epistemology*, p. 4.

45. Ibid., p. 80.

46. Ibid., p. 25.

47. I consider foundationalism to be a subset of what I have been calling classical epistemology.

48. Even Chisholm is a fallibilist. See Roderick Chisholm, *Theory of Knowledge*, 2d ed. (Englewood Cliffs, N.J.: Prentice Hall, 1977).

49. Duran, *Toward a Feminist Epistemology*, p. 13.

50. Ibid., p. 84.

51. Ibid., p. 75.

52. Ibid., p. 85.

53. Grosz, "Conclusion," p. 333.

54. Duran, *Toward a Feminist Epistemology*, p. 121.

55. For the purpose of this book, I mean discrimination against women. But the same would be true for minorities, other species, etc.

56. See E. R. Klein, "Is 'Normative Naturalism' an Oxymoron?" pp. 289–97.

57. Lorraine Code, *What Can She Know? Feminist Theory and the Construction of Knowledge* (Ithaca, N.Y.: Cornell University Press, 1991), pp. 53–55.

7

Pedagogy and University Politics: Getting Personal

Academic Institutions *are* profoundly patriarchic in how they reproduce knowledge in masculine bodies. Likewise, they are profoundly phallocentric in their reproduction of a particular version of theoretical discourse supportive of ideologies that discriminate against women.

Magda Gere Lewis[1]

To teach is to guide students through the course material in such a way that they come to form a series of rationally based true beliefs with regard to it.

Peter J. Markie[2]

It is not the aim of education to make the student feel good about himself or herself. On the contrary; if anything, a good education should lead to a permanent sense of dissatisfaction.

John Searle[3]

In the subtitle of this chapter, I am playing on the fact that the phrase "the personal is the political" has been "a caveat of the contemporary feminist movement."[4] An investigation of contemporary pedagogy and the impact feminism has had on it will occupy us here. I will argue that academic feminists have done more harm than good with respect to the education of our students, particularly our female students.

199

Feminism in the Academy: My Own Case

I begin this discussion with a few modest personal examples. The first is an account of how the feminists on my own campus reacted to my criticism of professional feminism. The stories are, of course, only evidentially anecdotal; nonetheless they tell of what I have confronted in the "scholarly" community both within and outside my particular institution.

PEDAGOGY

In the 1993 spring semester I offered an advanced (3000 level) course entitled "Feminist Philosophy." Below is the syllabus.

FEMINIST PHILOSOPHY
PHI 3930

Required Texts:
Gender and Science, Keller
The Man of Reason, Lloyd
Is Women's Philosophy Possible?, Holland
What Can She Know?, Code
Whose Science? Whose Knowledge?, Harding
Toward a Feminist Epistemology?, Duran
Who Knows?, Nelson

Course Description:
Is classical epistemology, philosophy of science, and the method of critical analysis itself essentially male-biased? This question is at the heart of feminist philosophy and, I believe, it is imperative that we address it.

This question needs serious attention; for so much is at stake, especially in such a volatile academic climate as the one surrounding the question of Political Correctness (P.C.) If the answer is yes, as is assumed by many feminists, then the whole character of philosophy must change. If philosophizing is itself male-biased, then every nonsexist and antisexist philosopher is morally obligated to replace his/her goals and methods (including the way we teach philosophy) with those prescribed by feminists.*

---

*Actually, this does not follow, at least not directly. What we may want to do is take the male-biased philosophy and substitute it for a gender-neutral philosophy or a feminist standpoint approach. The feminists opt for the second on the grounds that they believe that there is no such thing as a gender-neutral stance. Whether they are right about this will be the main topic of discussion in this class.

These changes would not take place only within the walls of philosophy departments. The ramifications of such a methodological shift would be far reaching. Given that every academic discipline is grounded in the same methodological commitments as the analytic philosopher (e.g., language, logic, and evidence), if philosophy falls to this kind of feminist criticism, the rest of the academy shall crumble with it.

Because of the important nature of the male-bias question, this class will be devoted solely to the quest for an answer.

Course Mechanics:

Students are expected to attend and be prepared for all classes.

(1) Students will be required to outline each book, article, or paper. Outlines are due at the beginning of the class period following the class period in which they were assigned. In addition, students will prepare critical questions to be asked in class. These assignments will count for 20% of the student's final grade.

(2) Students will be required to write a short critical paper* (approx. 10 pgs.) on any area of feminist philosophy—you must DEFEND feminism. This paper is due at the beginning of the class period before spring break. This paper will count for 20% of the student's final grade.

(3) Students will be required to present a revised version (a second draft) of their paper to the rest of the class. Presentation date to be determined—Once the date has been determined, students cannot make alterations without the permission of the instructor, and only if someone else is willing to swap their time-slot. The presentation will count for 20% of the student's final grade.

(4) Students will be required to write a short critical paper on each presentation. This paper will be due on the class period following the presentation and copies are to be turned in to me and the original presenter. This short paper will count for 20% of the student's final grade.

(5) Students will be required to hand in a third and final draft of their paper, taking peer criticism into account, at the beginning of the last class period. The final draft should be of conference quality and will count for 20% of the student's final grade.

NO LATE OUTLINES, PAPERS, OR PROJECTS WILL BE ACCEPTED.

---

*A critical paper:

(1) Make clear and concise normative claim—at least in the first paragraph, preferably in the first sentence.

(2) Attempt to defend that claim:

(a) Give reasons why one should take the claim seriously.

(b) Offer at least one possible counterclaim to the original claim, demonstrating why you believe that it fails (and therefore why you are rationally pressed to maintain the original claim).

As you can see, it was a very serious philosophy course. As it normally happens the first day of class found me in front of a number of students I had never seen before. Since I was unfamiliar with their work I asked that each be prepared to "do" serious philosophy. As such, anyone who had never taken an introductory course in philosophy should perhaps think of dropping out. No one moved. I then decided to go around the room and arbitrarily ask the new faces a question: What is philosophy?

It is important to first note that almost any attempt to answer the question would have sufficed, since it is the skills and courage of the method of critical analysis itself in which I was really interested. Most people attempted some answer and I encouraged their response in the usual way, i.e., with more questions. If the answer was, after a few minutes of dialogue, still inappropriate, for example, "I do not know," I gently but firmly suggested that the student enroll in my Introduction to Philosophy class instead of taking on the feminism course.

After the first class and sometime before the next session I was called into my chair's office and told that he had received a number of complaints concerning my style in the classroom, including complaints from professors! It turns out, I was informed, that six of the new students, all from the Women Studies Program, along with their two primary professors (who had not attended), found me to be "brusque." They were offended and wanted me reprimanded. My chair did not see fit simply to discuss the problem; in all his wisdom the event showed up on my yearly evaluation. It is important to note that I have been teaching for nearly fifteen years, and in this time I have received an overwhelming amount of superb evaluations from students at all levels. In addition, many of my former students personally thank me for my frank and demanding style. My chair knew this and for him to have referred to this isolated incident in such an important document was inappropriate, to say the least.

I believe this occurrence to be possibly indicative of three things: First, that "much of what students learn in women's studies classes is not disciplined scholarship but feminist ideology."[5] After all, if the six students described above were serious students, in any sense of the word, they would have seized the opportunity for philosophical challenge. Interestingly, the remaining "new faces" (some men, some women) who also had no philosophical training remained in the course and found it to be interesting and challenging. They voiced no complaints.

Second, that administrators, too wary to stand up to the wave of political correctness that has infected the academy, specifically in terms of what Christina Hoff Sommers calls "feminist colonization," are too ready to kneel at the altar of the "gender feminists." (An important distinction should be made between 'equity feminists'—those who embrace no special feminist doctrines, but merely want for women what they want for everyone, a "fair field and no favors"—and 'gender feminists'—those who believe they are in the vanguard of a conceptual revolution of historic proportions.[6]) Alas, my chair did not appreciate the irony of having a group of women complain to him, a man, about another woman who is an aggressive thinker and a demanding teacher. Instead of sending these people to see me in my office—a more appropriate course of action—he decided to handle this from his (white male) hierarchical position.

Third, either the academy simply does not recognize quality when it sees it in terms of tough-minded critical thinking aimed at getting at the truth, or it has bought into the insidious "new pedagogy" that "impugns all objectivity, even that of science."[7] When administrators have the gall to tell students that "learning and teaching have less to do with truth, reality, and objectivity than we assumed,"[8] and academics have a stronger commitment to difference than to truth—exemplified by papers like "Toward a Feminist Algebra"[9]—then it is time to reeducate the educators.

Unfortunately, it seems "American universities have adopted feminism . . . its relativistic underpinnings . . . and its fundamentalism."[10] Nowhere is this more obvious to me than at my own institution (although I know I am not alone). Never does a discussion about "teaching excellence" go by without at least one administrator piping up with his or her unique version of relativism: there can be no such criteria since what's excellent for one group of people may not be excellent for another. Of course, if the person is truly right, then what's the point of discussing teaching excellence at all?

In another instance, in the context of a candidate search, I was scorned at a faculty meeting for asking questions about the university's commitment to multiculturalism, a commitment that ranged from the usual diversity of race and sex to differences in philosophical orientation (e.g., analytic or continental, thereby making the whole commitment meaningless), and to a desire to hire a feminist scholar, someone who approached feminism the "right way."

SCHOLARSHIP

Academic freedom in the classroom and the committee room is not the only aspect of professional life that is being oppressed by gender feminism; scholarship is under attack as well.

In 1991, I answered a "Call for Papers" in the *American Philosophical Association's Proceedings,* which read as follows:

> Essays are sought for a volume concerned with the traditional problematics of knowledge as they have been understood in philosophy, including truth, justification, belief, agency, and power. It is imagined that these essays might deal strictly with contemporary epistemological issues or proceed by analysis of historical theories, figures, or periods.
>
> Although the volume will turn around traditional problematics, it is meant to be an inclusive one, excluding only sociological or other studies with little or no relation to traditional epistemological concerns. Certainly issues such as consensus, cognitive authority, and the relation of social and political power to the content and boundaries of knowledge would fall well within the purview of the volume.
>
> Also welcomed are critiques of traditional epistemology as anti-feminist, for example, because theoretical terms of analysis have been limited, excluding such factors as responsibility, interests, and other ethical values and concerns. Too, feminist epistemologies may require the violation of area boundaries, especially between epistemology and ethics, as well as of disciplinary boundaries between philosophy and sociology, politics, economics, literature, history, and art.
>
> As the working title ["Feminist Epistemologies"] suggests, it is not believed that there can be one feminist epistemology inasmuch as the feminist tenets are accepted that knowledge arises from social practices and that practices vary widely among groups of people. These tenets in turn raise issues of concern to the volume, viz., whether feminist epistemologies are necessarily relativist and, if so, whether feminists can find grounds from which to urge social and political changes as well as changes in our ways of producing knowledge.
>
> For further information call or write to either Linda Alcoff, Syracuse University, or Elizabeth Potter, Hamilton College.[11]

The above clearly calls for papers in all areas of epistemology. Although criticisms of traditional epistemology would be considered, there is nothing in the "call" that suggests that is all that will be considered.

I then sent the following, only two days after my timely receipt of the *Proceedings*:

> I am interested in acquiring further information concerning your forthcoming volume *Feminist Epistemologies*.
>
> I am a traditional (nonrelativistic and nonnaturalistic) epistemologist. I am also very committed to most of the political ideals of most feminists. Therefore, if there were good arguments defending the position that traditional epistemology is *essentially* male-biased, I would support every effort to destroy or reconstruct it. But such arguments have yet to be developed.
>
> If an essay defending traditional epistemic concepts (e.g., justification or rationality) from the charge of male-bias would be in keeping with the mission of your volume I would be most honored to contribute.

Here is the essence of the response I received from Alcoff:

> . . . Our volume is starting from the position, which we believe to be well-established, that the tradition of epistemology is no more free of male-bias than any other theoretical tradition in the West. . . . Though we start from the position, therefore, that gender matters, there is much work yet to be done to understand the way in which epistemology has been gendered male and the implications of this for particular epistemological formulations and for the self-conception of the field as a whole.[12]

She then wished me well, hoped I would read the book and become convinced that the project of simply espousing one side, the feminist epistemology issue, was worthwhile. The volume has since been published and it is filled with the usual feminist jeremiads of male-bias. The spirit of evenhandedness alluded to in the "call" was, it appeared, a charade.[13]

Apparently, so was the "call" in the *APA Newsletter* in spring 1993 asking the question, "Is There a Feminist Philosophy?" Why a charade? Here, once again, I sent a paper that, oddly, was misplaced for a number of months until the deadline had passed. Although the piece was sent registered mail to the contact person cited in the *Newsletter*, I was told that she no longer was the editor . . . and that she was off for the summer . . . and her secretary must have signed for it and then left it (stillborn) in the editor's mail box. By the time the new editor heard of the problem the deadline was long passed. She told me on the phone that "I was an unfortunate victim of the system."

I then submitted yet another paper to the *Newsletter*'s next "call" for "Doing Philosophy as Feminist." That piece, too, was returned with the following criticisms:

> I recommend that this piece be rejected (without qualification).
>
> Its key problem is that it operates with an extremely superficial and uninformed understanding of the feminist critique of rationality. That critique is far more diverse and much more complex than the author seems aware of. In particular, and most crucial is the failure of the author to make a significant "case" against feminist critiques of rationality.
>
> —Very few authors base their critiques on the *sexism* of male philosophers, as the author claims. Rather—as for example in Lloyd, Keller, Harding, and Bordo and many others—the critique is directed against the *masculinism* of their conceptions of reason. These are two very different things, as an author better versed in the literature would recognize.
>
> —Rarely do feminists call for the "dismissal" of reason. Rather, the argument is against the limitations (variously conceived by different writers) of dominant historical conceptions of reason, *notions* of rationality. Many writers explicitly call for the *reconstruction* of rationality; I don't know of anyone who says "let's get rid of reason" (anymore than anyone advocates "getting rid of dead white males" from the curriculum—another ridiculous, and common misconception about feminism). So, one is hardly barred from using rationality in order to critique or defend feminist arguments here (the linchpin of the author's claim that these arguments are "self-refuting"). Some feminist epistemological critiques might, however, underscore precisely the problems with the conception of rationality which appears to guide *this* piece—e.g., its acontextual, "logical flaw" orientation (as though one "fatal flaw" could invalidate a text, let alone a whole literature), its failure to become intimately acquainted with the object of critique before claiming to "know" it adequately.
>
> Since the author's conception of feminist epistemology is a caricature and a "straw woman," his/her argument against it is of no value to anyone interested in a serious consideration of whether or not the notion of "doing philosophy as a feminist" is beneficial or coherent.

Given the many direct quotations of feminists and my arguments in the preceding chapters, I encourage the reader to decide for herself. I would like to add, however, that when this issue of the *Newsletter* finally came out, there was not a single critical piece. It seems that, again, the only answer to questions concerning the beneficial nature of doing philosophy as a feminist, or even the coherence of such an approach, according to the feminists sitting on the editorial board, is yes.

Could it really be that no philosopher in the country critical of feminism is familiar enough with the material or careful enough not to build a "straw woman"? Or that no one save myself submitted a critical piece? Neither seems plausible.

The evidence of political manipulation showed itself pointedly in October 1993 when I became aware of a conference, sponsored by the New School for Social Research in New York City, entitled "Is Feminist Philosophy, Philosophy?"

After hearing about the conference, I called the program coordinator, Camille Atkinson, to register. (I had missed the "call for papers.") During the phone conversation I inquired about the program and asked if anyone at the conference would be presenting a paper which answers the conference title question with a no. The answer to my question was no. Why? Because, she said, all of the no proposals were "naively philosophical and simplistic."[14] I asked if she could tell me the name of anyone who made a no proposal and she said, "some Tibor guy."

Having known of only one "Tibor guy" in philosophy, I took a chance and dialed up Tibor Machan from Auburn University. Although we had never spoken, he was quite friendly and confirmed that he was, in fact, the "Tibor guy" who submitted to the conference. His proposal was, however, rejected. It is important to note that Machan is a very well respected author and editor of the philosophical journal *Reason Papers*. Below is a copy of his proposal.

Philosophy and Feminist Criticism

This paper argues that feminism—in its several versions—is a school of philosophy, as Marxism, existentialism, and objectivism are such schools. Feminism provides—or by implication embraces—certain answers to questions that arise in philosophy, thereby aspiring to be *the* correct philosophy. It sometimes raises new questions that are proposed to be included under the rubric of philosophy.

Feminism, however, is subject to philosophical scrutiny and criticism, just as are other schools. Thus feminism, too, must face the problematic nature of such philosophical criticism, namely, that it may itself embrace some assumptions and be incapable of being articulated outside some school of philosophy.

Nevertheless, the aspiration to find some objective, unbiased stance from which critical assessment of the content of some school of philosophy may be advanced, is legitimate. And it is only if that legitimacy is preserved that feminism, as other schools of philosophical thought, can continue to participate in the ongoing, possibly endless philosophical dialogue, one that aims to be self-corrective by means of the generation of different schools, all of which aspire to be philosophy proper.

This paper aims to provide grounds for the legitimacy of both philosophy *per se* and the aspiration of various schools of philosophical thought for becoming philosophy *per se*. It will be argued that philosophy is an ongoing dialogue with the goal of addressing questions that arise in ordinary life. These questions are not about special but very general topics such as what it is to be, what it is to consider the relationship of questioning beings in the world in all its conceivable facets, including what it is to know, to evaluate things and actions, to conduct oneself in the light of the answers to these questions as individuals and members of communities, etc.

It will next be argued that feminism, in its several varieties, is an identifiably distinctive coherent set of contributions to the above characterized philosophical endeavor. As such, it may be completely, partially, or not at all sound. That itself, however, must emerge from the dialogue itself.

Therefore, no tension exists between philosophy and feminism in any fundamental respect, although there may be some tension between certain facets of certain versions of feminism and the basic (yet unchangeable) tenets of the philosophical endeavor. The input of feminism has the potential to contribute to the possible changes in how philosophy will emerge following the phase of the dialogue in which feminists have taken a major part.[15]

Although unsure about the quality of the other proposals, I know that the above is anything but "naive and simplistic." It is insightful, philosophically provocative, and well written.

Finally, it is hard for me to believe that in the entire country (and yes, there were other critical entries), not one professional philosopher *critical of feminism* was talented enough to make the grade for this conference.

The point of these examples is not to whine but to illustrate through my own experiences that it is at least plausible, if not highly likely, that politics, not philosophy, is guiding a number of feminist conference and publication decisions. For a much broader and very well-documented account of the infiltration of gender feminism in the American academy, I urge you to read Christina Hoff Sommers's celebrated *Who Stole Feminism?* in which she documents the fact that many feminists (by intention or zealousness) have inflated evidence against them and infiltrated the academy in very destructive ways. I also recommend Noretta Koertge and Daphne Patai's *Professing Feminism: Cautionary Tales from Inside the Strange World of Women's Studies,* where they conclude "the ethos of contemporary women's studies not only would discourage young women from seeking a career in science, but also would make them feel morally and politically enlightened in remaining ignorant about science."[16]

In the rest of this chapter I will argue against the move to teach (specifically philosophy) feminist*ly*.

Teaching Philosophy Feminist*ly*

What does it mean to teach (philosophy) feminist*ly*? Throughout the years it seems to have meant different things to different people.

It could mean a *change in content*. One could incorporate the *works of women* into the traditional curriculum (e.g., putting Harding's books into a philosophy of science course along with Hempel, Kuhn, and others). This approach to feminist pedagogy is often called "mainstreaming."[17]

One could also tackle this task by incorporating works that are *feministly motivated*, i.e., "critical of the tradition."[18] For example, one could assign the critiques of traditional (male) philosophical works like Genevieve Lloyd's *The Man of Reason*, which (ostensibly) criticizes classical epistemology, or Andrea Nye's *Words of Power*, which attempts to criticize standard logic.

In addition, one could design a syllabus around the *works of women philosophers*, e.g., the collections of Martha Lee Osborne's *Women in Western Thought* or May Ellen Waithe's *A History of Women Philosophers, Vol. I*; or teach *about feminism*—liberal, Marxist, psychoanalytic, postmodern, etc.—using either an anthology or selected readings from each type of feminist.

Using a slightly different tact one could teach feminism as a change in content by discussing only contemporary *gender issues* (e.g., abortion, pornography, affirmative action, etc.), or focusing on how sex/gender plays itself out in a particular social structure (e.g., primary and secondary education[19]).

Finally, one could teach what is touted as *feminist philosophy* itself: feminist ethics (e.g., Nel Nodding's *Caring*), feminist philosophy of science (e.g., Evelyn Fox Keller's *Gender and Science*), or feminist epistemology (e.g., Jane Duran's *Toward a Feminist Epistemology*).

The problem with all of these ways of teaching, however, is twofold. First, none entail teaching philosophy feminist*ly* per se. They discuss feminism, in various forms, and then discuss philosophy, but none teach philosophy feminist*ly*. Doing this would require a change in form. (More will be said about this below.)

Second, and more importantly, what seems like legitimate scholarship in principle ends up being, in practice—in women's studies and philosophy departments across the country—nothing but claptrappism. Consider the following, carefully documented by Christina Hoff Sommers in *Who Stole Feminism?*:

> For the past few years I have reviewed hundreds of syllabi from women's studies courses, attended more feminist conferences than I care to remember, studied the new "feminist pedagogy," reviewed dozens of texts, journals, newsletters, and done a lot of late-into-the-night reading of e-mail letters that thousands of "networked" women's studies teachers send to one another. I have taught feminist theory. I have debated gender feminists on college campuses around the country, and on national television and radio. My experience with academic feminism and my immersion in the ever-growing gender feminist literature have served to deepen my conviction that the majority of women's studies classes and other classes that teach a "reconceptualized" subject matter are unscholarly, intolerant of dissent, and full of gimmicks. In other words, they are a waste of time. . . . The feminist classroom does little to prepare students to cope in the world of work and culture. It is an embarrassing scandal that, in the name of feminism, young women [and some men] in our colleges and universities are taking courses in feminist classrooms that subject them to a lot of bad prose, psychobabble, and "new age" nonsense . . . the feminist classroom *short-*

changes women students. It wastes their time and gives them bad intellectual habits. It isolates them, socially and academically.[20]

The news is worse for feminists, however. Many feminists have come to believe that "integrating feminist philosophy into them [philosophy courses] does not mean merely adding a feminist to the reading list. It goes much deeper than that. We must be willing to consider central methodological and substantive questions about the way we go about doing philosophy."[21] This *change in form* leads to even greater problems with respect to the legitimacy of this kind of education. And this I believe is even more seriously problematic.

There are two ways one can teach feminist*ly* by way of a change in form. One way is to teach any of the above "contents" while incorporating feminist values. The other is to teach traditional (male) "content"—philosophers, texts, or topics—while incorporating feminist values. In either case, I will call this fundamental change in approach, teaching philosophy feminist*ly*.

TEACHING FEMINIST*LY* DEFINED

Magda Gere Lewis identifies five practical strategies and techniques for teaching feminist*ly*.

> We look to share materials and teaching methodologies that bring women's experiences out of the shadows and make them legitimate curriculum content. We seek to share strategies on class-room practices that make the daily rigor of teaching less draining and more mutually supportive between students and teacher. We attempt to share in finding effective ways of making clear our political position not as an ideological construct but as a perspective or vantage point derived from our experience. We seek also to find ways of negotiating in our class-rooms the skepticism of students who have been well schooled in the ideological notions of the possibility of neutral social science research and educational practices. And, finally, though not insignificantly, we reach out for support from one another in those moments of despair and disillusionment when we are faced with that student who has come for the easy mark.[22]

To summarize, Lewis's five strategies and techniques are: (1) mutual support between teacher and other teachers and administrators, (2) mutual support between teachers and students, (3) making the feminist "perspective" derived from women's experience clear, (4) teaching students to challenge their belief in unbiasedness, and (5) emotional support.

The first desideratum seems to be completely legitimate. After all, educators should be able to turn to their colleagues and administrators for support, that is, as long as the support is for a legitimate course of study. Male-bashing, for example, would be illegitimate; and the use of the institution to simply propagate feminism would be, at best, questionable.[23]

The second needs more analysis. One way to feminist*ly* think about the relationship between the student and teacher is through the feminist ideal of "care."[24] To act as "one caring" includes, among other things, meeting the student directly, as a person with you as the one caring,[25] viewing the student as infinitely more important than the subject matter.[26] This may mean teachers will have to "choose words carefully and negotiate our analysis with the women students in ways that will not turn them [women] away from the knowledge they carry in their experience."[27] And, most importantly, the teacher must "nurture the student's ethical ideal, as a human being responsible for his words and acts."[28] "To reflect feminist values in teaching is to teach progressively, democratically, and with feeling."[29] As Nel Noddings claims:

> A teacher cannot "talk" this ethic. She must live it, and that implies establishing a relation with the student. Besides talking to him and showing him how one cares, she engages in cooperative practice with him. He is learning not just mathematics or social studies; he is also learning how to be one-caring. Everything we do, then, as teachers, has moral overtones. Through dialogue, modeling, the provision of practice, and the attribution of best motive, the one-caring as teacher nurtures the ethical ideal. She cannot nurture the student intellectually without regard for the ethical ideal unless she is willing to risk producing a monster, and she cannot nurture theoretical ideals without considering the whole self-image of which it is a part. For how he feels about himself in general—as student, as physical being, as friend—contributes to the enhancement or diminution of the ethical ideal. What the teacher reflects to him continually is the best possible picture consistent with reality. She does not reflect fantasy nor conjure up "expectations" as strategies. She meets him as he is and finds something admirable and, as a result, he may find the strength to become even more admirable. He is confirmed.[30]

Another way to teach philosophy feminist*ly* is to make the learning experience *noncompetitive*. Often the techniques used "emphasize peer discussion, group interaction, collective problem solving."[31]

With respect to evaluation, she says noncompetitive learning requires that instead of criticizing a work, feminist teachers should see how it fits "into the larger picture of feminist goals, and the broad view of social and political or ethical (or epistemological, metaphysical, etc.) thought."[32] Instead of using the Socratic method of directing a student to problems he/she may have misunderstood or overlooked, the feminist teacher is to emphasize group activity toward a "new understanding for all members in the class . . . a collective search for truth."[33]

But not a search for truth as an end, of course; when one teaches feminist*ly*, the search itself becomes the goal.

This is for two, interrelated reasons. The first is a commitment to the process; the second, a lack of commitment to truth itself. The first seems noncontroversial. The second, although recognized by Lewis (above) as the fourth desideratum of feminist pedagogy, is problematic and downright dangerous. Although criticisms of a lack of commitment to 'objectivity' have been dealt with in chapter 2, more will be said below about the pedagogical implications of rejecting the search for unbiasedness.

In addition, when one teaches feminist*ly*, one may want to put the course, at least to some degree, into the hands of the students, and teach *nonhierarchically*. This can be accomplished by setting up a democratic working environment, where students play an important role in developing every aspect of their classroom experience from determining what books they will read[34] to how often they should be in class to how they ought to be evaluated,[35] for what achievements,[36] and by whom. Feminists "deemphasize the role of the teacher and of texts and 'authorities', and rely heavily on student-directed learning."[37]

"Feminists are also unlikely to tolerate a theory that rejects or denies personal experience."[38] This is the point of Lewis's third desideratum. In the classroom feminist*ly* motivated teachers should integrate the cognitive and personal/affective forms of experience[39] and learning (e.g., have the students keep journals of their personal feelings about readings or their own experiences).

According to Lewis, this process is self-perpetuating. For once an examination of personal experience is begun, experiences of women's oppression gathered by way of consciousness investigation become themselves topics for oppression-investigation. "No gathering of women directed toward an articulation of these can escape the retelling of the brutalizations which women have experienced as an aspect of this process."[40]

Teaching feminist*ly* then is finally, and most fundamentally, the empowering of women by way of "consciousness raising." Under this kind of approach, "the sex/gender system appears to be a fundamental organizing principle of society and for that reason it becomes a primary object of analysis."[41] Teaching feminist*ly* requires that one recognize that "pedagogy, even radical pedagogy, does not easily translate into an education that includes women if we do not address the threat to women's survival and livelihood that a critique of patriarchy in its varied manifestations confronts."[42] In other words, according to the feminists who support this kind of teaching, the most important lesson a woman can learn is that she is oppressed by men and must fight back. Feminist pedagogues of this stripe all agree that teaching feminist*ly* "assumes that [feminist theory] is a part of an educational process that is connected to the feminist political struggle."[43]

CRITICISM OF TEACHING FEMINISTLY

Justifying one's teaching feminist*ly*—i.e., borrowing a phrase from Nel Noddings, as one caring, nonhierarchically, noncompetitively, emphasizing personal experience and feelings, and with a primary goal of feminist consciousness raising—is problematic. On the one hand the above aspect of "teaching feminist*ly*," as one who cares, which is legitimate and appropriate, is not the special bailiwick of feminism. On the other, the methods that are particularly feminist are neither pedagogically sound, especially for philosophy, nor, in the final analysis, good for women.

One Caring

Teaching as "one caring" is neither essential to feminism nor inconsistent with more classical teaching. For one thing, feminists have often acted in ways that do not seem to be as "one caring," especially to their male students, but also to female students who do not buy into the feminist political agenda.[44]

Nor is acting as one caring peculiarly feminist. I have always cared while I taught, and those professors whom I consider to be the best have done the same. At no time have I ever seen this as a commitment to feminism—the empowerment of women, but as my duty as a teacher—the empowerment of every citizen. The fact that pedagogical excellence, regardless of one's political motivations, requires that we care for our students should be obvious. Even our Hollywood interpretation of teaching excellence—e.g., *To Sir with Love*; "Welcome Back, Kotter"; *Stand and Deliver*; *Dead Poets Society*; *Goodbye, Mr. Chips*; *Educating Rita*; *The Blackboard Jungle*; and "Head of the Class" (ironically all of the teachers are men, and *Dead Poets Society* is a school for boys only)—articulates caring as its essence. The point is simple. Feminists have no special claim on caring.

The remaining characteristics of teaching feminist*ly*, namely, nonhierarchically, noncompetitively, emphasizing personal experience and feelings, and with a primary goal of feminist consciousness-raising, however, are dubious pedagogical ideals and not clearly good for women.

Teaching Nonhierarchically

In a general sense, it is not pedagogically sound to treat the student, the paradigmatic neophyte, as an equal to the teacher, a trained professional. Although there are certain fundamental ways in which they are equal (e.g., under the law and as moral agents), there are many ways in which they are different (amount of schooling, degrees, reasons for being in the classroom). Nor are these differences trivial in the context of the university. The reason professors are there, indeed the reason the university exists at all, is precisely because they have something to offer the student that the student neither has, nor can be acquired without the help of the professor. To believe otherwise diminishes the entire education process and the disciplines we are trying to impart.

But what precisely do the feminists mean by attempting to remove hierarchy from the classroom? Do they mean that the professor does not choose the required reading materials or the criteria for satisfactorily completing the course? If so, then the professor is not an educator, but merely a facilitator. Does it mean the professor should not evaluate the students at all or should do so in conjunction with the student's input on what it means for him/her to satisfy the criteria? If so, then the professor has given up responsibility for the student's education as well as her particular discipline.

Democracy in the classroom, at any level, undermines the point of pedagogy. Remember, viable democracies presuppose equality; and in the world of the classroom, teacher and student are not equals. If they were, then there would be no way to justify the fact that one person is the professor, is paid by the university to attend the class and act, in some way, as teacher. For the professor to give up her hierarchical position is to undermine her pedagogical duty.

Of course, she should not abuse her power in the hierarchy by using it to oppress students, e.g., belittle them as persons or deny them the ability to challenge and question the theories and perspectives of the professor (and their peers). Instead, the teacher must finesse the power of the hierarchical position so that she can retain a sense of educational excellence.

But perhaps all that is meant by a nonhierarchical classroom is to allow students the opportunity to work in groups, openly discuss their ideas, and challenge the professor to justify the course, its content, and its form. Well, these are certainly sound pedagogical principles, and I for one would certainly adhere to them; but I fail to see what is peculiarly feminist about these methods. Again, this is simply good pedagogy.

Teaching Noncompetitively

In the classroom, or even in the university as a whole, how is it possible to avoid competition? After all, if everyone is good enough to obtain the grade of "A" in a course, or complete the degree at a university, then the "A" and the degree itself become meaningless. Therefore, it must be, at least in principle, possible to fail to achieve these goals.

Such goals, then, must articulate themselves in meaningful, practical ways (e.g., write a ten-page paper arguing for . . .) that are verifiable and justifiable, at least from the standpoint of the discipline. (Educators cannot, for example, require that a criterion for getting an "A" is that the student have red hair. Although verifiable, there would be no way to justify this under the tradition of Western education. On the other hand, although it may be appropriate to give an "A" to the student who is the most intelligent and creative, there is no way to verify that the student has such gifts unless articulated in some way, e.g., by producing something.) But once such goals have been articulated, the professor must, at some point, recognize that while some students have achieved the goals, others have not. Put another way, the students end up, if not competing directly with each other, at least competing with the professor's idea of what it means to have achieved the goal in question. Competition, at some level, seems to be essential in education.

Often, however, feminists articulate their distaste for competition by claiming that there are no such things as standards of excellence in any particular discipline, for such standards require a commitment to traditional concepts of objectivity and classical accounts of epistemology that have ostensibly been shown to be male-biased. This tack clearly has an underlying commitment to some form of relativism (see chapter 3).

More importantly for this discussion, however, a relativistic attitude undermines education itself. If the expression of each individual student's personal experiences and feelings is the goal of an education, then why bother, again, training professionals—Ph.D.s, for example, in philosophy or literature—to monitor these psychological states; and why should this be done in a university setting under the guise of gaining an "education"?

But of course this is not the goal of education. The point is to enable the student to become a better citizen and a critical thinker (in the best sense of that term); to train individuals to think critically about their own beliefs and those embedded in societies and cultures. And although it may be pedagogically efficient to begin with the student's personal experience in getting one to begin this process, to aim for this as an end is absurd. Both the student and the professor must believe that certain kinds of beliefs are simply better than others, and that it is through education that one can acquire those beliefs that are better.

Of course, this does not mean that the professor should ignore a student's feelings, but that it is the professor's duty, at the very least, to demonstrate that feelings cannot go unchecked by rationality, that they may lead him to a disrespect for the evidence and, therefore, unjustified beliefs. One can respect the open-mindedness of a critical thinker without accepting the wide-mindedness of a person who believes that everyone's thoughts and feelings are equally justifiable. The job of the pedagogue is to encourage the former, not the latter. However, in order to maintain the distinction, the teacher must be committed to the belief that there are educational goals (for their respective disciplines) and that while some students achieve them, others, despite their best efforts, do not.

Again, a commitment to one's discipline and the educational ideals it has established throughout the years does not entail an adherence to the straw position that the professor must value those ideals above the individual to whom those ideals are to be imparted. Precisely the opposite is the case. Ideals are established, and continue to be reaffirmed, precisely because pedagogues believe that it is by way of their maintenance that we truly educate our students and make the world a better place.

Consciousness-Raising as a Good

'Consciousness-raising' is defined in a number of ways: (1) "Consciousness-raising is the major technique of analysis, structure of organization, method of practice, and theory of social change of the women's movement";[45] (2) "consciousness-raising types of education, like assertiveness training and counseling programs that advocate the goal of economic independence for women";[46] (3) "women need to develop an analogous true consciousness of their own oppressed condition, in the process shedding 'false consciousness,' of 'male-identified' ideologies that serve male, ruling-group interests."[47]

My question is simply to ask, is this goal, construed as the empowerment of women to the exclusion of men, legitimate?

First, I would like to confess that I have tried it. In 1989, while still a believer in academic feminism, I taught my first feminist philosophy course and took seriously the idea of teaching feminist*ly*. I chose the texts carefully: Bleier's *Science and Gender*, Mill's *The Subjection of Women*, Tong's *Feminist Thought*, Gilligan's *In a Different Voice*, Noddings's *Caring*, Keller's *Reflections in Gender and Science*, Lloyd's *The Man of Reason*, and Grimshaw's *Philosophy and Feminist Thinking*.[48] (At the time these books were the gold standard.)

I also took seriously what it would mean to challenge the methods of traditional philosophy and attempt to teach feminist*ly*. In order to achieve both the objective of teaching philosophy (something I had done for a number of years) and the objective of teaching philosophy feminist*ly* (something I had never done before), I incorporated the writing of a daily journal as a means of self-expression and additional noncritical evaluation. This, I believed at the time, allowed the student to express her feelings about the books, topics, world around her, classroom experience, and so forth, without putting her critical comments at risk. The student was graded "loosely" in terms of how well she followed the assignment (and the amount of credit given for the journal was determined by the student at the beginning of the course), and on how conscientiously and sincerely she attempted to analyze and develop feelings about sexism and feminism. My comments in these journals were infrequent and were intended only to nurture. These comments usually took the form of questions, urging the student to further her investigation.

The upshot of this is that by the end of the semester the students did not learn philosophy, even when compared to the students in my typical introduction to philosophy class, let alone my more advanced courses. And whatever consciousness they gained was so incredibly painful that it was hard for me to defend the claim that it was, in fact, in their best interest to address it at the time. Most of the women in the class were too young and intellectually and emotionally unprepared to accept their new plight as, ostensibly, the oppressed. This supposed fact made many of them miserable, insecure, and even a bit fearful and paranoid. They not only feared men, but they saw sexism in every aspect of their lives. As Christina Hoff Sommers has pointed out,[49] the adoption of a feminist ideology may not result in personal happiness. If she is indeed right, then we must ask ourselves, what is the point? If truth is supposed to hurt, why not stick with the old male one? More importantly, do we as feminists or teachers really have a duty to raise the feminist consciousness of our women students?

It seems that I fell into the pedagogical trap articulated by Koertge and Patai:

In the name of being "supportive" to women, the therapeutic aim of feminist pedagogy too often colludes in inculcation the attitude of "learned
helplessness" so deplored by our earlier, tougher, feminist foremothers.[50]

The greatest regret I have from my one semester of consciousness-
raising was not that the students were unhappy, but that I gave up the
chance to teach students—all students—how to think critically. As far as
I'm concerned, this and only this is the duty of the philosopher and the
true test of educational excellence.

CRITICAL THINKING AS THE EDUCATIONAL IDEAL

Is critical thinking really an educational ideal and can it be made consistent with feminist political goals, specifically the empowerment of women?
The educational ideal of critical thinking "promulgates the development in students of autonomy, self-sufficiency, the skills of reason assessment, and the attitudes, dispositions, habits of mind, and character
traits of the critical spirit, and erects those features of persons as the fundamental guidelines for the evaluation and transformation of society."[51]
Can this be justified as the educational ideal?
Harvey Siegel, in his book *Educating Reason*, offers four kinds of justification: Respect for students as persons, self-sufficiency and preparation for
adulthood, initiation into the rational traditions, and the ideal of democracy.

The first consideration is simply that we are morally obliged to treat students (and everyone else) with respect. If we are to conduct our interper-
sonal affairs morally, we must recognize and honor the fact that we are dealing with other persons who as such deserve respect—that is, we must show
respect for persons. This includes the recognition that other persons are of
equal moral worth, which entails that we treat other persons in such a way
that their moral worth is respected. This in turn requires that we recognize
the needs, desires, and legitimate interests of other persons to be as worthy of consideration as our own. In our dealings with other persons, we must
not grant our interests more weight, simply because they are *our* interests,
than the interests of others. The concept of respect for persons is a Kant-
ian one, for it was Kant who urged that we treat others as *ends* and not
means. This involves recognizing the equal worth of persons. Such worth
is the basis of the respect which all persons are due. . . . The general moral
requirement to treat persons with respect thus applies to the teacher's

dealing with her students simply because those students are persons and so are deserving of respect. . . .

The second reason for taking critical thinking to be a worthy educational ideal has to do with education's generally recognized task of preparing students to become competent with respect to those abilities necessary for the successful management of adult life.[52]

Since we do not know what students will be in that adult life, we must prepare them for any and every possible life. We must make them autonomous.

> To thus empower the student is to raise her, in the most appropriate sense of the term, to her "fullest potential," for any such potential surely includes the power to shape and choose, and to attain, possible potentials. . . . To help students to become critical thinkers is to "encourage them to ask questions, to look for evidence, to seek and scrutinize alternatives, to be critical of their own ideas as well as those of others" [Scheffler, *Reason and Teaching*, p.143]. . . . By encouraging critical thinking, then, we teach the student what we think is right, but we encourage the student to scrutinize our reasons and judge independently the rightness of our claims. In this way the student becomes a competent judge; more importantly for the present point, the student becomes an independent judge.[53]

For Siegel, critical thinking is "coextensive"[54] with rationality, which is, in turn, interested in reasons. Therefore, the third justification for critical thinking as the educational ideal is simply that we have a duty to initiate students "into the rational traditions."[55]

> Such initiation consists in part in helping the student to appreciate the standards of rationality which govern the assessment of reasons (and so proper judgment) in each tradition, then we have a third reason for regarding critical thinking as an educational ideal. Critical thinking, we have seen, recognizes the importance of getting students to understand and appreciate the role of reasons in rational endeavor, and of fostering in students those traits, attitudes and dispositions which encourage the seeking of reasons for grounding judgment, belief, and action. If education involves initiation into the rational traditions, then we should take critical thinking to be an educational ideal because so taking it involves fostering in students those traits, dispositions, attitudes and skills which are conducive to the successful initiation of students into the rational traditions.[56]

Of course proponents of teaching feminist*ly* may claim that these "rational ideals" are precisely what need to be avoided. Given the feminist criticisms (see chapter 2) of reason, rationality, and classical epistemology, such "ideals" may be viewed as only seemingly value-neutral when in fact they are male-biased. With this kind of criticism in mind such a theoretical appeal would probably go unheeded.

But what if we take a more pragmatic, even practical, approach to pedagogy and consider the relationship between critical thinking and democracy? According to Israel Scheffler, democracy ideally

> aims so to structure the arrangements of society as to rest them ultimately upon the freely given consent of its members. Such an aim requires the institutionalization of reasoned procedures for the critical and public review of policy; it demands that judgments of policy be viewed not as the fixed privilege of any class or elite but as the common task of all, and it requires the supplanting of arbitrary and violent alteration of policy with institutionally channeled change ordered by reasoned persuasion and informed consent.[57]

In a democratic society—one in which our students end up voting for policies via our representatives—educators have a duty to empower our students with the most useful tools for making the best decisions they can. Until the feminist critics of reason have won the day, critical thinking remains education's central task.

Critical thinking, which is synonymous with a commitment to rationality, ought to maintain its place as *the* educational ideal because it has at its heart the development of self-sufficient, responsible members of society who have respect for themselves and everyone else in their community.

Is this commitment consistent with teaching feminist*ly*? No, not if from a feminist perspective there are only two ways to resolve opposition of beliefs: (1) by claiming that each person has her own perspective and all opinions are equally valid, or (2) by giving preference to the opinion of the person who is most oppressed.[58]

I see no further positive argument that needs expressing. After all, if the above arguments for empowering students is accepted, then it would follow trivially that women would be empowered as well. Unless, of course, there were some reasons why women would be exempt.

One reason, alluded to in chapter 4, could be that women are, in fact, fundamentally different from men, in such a way that they are unable to achieve the level of critical thinking required for their ability to really act as rational, autonomous citizens. Although I will not engage in the biological research necessary to demonstrate either the truth or falsity of such a claim, I will point out that such a belief would be problematic for feminists. For if true, men could discriminate against women and, due to their inability to achieve the same level of rationality, such discrimination would be justified.

The other reason, discussed in chapter 2, is that the ideal of rationality is problematic, not because women are incapable of achieving it, but because the ideal is so essentially male that it is self-alienating for women to even try to embrace it.[59]

Again, both of the above have been challenged. More importantly for this discussion, even if it were demonstrated that there *is* and/or *should* be a separate "women's way of knowing," such knowledge would be impotent in this feminist-declared man's world. I always found it odd that the same feminists who call for changes in the classroom, do so with the strength of the Ph.D.s they earned the old-fashioned way. Why do they not want their students to have the same training that has empowered them?

While I spend hours strengthening my students' critical reasoning skills—building in my own obsolescence—my colleagues who do anything less create generations of students unable to compete either with them or the students I (and the other traditionalists) produce. Christina Hoff Sommers asks if academic feminists like women; I ask if those who teach feminist*ly* really like their own students.

As Koertge and Patai so eloquently remind us:

> Girls, as they grow up, need to overcome the well-meaning but often ill-advised overprotectiveness of their parents, which sends them the message that they are not quite competent. Do they go to university only to have this message repeated to them in women's studies programs?[60]

Or, if I may add, in any classroom where philosophy (or any topic) is being taught feminist*ly*?

In conclusion, my own experiences with feminists in academe has not been particularly fulfilling. As a woman I liken their sisterhood to a bad sorority—one has to look and think like they do to be accepted. As a philosopher, the situation is worse. Where feminists are in power—specific universities or editorial boards—my work and accomplishments have been systematically ignored.

I realize that these women have worked hard for a voice; and I do not begrudge them this. But now that they have power, it's time to use it to help all women.

If feminists in the academy want to do more than just feather their own nests, they should listen to all women, even those who sing a distant song. There is one thing worse than not having a voice at all and that is having one that no one listens to.

Notes

1. Magda Gere Lewis, "The Challenge of Feminist Pedagogy," *Queen's Quarterly* 96, no. 1 (Spring 1989): 127.

2. Peter J. Markie, *A Professor's Duties: Ethical Issues in College Teaching* (Lanham, Md.: Rowman and Littlefield, 1994), p. 3.

3. John Searle, "Is There a Crisis in American Higher Education?" *Bulletin of the American Academy of Arts and Sciences* 46, no. 4 (January 1993), p. 47.

4. Elizabeth A. Meese, "The Political Is the Personal: The Constructing of Identity in Nadine Gordimer's *Burger's Daughter*," in *Feminism and Institutions*, ed. Linda Kaufman (Cambridge: Basil Blackwell, 1989), pp. 251–60.

5. Christina Hoff Sommers, *Who Stole Feminism?* (New York: Simon and Schuster, 1994), p. 51.

6. Ibid.

7. Ibid., 109.

8. Ibid.

9. Mary Anne Campbell and Randall Campbell, "Toward a Feminist Algebra," Mathematical Association of America (1993), MAA Abstract No. 878–00–1035.

10. Paul R. Gross and Norman Levitt, *Higher Superstition: The Academic Left and Its Quarrels with Science* (Baltimore: The Johns Hopkins University Press, 1994), pp. 107–11.

11. *APA Proceedings* 63, no. 7 (June 1990): 91.

12. Letter dated August 14, 1990.

13. Many pieces are cited in chapter 2.

14. Camille Atkinson, phone conversation, September 29, 1993.

15. Machan sent me a copy of his proposal in personal correspondence, August 18, 1994.

16. Noretta Koertge, "Point of View: Are Feminists Alienating Women from the Sciences?" *The Chronicle of Higher Education* (September 14, 1994): A80.

17. Ann Garry, "Integrating Feminist Philosophy into Traditional Philosophy Courses: Rethinking a Philosophy Syllabus," *APA Newsletter* (April 1988): 17.

18 Bat-Ami Bar On, "Balancing Feminism and the Philosophical Canon," *APA Newsletter* (April 1988): 24.

19. See, e.g., Kathleen Weiler, *Women Teaching for Change: Gender, Class and Power* (Massachusetts: Bergin and Garvey, 1988).

20. Sommers, *Who Stole Feminism?* pp. 90–91.

21. Garry, "Integrating Feminist Philosophy," p. 17.

22. Lewis, "Challenge of Feminist Pedagogy," p. 127.

23. Again, see all of C. H. Sommers's work.

24. Nel Noddings, *Caring: A Feminist Approach to Ethics and Moral Education* (Berkeley: University of California Press, 1986), especially pp. 175–201.

25. Ibid., p. 177.

26. Ibid., p. 176.

27. Magda Lewis, "Interrupting Patriarchy: Politics, Resistance, and Transformation," *Harvard Education Review* 60, no. 4 (1990): 474.

28. Noddings, *Caring*, p. 178.

29. Nancy Schniedewind, "Feminist Values: Guidelines for Teaching Methodology in Women's Studies," *Radical Teacher* 18 (n.d.): 28.

30. Noddings, *Caring*, p. 179.

31. Ruth Ginzberg, "Teaching Feminist Logic," *APA Newsletter* 88, no. 2 (1989): 58.

32. Susan Sherwin, "Philosophical Methodology and Feminist Methodology: Are They Compatible?" in *Women, Knowledge and Reality*, ed. A. Garry and M. Pearsall (London: Unwin Hyman, 1984), p. 30.

33. Ibid.

34. See the struggle of Thomas Wartenberg, "Teaching Women Philosophy," *Teaching Philosophy* 11, no. 1 (1988): 15–24.

35. Ginzberg, "Teaching Feminist Logic."

36. Let us hope, however, that one "achievement" that would not be voted on would be the grading down of male students who refuse to use gender-neutral pronouns, which was the decree of choice by a number of feminists who attended a workshop entitled "White Male Hostility in the Feminist Classroom." See Christina Hoff Sommers, *Who Stole Feminism?* p. 91.

37. Ginzberg, "Teaching Feminist Logic," p. 58.

38. Sherwin, "Philosophical Methodology," p. 29.

39. Margo Cully, "The Politics of Nurturance," states that "the feminist classroom is the place to . . . welcome the intrusion/infusion of emotionality—love, rage, anxiety, eroticism" (p. 19).

40. Lewis, "Challenge of Feminist Pedagogy," pp. 118–19.

41. Ruth Pierson, "Two Marys and a Virginia: Historical Moments in the Development of a Feminist Perspective on Education," in *Women and Education: A*

Canadian Perspective, ed. J. Gaskell and A. McLaren (Calgary, Alberta, Canada: Detselig Enterprises, 1987), p. 203.

42. Lewis, "Challenge of Feminist Pedagogy," p. 473.

43. Charlotte Bunch, "Not by Degrees: Feminist Theory and Education," in *Learning Our Way: Essays in Feminist Education*, ed. C. Bunch and S. Pollack (Trumansburg, N.Y.: The Crossing Press, 1983), p. 255.

44. Christina Hoff Sommers, "Do These Feminists Like Women?" *Journal of Social Philosophy* 21 (1990): 66–74.

45. Catharine MacKinnon, "Feminism, Marxism, Method and the State: An Agenda for Theory," *Signs* 7 (1982): 5.

46. Ann Ferguson, "A Feminist Aspect Theory of the Self," in *Women, Knowledge and Reality: Explorations in Feminist Philosophy* (Boston: Unwin Hyman, 1989), p. 96.

47. Josephine Donovan, *Feminist Theory: The Intellectual Traditions of American Feminism* (New York: F. Ungar Publishing Company, 1985), p. 85.

48. For a much more detailed account of the events of this course and the justifications for each choice of required reading see E. R. Klein, "One Should Not Teach Philosophy Feministly," *Social Epistemology* (forthcoming, 1996).

49. Christina Hoff Sommers, "Feminist Philosophers Are Oddly Unsympathetic to the Women They Claim to Represent," *Chronicle of Higher Education* (October 11, 1989): B2–B3.

50. Noretta Koertge and Daphne Patai, *Professing Feminism: Cautionary Tales from Inside the Strange World of Women's Studies* (New York: Basic Books, 1994), p. 107.

51. Harvey Siegel, *Educating Reason* (New York: Routledge, 1988), p. 55.

52. Ibid., pp. 56–57, without note.

53. Ibid., pp. 57–58.

54. Ibid., p. 59.

55. Ibid.

56. Ibid., pp. 59–60.

57. Israel Scheffler, "Moral Education and the Democratic Ideal," in *Reason and Teaching* (New York: Bobbs-Merrill, 1973), p. 137.

58. Paraphrased from Koertge and Patai, *Professing Feminism*, p. 107.

59. See Jane Rolan Martin's series of critiques of traditional education, specifically critical reasoning, in: "Needed: A New Paradigm for Liberal Education," in *Philosophy and Education: The Eighteenth Yearbook of the National Society for the Study of Education*, ed. Jonas F. Soltis (Chicago: University of Chicago Press, 1981), pp. 37–59; idem, "Sophie and Emilie: A Case Study of Sex Bias in the History of Educational Thought," *Harvard Educational Review* 51 (August 1981): 357–72; idem, "Two Dogmas of the Curriculum," *Synthese* 51 (April 1983): 5–20; idem, "The Ideal of the Educated Person," in *Philosophy of Education 1981: Proceedings of the Thirty-seventh Annual Meeting of the Philosophy of Education Society*, ed. Daniel R. DeNicola (Normal, Ill.: Philosophy of Education Society, 1982), pp. 3–20; idem, "Excluding Women from the Educational Realm," *Harvard Educational Review* 52 (May 1982): 133–48.

60. Koertge and Patai, *Professing Feminism*, p. 114.

Conclusion

Feminism Is Not Philosophy

> It may be true that all things which are good are *also* something else, just as it is true that all things which are yellow produce a certain kind of vibration in the light. And it is a fact, that Ethics aims at discovering what are those other properties belonging to all things which are good. But far too many philosophers have thought that when they named those other properties they were actually defining good; that these properties, in fact, were simply not 'other', but absolutely and entirely the same with goodness. This view I propose to call the 'naturalistic fallacy' and of it I shall now endeavor to dispose.
>
> G. E. Moore[1]

In the 1988 article, "How Can Philosophy Be Feminist?" Alison M. Jaggar offers a number of possible ways in which philosophy can be done as a feminist: (1) reevaluate the work of women throughout the history of philosophy and the reasons why their "contribution has been overlooked,"[2] (2) resolve questions "about women's nature and place in society,"[3] (3) reassert "the philosophical significance of questions that have come to be viewed primarily as women's concerns,"[4] and (4) "question even the possibility of philosophy that is unbiased . . . seeking perennial truths . . . [via] a method of universal reason."[5] Of the four genres the first three suggest that feminists *philosophically* attend to feminism as *content*: the study of women, their works, and concerns. The fourth, however, suggests that feminists *feministly* attend to philosophy as *form*: the assault on method, and perhaps even "the abandonment of philosophy altogether."[6] I will argue that Doing Philosophy Feminist*ly* (DPF), is philosophically problematic and, ultimately, inimical to women.

DPF: The Initial Problem

DPF springs from the assumption that philosophy qua method of critical analysis, via "its privileging of reason and in the way that it has construed rationality,"[7] is essentially male-biased. Therefore, it is claimed that the "general ground rules for philosophizing" should be:

1. All our thought processes must be grounded in social and historical reality.

2. One must take experience seriously, including the experience of feelings, emotions, and perceptions.

3. One must look carefully for nontraditional sources of philosophical insight.

4. Always bear in mind the source and political implications of one's theories and other philosophical activities; these will be best and truest to the overarching goals of feminism when they are geared toward social reform or liberatory changes for all peoples.[8]

This supposition and its antecedent political program, however, are immune from philosophical criticism. A paradox arises when one sees the question: How can one offer *reasons* against a position if the commitment to reason is itself viewed as "the pretension of a distinctively masculine intellect"[9] or if "reasons" must be grounded in history or skewed toward the oppressed? Having dismissed the notion of reason as male-biased or "situated" in some political agenda, it is unclear how one can, in principle, offer a rationale for DPF without succumbing to self-refutation.

Again, as shown above, relativism (chapter 3) becomes the underlying "grounding" with all its logical and pragmatic problems, and naturalism (chapters 4, 5, and 6) can neither pull its needed normative weight nor support feminist goals.

Given that, in the final analysis, one can neither offer reasons in support of DPF (without simultaneously rejecting it) nor offer reasons against DPF (on the grounds that reasons are always male-biased), I claim that we have no reason to take DPF to be a serious philosophical enterprise.

DPF: Is It Oxymoronic?

Perhaps the reason one should not embrace DPF is that one, consistently, cannot. Perhaps what is peculiarly feminist about "feminist philosophy" is not particularly philosophical; and what is philosophical is not particularly feminist.[10]

FEMINIST BUT NOT PHILOSOPHY

In the good old days advocates of DPF were easy to identify. Their theories were brightly characterized by notions which insisted both that the content of Western philosophy, specifically, the notions of 'reason' and 'rationality', and its form, the process of critical analysis, were essentially male-biased.

As I pointed out in chapter 2, Genevieve Lloyd claimed that "our trust in a Reason that knows no sex has been largely self-deceiving";[11] that "rationality has been conceived as transcendence of the feminine."[12] In addition, Nancy J. Holland stated that all of contemporary analytic philosophy is committed to a "self-definition that identifies it as necessarily men's philosophy."[13] Lorraine Code wrote that "mainstream epistemology masks the facts of its derivation from and embeddedness in a specific set of interests: the interests of a privileged group of white men."[14] Finally, Karen J. Warren points out that numerous feminist philosophers have maintained "the hypothesis that mainstream Western conceptions of reason and rationality are distinctively male or masculine perspectives.[15] (Some feminists have even suggested that there is a peculiarly "woman's way of knowing."[16])

These comments, though I believe I demonstrated to be unjustified, are at least provocative and brazenly feminist. Certainly the Eve Browning Cole program outlined on page 228 is nothing if not feminist. Nevertheless, none of the above recommendations speak to philosophy proper.

NOT PARTICULARLY FEMINIST

In the good old days, what was most feminist about feminist philosophy was barely philosophical. Those days, however, may be gone. Now whenever I use the above kinds of quotations I am called naive and told that today's feminists do not merely adopt a "standpoint" while rejecting reason or analysis, and certainly they do not ask for the "abandonment of philosophy altogether."[17] Unfortunately, there seems to be little textual evidence of this.[18]

Furthermore, what now? What of interest is left? What remains of DPF that is peculiarly feminist?

The absence of a peculiarly feminist aspect to DPF is even more noticeable in the work of those feminists, especially feminist epistemologists, committed to saving philosophy from their sisters' more radical claims by unearthing feminist veins in nearly every classical thesis, from Platonic Realism to Quinian Empiricism.[19] Unfortunately, if these more moderate feminists are successful, not only will they have demonstrated that philosophy does not need to be done feminist*ly*, they will have shown that feminism does not even need women. This, as I have said before, is a curious way indeed of promoting the feminist political agenda.

DPF: The Metalevel Problem

All of the above, however, is often viewed by feminists as unsympathetic and simplistic. But if the supporters of DPF are correct that the philosophical method is itself at the very least "gender coded,"[20] that the incessant need for rational support, perhaps even the most bare-bones account of rationality—a commitment to logical consistency,[21] or modus ponens*—is itself simply a politico-patriarchal ploy to oppress women, then that response holds little weight.

The evidence offered in favor of this kind of metalevel bias as I argued earlier is primarily historical. Supporters of DPF argue that: (1) men have been responsible for the development of (Western) philosophy; (2) given that men have acted in a sexist manner, that is, they have used these philosophical constructs to oppress women, it follows that (3) philosophical constructs, e.g., 'objectivity' and 'rationality', must be male-biased.

Male-biasness, though historically accurate, is not a necessity but, as shown in chapters 1 and 2, an unfortunate contingency. Clearly, not all men *must* be sexist. Furthermore, not all philosophy (or science) *must* be used in an oppressive manner. To believe so is to entertain a category mistake. Philosophy *qua* method is not the kind of thing that can be oppressive. In short, methods don't oppress women, (sexist) men do.

Ironically, it is the feminists themselves who best illustrate this point. While arguing for DPF, they are, in fact, doing "male" philosophy by making claims, offering reasons, etc. The method is the same, only the goal—the empowerment of women only—has changed.

An appeal to the (oppressive) nature of men and the (male-oriented) history of philosophy is not the only maneuver open to the DPF enthusiast, however. Another strategy is to claim that the real problem lies not with the male inability to transcend bias, but with the fact that there is nothing to transcend to. Thus the reason for showing the problems with relativism in chapter 3.

Again, not only does relativism suffer from a number of logical and pragmatic problems, but, if true, it is true for the supporters of DPF as well. Unfortunately, relativism entails the possibility of some very pernicious consequences for women. One such consequence is that it would be difficult to argue in favor of anything, including the empowerment of women.[22] The ability to argue that women have been oppressed and ought not be requires precisely the kinds of objective facts and reasoned values supporters of relativism claim do not exist. Another consequence would be the ease with which one could defend any and every action, since there

---

*$P > Q$

$\dfrac{P}{Q}$, the 'affirming mode', if p then q, p, therefore q.

would be no way to adjudicate the rightness of one action over another. Relativism can only lead to epistemological and moral nihilism, a world where oppressed women can offer no reasons why they ought not be.

Therein lies the philosophical folly of DPF. Legitimate philosophy must be committed at some level to reasons. I say "at some level" because I want to allow for the *philosophical* criticism of reason and politics. For philosophy to consistently live up to its own ideals, everything (although not everything at once) must be criticizable, even the method of critical analysis itself. Unfortunately, radical feminist claims like those offered above suffer the same syndrome as fundamentalist religious claims: they cannot countenance rationale challenge. How can one philosophically criticize claims or offer *reasons* why a position is incorrect if *the commitment to reason* is itself viewed as "male" and, therefore, illegitimate?[23] When criticism is intolerable, philosophy, in principle, becomes impossible.

Of course I may have yet to take the feminist perspective seriously in that what they are really aiming to do is deconstruct[24] philosophy—*qua* method—itself. To this I respond with two questions, both sincere: How? and Why? The first question is motivated simply by a desire for understanding. I fail to see how a complete elimination of classical philosophical tools will allow anything at all to be built in its place.

Living on a barrier island I have often wondered what would happen if a hurricane destroyed my home. Of course, the simple answer is to use my insurance money to rebuild it from the ground up. But what if the ground on which the house now stands is itself no longer there, i.e., reclaimed by the ocean? On what do I build? The point is that there comes a time at which clearing away the old in order to make room for the new has gone too far. I believe this limit (*un*critical mass) is reached once the feminists demolish not only particular philosophical accounts of rationality, but the commitment to rationality itself and its bare-bones grounding in the law of noncontradiction. In a similar vein, why do feminists insist upon calling whatever is left after their destruction of philosophy, 'philosophy'? If the commitment to criticize is gone, so is the philosophy.

The supporters of DPF should realize that at the heart of their program is politics, and politics is *not* philosophy. This is not to say that "epistemology is by nature apolitical and hence can't be feminist," nor that "being objective is incompatible with any form of political commitment."[25]

Of course one can maintain an attitude of objectivity regarding feminist political commitments, but not while *simultaneously* criticizing the concept of 'objectivity'. While objectivity is being challenged for political reasons, it cannot then be said that this particular political commitment—this standpoint—is being objectively embraced.

My point, furthermore, is *not* that epistemology can't be feminist; on the contrary, I believe it *is*. This is precisely why I do not think that women need to invest in their own; the classical concepts, when properly applied, will work just fine at eliminating bias and promoting justice and equality for women. The reverse, however, seems false. While epistemology, i.e., classical epistemology *can* be feminist, feminism—with its uncritical standpoint—*can't* be epistemology. Feminism focuses on one goal: the empowerment of women. The question about the goodness of the goal itself is never, within the confines of feminist scholarship, challenged. Like religious belief[26] it is something sacred, a faith that believers will not—by their own lights cannot—challenge from within.

Philosophy on the other hand is fundamentally different, for it holds nothing sacred. Everything can—and should be—(though not all at once)[27] challenged and questioned.

The very act of questioning, so essential to philosophy (for nothing else separates it from all other fields of inquiry), emphasizes the demarcation between philosophy and politics. As long as one is within her right to ask, Ought I to follow this politic?; Ought I to do philosophy?; and even Ought I to maintain a distinction between politics and philosophy? the bifurcation between politics and philosophy prevails.

With respect to DPF, whether friend or foe the argument presents itself in the following way: once I ask, Ought one do philosophy feminist*ly*? (and one must, at some point, ask this question), I have ceased to do philosophy *as* a feminist; I am, instead, doing philosophy as a philosopher.

In the final analysis, Doing Philosophy Feministly is at best committed to relativism or dogmatism, which are both philosophically problematic and harmful to women, and at worst oxymoronic in nature. Insofar as DPF is provocative and politically potent, in its criticism of reason and analysis, it is dogmatic and therefore not properly philosophical. Insofar as DPF retreats from its sex/gender stance, it ceases to play its essential political role.

Philosophy Is Not Politics

Perhaps one can, sympathetically, take a more fundamental look at the break between philosophy and politics itself which drives much of this discussion. Perhaps we need to take a look at the legitimacy of the "is/ought" distinction.

'IS' VERSUS 'OUGHT'

In *Principia Ethica* G. E. Moore argued that the fundamental entity of ethics, 'good', is simple and indefinable;[28] it cannot be defined by, or reduced to, anything else. Any attempt to do so would commit the now infamous "naturalistic fallacy": construing that the 'is' of attribution is an 'is' of identity.

For Moore, simply pointing to the fact, for example, as Mill does in *Utilitarianism*, that humans *desire* pleasure, does not entail that pleasure *is* desirable or worthy of our desire, i.e., good. At best one can say that what we, in fact, desire is simply what we, in fact, desire; what is good *is* what is good. ('Good' here is being used substantively, not adjectivally.)

> When we say that an orange is yellow, we do not think our statement binds us to hold that 'orange' means nothing else than 'yellow', or that nothing can be yellow but an orange. . . . Why, then, should it be different with 'good'? Why, if good is good and indefinable, should I be held to deny that pleasure is good? Is there any difficulty in holding both to be true at once? On the contrary, there is no meaning in saying that pleasure is good, unless good is something different from pleasure.[29]

The fundamental distinction between 'good' and everything else must, according to Moore, be maintained. If not, the naturalistic fallacy arises.

This fallacy has contributed to the development of certain misguided accounts of ethics, specifically: (1) that what is natural is good,[30] (2) that nothing is good except pleasure,[31] (3) that everything that exists is in nature,[32] and (4) that our duty is defined by that action which causes more good to exist in the universe than any possible alternative.[33] In so doing, Moore sets the stage for all future criticism of anyone who attempts to break down the is/ought distinction. If 'good' is indefinable, then no amount of naturalizing will be enough.[34] The gap may be narrowed, even made "so narrow that it can be crossed in many cases by employing something that is no more than a mere truism,"[35] but it will, nonetheless, always remain.

THE RAMIFICATIONS FOR FEMINISM

If there always remains a gap between 'is' and 'ought', then one is within her rights to ask the open question: Yes, I know that feminism attempts to empower women—but, is this right? Should women be empowered at, for example, the expense of educational excellence, truth, or justice? Can we even call this empowerment? Which form of "education" is best?

Once the question is asked, the door is open, at least if we are intellectually honest, for the answers to come down against feminism. Those adherents to the feminist party line must realize that they will now have to defend their agendas, not merely presuppose them in theory and then impose them in practice.

Last Words

Since we can do philosophy, simpliciter, I urge that we ought. Insofar as we are doing philosophy feminist*ly* we violate the philosophical enterprise, compromise our professionalism, and indoctrinate, not teach, our students. While we all must strive to recognize women's contributions to philosophy, we should remember to always keep a close eye on feminism and never allow ourselves to be seduced by philosophy feminist*ly*.

Practically speaking, I propose the start of third-generation feminism with a cry to return to traditional science and classical epistemology. Sexism, from men or women, can be defeated and equal opportunity can be achieved only by stepping back to such basics: by tempering feminism under the fire of objective evidence and rational argumentation.

Given the arsonist nature of my project, it is perhaps inevitable that this monograph end in anticlimax—a quick flameout of the sustained critical analysis of feminist philosophy that was my goal. My intention was never to develop a positive account of classical philosophy—after all, that has already been provided by the masters of the discipline—but only to subject feminist philosophy to the systematic rigor of analysis. This I believe I have done.

My greatest hope is that my work will set the stage for a renaissance in philosophy. Once the destructive influences of feminist philosophy have been conflagrated, true feminists can get on with the business at hand—the empowerment of women through traditional commitments to objectivity and classical accounts of reason.

Notes

1. G. E. Moore, *Principia Ethica* (New York: Cambridge University Press, 1982), p. 10.

2. Alison M. Jaggar, "How Can Philosophy Be Feminist?" *APA Newsletter on Feminism* (April 1988): 5–6.

3. Ibid., p. 5.

4. Ibid., p. 6.

5. Ibid., p. 7.

6. Ibid.

7. Ibid., p. 6.

8. Eve Browning Cole, *Philosophy and Feminist Criticism* (New York: Paragon House, 1993), pp. 14–19.

9. Jaggar, "How Can Philosophy Be Feminist?" p. 7.

10. At the Is Feminist Philosophy, Philosophy? conference at the New School for Social Research, two feminists (Patricia S. Mann and Jana L. Sawicki) made points similar to this. Mann answered the question: Is feminist philosophy, philosophy? by saying "who cares?"—feminists should wean themselves from having to call themselves philosophers. And Sawicki said that she is more interested in what philosophy can do for feminism than whether or not feminism is philosophy. Her stated goal is to "pack philosophy departments with feminists."

11. Genevieve Lloyd, *The Man of Reason* (London: Methuen, 1984), p. x.

12. Ibid., p. 104.

13. Nancy J. Holland, *Is Women's Philosophy Possible?* (Savage, Md.: Rowman and Littlefield, 1990), p. 3.

14. Lorraine Code, *What Can She Know? Feminist Theory and the Construction of Knowledge* (Ithaca, N.Y.: Cornell University Press, 1991), p. x.

15. Karen J. Warren, "Male-Gender Bias and Western Conceptions of Reasons and Rationality," *APA Newsletter* 8, no. 2 (1989): 48.

16. See A. Garry and M. Pearsall, *Women, Knowledge and Reality* (London: Unwin Hyman, 1984).

17. Jaggar, "How Can Philosophy Be Feminist?" p. 7.

18. Even the most state-of-the-art writings claim that "feminist philosophers have become painfully aware of the degree to which traditional philosophy overlooks or trivializes women's interest, issues, concerns, and persons. . . . Among the neglected 'female-associated' elements in many of traditional philosophy's canonical texts are the concrete, particular, and subjective." Nancy Tuana and Rosemary Tong, eds., "Introduction," in *Essential Readings in Theory, Reinterpretation, and Application* (Boulder, Colo.: Westview Press, 1995), p. 2.

19. This is the point of most of the essays in Louise M. Antony and Charlotte Witt, *A Mind of One's Own* (Boulder, Colo.: Westview Press, 1993).

20. Tuana and Tong, "Introduction."

21. For examples of feminist critiques of logic itself, see Ruth Ginzberg, "Feminism, Rationality and Logic," *APA Newsletter* 88, no. 2 (1989): 34–39; Andrea Nye, *Words of Power: A Feminist Reader of the History of Logic* (New York: Routledge, 1990).

22. See E. R. Klein, "Criticizing the Feminist Critique of Objectivity," *Reason Papers* 18 (Fall, 1993): 57–70.

23. Alison Jaggar, for example, once viewed the commitment to reason as "the pretension of a distinctively masculine intellect." Jaggar, "How Can Philosophy?" p. 7.

24. I do not mean deconstruction as a philosophical program, but rather to *destruct* prevailing theories.

25. Richard Campbell in informal discussion, Summer 1995.

26. My colleagues David Fenner and Kenton Harris make an even stronger analogy, claiming that feminists, like theists, come to believe in the cause only via something like a religious conversion.

27. Even 'reason' can be challenged, but in doing so we must proceed carefully so as not to fall into fundamentalist pitfalls or dogmatic traps. When challenged, it cannot be within the confines of any particular political camp. It must be done purely, motivated only by the desire to reach truth, or at least another level of understanding.

28. Moore, *Principia Ethica*, pp. 8–9.

29. Ibid., p. 14.

30. Ibid., pp. 37–58.

31. Ibid., pp. 59–109.

32. Ibid., pp. 110–41.

33. Ibid., pp. 142–82.

34. Some examples, of course, of naturally occurring bad things could be AIDS and cancer.

35. Nicholas Rescher, *Baffling Phenomena* (Savage, Md.: Rowman and Littlefield, 1991), p. 46.

Bibliography

Addelson, Kathryn Pyne. "Knower/Doers and Their Moral Problems." In *Feminist Epistemologies*, edited by Linda Alcoff and Elizabeth Potter, 265–94. New York: Routledge, 1993.

Aisenberg, Nadya, and Mona Harrington. *Women of Academe: Outsiders in the Sacred Grove.* Amherst: University of Massachusetts, 1988.

Alcoff, Linda, and Elizabeth Potter. "Introduction: When Feminism Intersects Epistemology." In *Feminist Epistemologies*, edited by Linda Alcoff and Elizabeth Potter, 1–14. New York: Routledge, 1993.

Amt, Emilie M. *Women's Lives in Medieval Europe.* New York: Routledge, 1993.

Antony, Louise. "Quine as Feminist: The Radical Import of Naturalized Epistemology." In *A Mind of One's Own*, edited by Louise M. Antony and Charlotte Witt, 185–226. Boulder, Colo.: Westview Press, 1993.

Antony, Louise M., and Charlotte Witt, eds. *A Mind of One's Own: Feminist Essays on Reason and Objectivity.* Boulder, Colo.: Westview Press, 1993.

Atherton, Margaret. "Cartesian Reason and Gendered Reason." In *A Mind of One's Own: Feminist Essays on Reason and Objectivity*, edited by Louise M. Antony and Charlotte Witt. Boulder, Colo.: Westview Press, 1993.

Bar On, Bat-Ami. "Balancing Feminism and the Philosophical Canon." *APA Newsletter* (April 1988): 23–25.

Bayley, James E. "Introduction." In *Aspects of Relativism*, edited by James E. Bayley, 1–24. Lanham, Md.: University Press of America, 1992.

Baenninger, Maryanne, and Nora Newcombe. "Environmental Input to the Development of Sex-Related Differences in Spatial and Mathematical Ability." *Learning and Individual Differences* 7, no. 4 (1995): 363–79.

Belenky, Mary F., et al., eds. *Women's Ways of Knowing: The Development of Self, Voice and Mind.* New York: Basic Books, 1986.

Bernstein, J. M. *Beyond Objectivism and Relativism: Science, Hermeneutics and Practice.* Philadelphia: University of Pennsylvania Press, 1983.

Birke, Lynda. *Women, Feminism and Biology: The Feminist Challenge.* New York: Methuen Press, 1986.

Bishop, Sharon, and Marjorie Weinzweig, eds. *Philosophy and Women.* Belmont, Calif.: Wadsworth, 1979.

Bleier, Ruth. *Science and Gender: A Critique of Biology and Its Theories on Women.* New York: Pergamon Press, 1984.

Blum, Lawrence A. *Friendship, Altruism, and Morality.* Boston: Routledge and Kegan Paul, 1908.

Bordo, Susan. "The Cartesian Masculinization of Thought." In *Sex and Scientific Inquiry,* edited by S. Harding and J. F. O'Barr, 247–64. Chicago: University of Chicago Press, 1987.

———. *The Flight to Objectivity.* Albany: State University of New York Press, 1987.

———. "The View from Nowhere and the Dream of Everywhere: Heterogeneity, Adequation and Feminist Theory." *APA Newsletter* 88, no. 2 (1989): 19–25.

Braidotti, Rosie. "Feminism and Modernity." *Free Inquiry* 15, no. 2 (Spring 1995): 24–28.

Brown, Harold I. *Perception, Theory and Commitment.* Chicago: Precedent Publication Inc., 1977.

Bunch, Charlotte. "Not by Degrees: Feminist Theory and Education." In *Learning Our Way: Essays in Feminist Education,* edited by C. Bunch and S. Pollack, 248–60. Trumansburg, N.Y.: The Crossing Press, 1983.

Campbell, Mary Anne, and Randall Campbell. "Toward a Feminist Algebra." Paper presented at a meeting of the Mathematical Association of America, San Antonio, 1993. MAA Abstract No. 878–00–1035.

Caraway, Carol. Review of *Who Knows? From Quine to a Feminist Empiricism* by Lynn Hankinson Nelson. *Teaching Philosophy* 14, no. 2 (June 1991): 221–24.

Carnap, Rudolph. "Testability and Meaning." *Philosophy of Science* 3 (1936): 419–71.

———. "Empiricism, Semantics and Ontology." In *Semantics and the Philosophy of Language,* edited by Leonard Linsky, 208–28. Urbana, Ill.: University of Illinois Press, 1952.

———. *Der Logische Aufbeu der Welt* (The Logical Structure of the World: Pseudo Problems in Philosophy), translated by Rolf H. George. Berkeley: University of California Press, 1967.

Chandler, John. "Androcentric Science? *The Science Question in Feminism*," *Inquiry* 30 (1987): 317–32.

———. "Feminism and Epistemology." *Metaphilosophy* 21, no. 4 (1990): 367–81.

Chomsky, Noam. Review of B. F. Skinner's *Verbal Behavior* (New York: Appleton-Century-Crofts, 1957). In *Language* 35, no. 1 (January/February 1958): 26–55.

———. "Quine's Empirical Assumptions." In *Words and Objections: Essays on the Work of W. V. Quine,* edited by Donald Davidson and Jaakko Hintikka, 53–68. Dordrecht, Holland: D. Reidel Publishing Co., 1969.

———. *Rules and Representations.* New York: Columbia University Press, 1980.

Code, Lorraine. "Experience, Knowledge, and Responsibility." In *Women, Knowledge, and Reality,* edited by A. Garry and M. Pearsall. London: Unwin Hyman, 1984.

———. *Epistemic Responsibility.* Hanover, N.H.: University Press of New England, 1987.

———. "The Impact of Feminism on Epistemology." *APA Newsletter* 88, no. 2 (1989): 25–29.

———. *What Can She Know? Feminist Theory and the Construction of Knowledge.* Ithaca, N.Y.: Cornell University Press, 1991.

———. "Taking Subjectivity into Account." In *Feminist Epistemologies,* edited by Linda Alcoff and Elizabeth Potter, 15–48. New York: Routledge, 1993.

Cole, Eve Browning. *Philosophy and Feminist Criticism.* New York: Paragon House, 1993.

Cornell, Drucilla, and Adam Thurschell. "Feminism, Negativity, Intersubjectivity." In *Feminism as Critique,* edited by Seyla Benhabib and Drucilla Cornell, 143–62. Minneapolis: University of Minnesota Press, 1987.

Cully, Margo, et al. "The Politics of Nurturance." In *Gendered Subjects: The Dynamics of Feminist Teaching,* edited by Margo Cully and Catherine Protuges, 11–20. Boston: Routledge and Kegan Paul, 1985.

Damer, T. Edward. *Attacking Faulty Reasoning: A Practical Guide to Fallacy-Free Arguments.* Belmont, Calif.: Wadsworth, 1995.

Derrida, Jacques. *De la grammatologie.* Paris: Editions de Minuit, 1967.

———. *Positions,* edited and annotated by Alan Bass. Chicago: University of Chicago Press, 1981.

Descartes, R. *Meditations on First Philosophy,* translated by Laurence J. LaFleur. New York: Macmillan, 1951.

Dinnerstein, Dorothy. *The Mermaid and the Minotaur: Sexual Arrangements and Human Malaise.* New York: Harper and Row, 1977.

Donovan, Josephine. *Feminist Theory: The Intellectual Traditions of American Feminism.* New York: F. Ungar Publishing Co., 1985.

Duhem, Pierre. *The Aim and Structure of Physical Theory,* translated by Philip P. Wiener. Princeton, N.J.: Princeton University Press.

Duran, Jane. *Toward a Feminist Epistemology.* Savage, Md.: Rowman and Littlefield, 1991.

Dwyer, Susan, ed. "Men's Pornography: Gay vs Straight." In *The Problem of Pornography*. New York: Wadsworth, 1995.

Einstein, Albert. "Reply to Criticisms." In *Philosopher-Scientist*, edited by Paul Arthur Schilpp, 676–78. Evanston, Ill.: Library of Living Philosophers, 1949.
Erwin, Edwin. "The Confirmation Machine." In *Boston Studies in the Philosophy of Science*, Vol. 7, edited by Roger C. Buck and Robert S. Cohen, 306–21. Dordrecht, Holland: Reidel Publishing Co., 1971.

Fausto-Sterling, Anne. "The Five Sexes: Why Male and Female Are Not Enough." *Science* (March/April, 1993): 20–25.
Fee, Elizabeth. "A Feminist Critique of Scientific Objectivity." *Science for the People* (July/August 1982): 5–33.
Fenner, D. E. W. "Naturalism, Mechanism, and Determinism." Unpublished manuscript.
Ferguson, Ann. "A Feminist Aspect Theory of the Self." In *Women, Knowledge, and Reality: Explorations in Feminist Philosophy*, 93–107. Boston: Unwin Hyman, 1989.
Feyerabend, Paul. *Against Method*. London: Verso, 1975.
———. *Farewell to Reason*. New York: Verso, 1987.
Flax, Jane. "The Conflict between Nurturance and Autonomy in Mother-Daughter Relationships and within Feminism." In *Women and Mental Health*, edited by E. Howell and M. Bayes, 51–69. New York: Basic Books, 1981.
———. "Political Philosophy and the Patriarchal Unconscious: A Psychoanalytic Perspective on Epistemology and Metaphysics." In *Discovering Reality: Feminist Perspectives on Epistemology, Metaphysics, Methodology and the Philosophy of Science*, edited by Sandra Harding and Merrill Hintikka, 245–81. Dordrecht, Holland: Reidel Publishing Co., 1983.

Garry, Ann. "Pornography and Respect for Women." *Social Theory and Practice* 4 (Summer 1978): 395–442.
———. "Integrating Feminist Philosophy into Traditional Philosophy Courses: Rethinking a Philosophy Syllabus." *APA Newsletter* (April 1988): 17–20.
Garry, Ann, and Marilyn Pearsall, eds. *Women, Knowledge, and Reality: Explorations in Feminist Philosophy*. Boston: Unwin Hyman, 1984.
Gatens, Moira. *Feminism and Philosophy: Perspectives on Difference and Equality*. Indianapolis: Indiana University Press, 1991.
Gettier, Edmund. "Is Justified True Belief Knowledge?" *Analysis* 23, no. 6 (1963): 121–23.
Gibson, Roger F. *The Philosophy of W. V. Quine*. Tampa, Fla.: University Press of Florida, 1982.
———. "Translation, Physics, and Facts of the Matter." In *The Philosophy of W. V. Quine*, edited by Edwin Hahn and Paul Arthur Schilpp, 139–54. La Salle, Ill.: Open Court Press, 1986.

Gibson, Roger F. "Quine on Naturalism and Epistemology." *Erkenntnis* 27 (1987): 57–78.

———. *Enlightened Empiricism.* Tampa, Fla.: University Press of Florida, 1988.

Gilligan, Carol. *In a Different Voice.* Cambridge, Mass.: Harvard University Press, 1982.

Ginzberg, Ruth. "Feminism, Rationality and Logic." *APA Newsletter* 88, no. 2 (1989): 34–39.

———. "Teaching Feminist Logic." *APA Newsletter* 88, no. 2 (1989): 58–62.

Goldman, Alan H. *Justice and Reverse Discrimination.* Princeton, N.J.: Princeton University Press, 1979.

Goldman, Alvin I. "A Causal Theory of Knowing." *Journal of Philosophy* 64, no. 12 (1967): 355–72.

———. "What Is Justified Belief?" In *Naturalizing Epistemology,* edited by Hilary Kornblith, 91–114. Cambridge, Mass.: The MIT Press, 1979.

———. *Epistemology and Cognition.* Cambridge, Mass.: Harvard University Press, 1986.

Goodman, Nelson. *Fact, Fiction and Forecast,* 4th ed. Cambridge, Mass.: Harvard University Press, 1983.

Grimshaw, Jean. *Philosophy and Feminist Thinking.* Minneapolis: University of Minnesota Press, 1986.

Gross, Paul R., and Norman Levitt. *Higher Superstition: The Academic Left and Its Quarrels with Science.* Baltimore: The Johns Hopkins University Press, 1994.

Grosz, Elizabeth. "Conclusion: A Note on Essentialism and Difference." In *Feminist Knowledge: Critique and Construct,* edited by S. Gunew, 332–44. New York: Routledge 1990.

———. "Philosophy." In *Feminist Knowledge: Critique and Construct,* edited by S. Gunew, 147–74. New York: Routledge, 1990.

———. "Bodies and Knowledge: Feminism and the Crisis of Reason." In *Feminist Epistemologies,* edited by Linda Alcoff and Elizabeth Potter, 187–216. New York: Routledge, 1993.

Grünbaum, Adolf. "The Falsifiability of Theories: Total or Partial? A Contemporary Evaluation of the Duhem-Quine Thesis." *Synthese* 14 (1962): 17–34.

———. "Can We Ascertain the Falsity of a Scientific Hypothesis?" In *Observation and Theory in Science,* edited by M. Mandelbaum, 69–129. Baltimore: The Johns Hopkins University Press, 1971.

Gunew, Sneja. "Feminist Knowledge: Critique and Construct." In *Feminist Knowledge: Critique and Construct,* edited by S. Gunew, 13–35. New York: Routledge, 1990.

Haack, Susan. "Recent Obituaries of Epistemology." *American Philosophical Quarterly* 27, no. 3 (1990): 199–212.

———. "Critical Notice on Lorraine Code's *Epistemic Responsibility.*" *Canadian Journal of Philosophy* 21, no. 1 (1991): 91–107.

Haack, Susan. "Science 'From a Feminist Perspective.'" *Philosophy* 67 (1992): 5–18.

Halberg, Margareta. "Feminist Epistemology: An Impossible Project?" *Radical Philosophy* 53 (1989): 3–7.

Harding, Sandra. "Why Has the Sex-Gender System Become Visible Only Now?" In *Discovering Reality: Feminist Perspectives in Epistemology, Metaphysics, Methodology and Philosophy of Science,* edited by S. Harding and M. Hintikka. Dordrecht, Holland: Reidel Publishing Co., 1983.

———. "Feminist Justificatory Strategies." In *Women, Knowledge, and Reality,* edited by A. Garry and M. Pearsall, 189–201. London: Unwin Hyman, 1984.

———. *The Science Question in Feminism.* Ithaca, N.Y.: Cornell University Press, 1986.

———. "The Instability of the Analytical Categories of Feminist Theory." In *Sex and Scientific Inquiry,* edited by S. Harding and J. F. O'Barr, 283–302. Chicago: University of Chicago Press, 1987.

———. "Practical Consequences of Epistemological Choices." *Consciousness and Cognition* 21 (1988): 153–55.

———. "Responding to Smith's Criticism." *APA Newsletter* 88, no. 3 (1989): 46–49.

———. "Starting from Women's Lives: Eight Resources for Maximizing Objectivity." *Journal of Social Philosophy* 21 (1991): 140–49.

———. *Whose Science? Whose Knowledge? Thinking from Women's Lives.* Ithaca, N.Y.: Cornell University Press, 1991.

———. "Rethinking Standpoint Epistemology: What Is Strong Objectivity?" In *Feminist Epistemologies,* edited by Linda Alcoff and Elizabeth Potter, 49–82. New York: Routledge, 1993.

Harris, James F. *Against Relativism.* LaSalle, Ill.: Open Court, 1992.

Haslanger, Sally. "Doing Philosophy as a Feminist." *APA Newsletter* 91, no. 1 (1992): 112–15.

Hausheer, Herman. "Epistemological Subjectivism." In *Dictionary of Philosophy,* edited by D. D. Runes. Totowa, N.J.: Littlefield, Adams and Co., 1962.

Hawkesworth, Mary E. "Knowers, Knowing, Known: Feminist Theory and Claims of Truth." *Signs* 14, no. 3 (1989): 533–57.

Held, Virginia. "Developing Feminist Philosophy." *APA Newsletter* 91, no. 1 (1989): 118–20.

Heldke, Lisa. "Foundation and Relativism: The Issue for Feminism." *APA Newsletter* 88, no. 2 (1989): 39–42.

Holland, Nancy J. *Is Woman's Philosophy Possible?* Savage, Md.: Rowman and Littlefield, 1990.

Honderich, Ted, ed. *The Oxford Companion to Philosophy.* New York: Oxford University Press, 1995.

Humm, Maggie. *Dictionary of Feminist Theory.* Hertfordshire, U.K.: Wheatsheaf, 1989.

Jaggar, Alison M. *Feminist Politics and Human Nature.* Totowa, N.J.: Rowman and Allenheld, 1983.

————. "Love and Knowledge: Emotion in Feminist Epistemology." In *Women, Knowledge, and Reality,* edited by A. Garry and M. Pearsall, 129–56. London: Unwin Hyman, 1984.

————. "How Can Philosophy Be Feminist?" *APA Newsletter on Feminism* (April 1988): 4–8.

————. "Love and Knowledge: Emotion in Feminist Epistemology." In *Gender-Body-Knowledge: Feminist Reconstructions on Being and Knowing,* edited by Alison M. Jaggar and Susan Bordo. New Brunswick, N.J.: Rutgers University Press, 1989.

Jehlen, Myra. "Archimedes and the Paradox of Feminist Criticism." In *The Signs Reader: Women, Gender and Scholarship,* edited by E. Abel and E. K. Abel, 69–95. Chicago: University of Chicago Press, 1983.

Kahneman, David, Paul Slonic, and Amos Tversky. *Judgment Under Uncertainty: Heuristics and Biases.* Cambridge: Cambridge University Press, 1982.

Kant, Immanuel. *Critique of Pure Reason,* translated by Norman Kemp Smith. New York: St. Martin's Press, 1929.

Keller, Evelyn Fox. "Feminism and Science." In *Women, Knowledge, and Reality,* edited by A. Garry and M. Pearsall, 175–88. London: Unwin Hyman, 1984.

————. *Reflections on Science and Gender.* New Haven, Conn.: Yale University Press, 1985.

Kim, Jaegwon. "What Is Naturalized Epistemology?" *Philosophical Perspectives* 2 (1988): 381–405.

Klein, E. R. "Should Epistemology Be Naturalized? A Metaepistemological Investigation." Ph.D. diss., University of Miami, 1989.

————. "Is 'Normative Naturalism' an Oxymoron?" *Philosophical Psychology* 5, no. 3 (1992): 289–97.

————. "Criticizing the Feminist Critique of Objectivity." *Reason Papers* 18 (Fall 1993): 57–70.

————. "One Should Not Teach Philosophy Feministly." *Social Epistemology* (1996), forthcoming.

Koertge, Noretta. "Point of View: Are Feminists Alienating Women From the Sciences?" *The Chronicle of Higher Education* (September 14, 1994): A80.

Koertge, Noretta, and Daphne Patai, eds. *Professing Feminism: Cautionary Tales from Inside the Strange World of Women's Studies.* New York: Basic Books, 1994.

Kordig, Carl R. *The Justification of Scientific Change.* Dordrecht, Holland: Reidel Publishing Co., 1971.

Kornblith, H. "Introduction: What is Naturalistic Epistemology?" In *Naturalizing Epistemology,* edited by H. Kornblith, 1–14. Cambridge, Mass.: MIT Press, 1985.

Kouranay, Janet A., James Sterba, and Rosemary Tong, eds. *Feminist Philosophies.* Englewood, N.J.: Prentice-Hall, 1992.

Kuhn, Thomas. *The Structure of Scientific Revolutions.* Chicago: University of Chicago Press, 1970.

———. *The Essential Tension.* Chicago: University of Chicago Press, 1977.

———. "Commensurability, Comparability, Communicability." In *Philosophy of Science Association, Vol. 2,* edited by P. Asquith and T. Nichols, 669–88. East Lansing, Mich.: Philosophy of Science Association, 1983.

Leck, Glorianne M. "Feminist Pedagogy, Liberation Theory, and the Traditional Schooling Paradigm." *Educational Theory* 37, no. 3 (1987): 343–54.

Lewis, Magda. "The Challenge of Feminist Pedagogy." *Queen's Quarterly* 96, no. 1 (Spring 1989): 117–31.

———. "Interrupting Patriarchy: Politics, Resistance, and Transformation." *Harvard Education Review* 60, no. 4 (1990): 467–88.

Lewontin, R. C. "Women Versus the Biologists." *New York Times Review of Books* (April 7, 1994): 31–35.

Lloyd, Genevieve. *The Man of Reason.* London: Methuen, 1984.

———. *Man of Reason,* 2d ed. Minneapolis: University of Minnesota Press, 1993.

Longino, Helen E. "Can There Be a Feminist Science?" In *Women, Knowledge, and Reality,* edited by A. Garry and M. Pearsall, 203–16. London: Unwin Hyman, 1984.

———. *Science as Social Knowledge.* Princeton, N.J.: Princeton University Press, 1990.

———. "Subjects, Power and Knowledge: Description and Prescription in Feminist Philosophies of Science." In *Feminist Epistemologies,* edited by Linda Alcoff and Elizabeth Potter, 101–20. New York: Routledge, 1993.

MacKinnon, Catharine. "Feminism, Marxism, Method and the State: An Agenda for Theory." *Signs* 7 (1982): 514–44.

Martin, Jane Rolan. "Needed: A New Paradigm for Liberal Education." In *Philosophy and Education: The Eighteenth Yearbook of the National Society for the Study of Education,* edited by Jonas F. Soltis, 37–59. Chicago: University of Chicago Press, 1981.

———. "Sophie and Emilie: A Case Study of Sex Bias in the History of Educational Thought." *Harvard Educational Review* 51 (August 1981): 357–72.

———. "Excluding Women from the Educational Realm." *Harvard Educational Review* 52 (May 1982): 133–48.

———. "The Ideal of the Educated Person." In *Philosophy of Education 1981: Proceedings of the Thirty-seventh Annual Meeting of the Philosophy of Education Society,* edited by Daniel R. DeNicola, 3–20. Normal, Ill.: Philosophy of Education Society, 1982.

———. "Two Dogmas of the Curriculum." *Synthese* 51 (April 1983): 5–20.

Medawar, Peter Brian. *Induction and Intuition in Scientific Thought.* Philadelphia: American Philosophical Society, 1969.

Merchant, Carolyn. *The Death of Nature: Women, Ecology and the Scientific Revolution.* San Francisco: Harper and Row, 1980.

Minnich, Elizabeth. "Friends and Critics: The Feminist Academy." *Proceedings of the Fifth Annual GLCA Women's Studies Conference,* November 1979.

Moore, G. E. *Principia Ethica.* New York: Cambridge University Press, 1982.

Murphy, Claudia. "Feminist Epistemology and the Question of Relativism." In *Aspects of Relativism,* edited by James E. Bayley, 133–39. Lanham, Md.: University Press of America, 1992.

Nelson, Lynn Hankinson. *Who Knows? From Quine to a Feminist Empiricism.* Philadelphia: Temple University Press, 1990.

———. "Epistemological Communities." In *Feminist Epistemologies,* edited by Linda Alcoff and Elizabeth Potter, 121–60. New York: Routledge, 1993.

Newton-Smith, W. H. *The Rationality of Science.* London: Routledge and Kegan Paul, 1981.

Noddings, Nel. *Caring: A Feminist Approach to Ethics and Moral Education.* Berkeley: University of California Press, 1986.

Nye, Andrea. *Words of Power: A Feminist Reading of the History of Logic.* New York: Routledge, 1990.

Oliver, Kelly. "Toward Thoughtful Dialogue in the Classroom: Feminist Pedagogy." *APA Newsletter* 89, no. 1 (1989): 82–87.

Pateman, Carole. "Introduction: The Theoretical Subversiveness of Feminism." In *Feminist Challenges,* edited by C. Pateman and E. Gross, 1–12. Chicago: Northeastern University Press, 1987.

Pierson, Ruth. 1987, "Two Marys and a Virginia: Historical Moments in the Development of a Feminist Perspective on Education." In *Women and Education: A Canadian Perspective,* edited by J. Gaskell & A. McLaren, 203–22. Calgary, Alberta, Canada: Detselig Enterprises.

Pinnick, Cassandra L. "Feminist Epistemology: Implications for Philosophy of Science." *Philosophy of Science* 61 (1994): 646–57.

Plato. *Meno,* translated by W. K. C. Guthrie.

———. *Theaetetus,* translated by F M. Cornford.

Potter, Elizabeth. "Gender and Epistemic Negotiation." In *Feminist Epistemologies,* edited by Linda Alcoff and Elizabeth Potter, 187–216. New York: Routledge, 1993.

Putnam, Hilary. *Reason, Truth and History.* New York: Cambridge University Press, 1981.

Quine, W. V. "Truth by Convention." In *Philosophical Essays for A. N. Whitehead*, edited by O. H. Lee, 90–124. New York: Lengmeus, 1936.

———. "Two Dogmas of Empiricism." In *From a Logical Point of View*, 20–46. New York: Harper and Row, 1953.

———. *Word and Object*. Cambridge, Mass.: Harvard University Press, 1960.

———. "Carnap and Logical Truth." In *The Philosophy of Rudolph Carnap*, edited by Paul Arthur Schilpp, 385–406. La Salle, Ill.: Open Court Press, 1963.

———. "Posits and Reality." In *The Ways of Paradox and Other Essays*, 246–54. Cambridge, Mass.: Harvard University Press, 1966.

———. "The Scope and Language of Science." In *The Ways of Paradox and Other Essays*, 228–45. Cambridge, Mass.: Harvard University Press, 1966.

———. *The Ways of Paradox and Other Essays*. Cambridge, Mass.: Harvard University Press, 1966.

———. "Epistemology Naturalized." In *Ontological Relativity and Other Essays*, 69–90. New York: Columbia University Press, 1969.

———. "Natural Kinds." In *Ontological Relativity and Other Essays*, 114–38. New York: Columbia University Press, 1969.

———. "Ontological Relativity." In *Ontological Relativity and Other Essays*, 26–68. New York: Columbia University Press, 1969.

———. *Ontological Relativity and Other Essays*. New York: Columbia University Press, 1969.

———. "Replies." In *Words and Objections: Essays on the Work of W. V. Quine*, edited by Donald Davidson and Jaakko Hintikka, 292–352. Dordrecht, Holland: D. Reidel Publishing Co., 1969.

———. "On the Reasons for the Indeterminacy of Translations." *Journal of Philosophy* 67 (1970): 179–83.

———. *The Roots of Reference*. LaSalle, Ill.: Open Court Press, 1973.

———. "The Nature of Natural Knowledge." In *Mind and Language*, edited by S. Guttenplau, 67–81. Oxford: Clarendon Press, 1975.

———. "On Empirically Equivalent Systems of the World." *Erkenntnis* 9 (1975): 313–28.

———. "Letters to Professor Grünbaum." In *Can Theories Be Refuted? Essays on the Duhem-Quine Thesis*, edited by S. Harding. Dordrecht, Holland: D. Reidel Publishing Co., 1976.

———. "Cognitive Meaning." *The Monist* 62 (1979): 129–42.

———. "Five Milestones of Empiricism." In *Theories and Things*, 67–72. Cambridge Mass.: Harvard University Press, 1981.

———. "On the Nature of Moral Values." In *Theories and Things*, 55–66. Cambridge, Mass.: Harvard University Press, 1981.

———. "Russell's Ontological Development." In *Theories and Things*, 73–85. Cambridge, Mass.: Harvard University Press, 1981.

———. *Theories and Things*. Cambridge, Mass.: Harvard University Press, 1981.

———. "Things and Their Place in Theories." In *Theories and Things*, 1–23. Cambridge, Mass.: Harvard University Press, 1981.

Quine, W. V. "Relativism and Absolutism." *The Monist* 67 (1984): 293–96.
———. "Reply to Hilary Putnam." In *The Philosophy of W. V. Quine*, edited by Edwin Hahn and Paul Arthur Schilpp, 427–32. Lasalle Ill.: Open Court Press, 1986.
———. "Reply to Morton White." In *The Philosophy of W. V. Quine*, edited by Edwin Hahn and Paul Arthur Schilpp, 663–65. LaSalle, Ill.: Open Court Press, 1986.
———. "Reply to Robert Nozick." In *The Philosophy of W. V. Quine*, edited by Edwin Hahn and Paul Arthur Schilpp, 364–68. LaSalle, Ill.: Open Court Press, 1986.
———. "Reply to Roger F. Gibson." In *The Philosophy of W. V. Quine*, edited by Edwin Hahn and Paul Arthur Schilpp, 155–58. LaSalle, Ill.: Open Court Press, 1986.
———. "Indeterminacy of Translation Again." *Journal of Philosophy* 84 (1987): 5–10.
———. *Quiddities.* Cambridge, Mass.: Harvard University Press, 1987.
———. *Pursuit of Truth.* Cambridge, Mass.: Harvard University Press, 1990.
———. "In Praise of Observation Sentences." *Journal of Philosophy* 90, no. 3 (March 1993): 107–16.
Quine, W. V., and J. S. Ullian. *The Web of Belief.* New York: Random House, 1978.

Rachels, James. *The Elements of Moral Knowledge.* New York: McGraw-Hill, 1986.
———. *The Right Thing to Do.* New York: McGraw-Hill, 1989.
Reichenbach, Hans. *The Rise of Scientific Philosophy.* Berkeley: University of California Press, 1959.
Rescher, Nicholas. *Baffling Phenomena.* Savage, Md.: Rowman and Littlefield, 1991.
Richards, Janet Radcliffe. *The Skeptical Feminist.* Harmondsworth, U.K.: Pelican, 1982.
Rorty, Richard. *Contingency, Irony, Solidarity.* Cambridge: Cambridge University Press, 1989.
———. *Philosophy and the Mirror of Nature.* Princeton, N.J.: Princeton University Press, 1979.
Rose, Hilary. "Hand, Brain, and Heart: A Feminist Epistemology for the Natural Science." *Signs: Journal of Women in Culture and Society* 9, no. 3 (1983): 73–90. Reprinted in *Sex and Scientific Inquiry*, edited by S. Harding and J. F. O'Barr, 265–82. Chicago: University of Chicago Press, 1987.
Rushton, J. Phillippe. *Race, Evolution and Behavior.* New Brunswick, N.J.: Transaction Press, 1995.

Scaltsas, Patricia Ward. "Is There Time To Be Equal? Plato's Feminism." *APA Newsletter* 90, no. 1 (1990): 108–10.
Scheffler, Israel. *Science and Subjectivity.* Indianapolis: Bobbs-Merrill, 1967.
———. "Vision and Revolution: A Postscript to Kuhn." *Philosophy of Science* 39 (1972): 366–74.
———. "Moral Education and the Democratic Ideal." In *Reason and Teaching*, 136–45. New York: Bobbs-Merrill, 1973.

Schniedewind, Nancy. "Feminist Values: Guidelines for Teaching Methodology in Women's Studies." *Radical Teacher* 18 (n.d.): 28.

Schuh, Sandra. "A Closer Moral Look at Pornography." Paper presented at the Florida Philosophical Association, 1990.

Schwartz, Lewis M. *Arguing About Abortion.* Belmont, Calif.: Wadsworth, 1992.

Searle, John. "Indeterminacy, Empiricism, and the First Person." *Journal of Philosophy* 84 (1987): 123–46.

———. "Is There a Crisis in American Higher Education?" *Bulletin of the American Academy of Arts and Sciences* 46, no. 4 (January 1993): 47.

Sherwin, Susan. "Philosophical Methodology and Feminist Methodology: Are They Compatible?" In *Women, Knowledge, and Reality,* edited by A. Garry and M. Pearsall, 21–36. London: Unwin Hyman, 1984.

———. "Feminist Knowledge, Women's Liberation, and Women's Studies." In *Feminist Knowledge: Critique and Construct,* edited by S. Gunew, 36–55. New York: Routledge, 1990.

Shrader-Frechette, Kristin. Review of *The Science Question in Feminism* by Sandra Harding. *Synthese* 76 (1988): 441–46.

Siegel, Harvey. "Justification, Discovery and the Naturalizing of Epistemology." *Philosophy of Science* 47 (1980): 297–321.

———. "Genderized Cognitive Perspectives and the Redefinition of Philosophy of Education." *Teachers College Record* 85, no. 1 (1983): 100–19.

———. "Empirical Psychology, Naturalized Epistemology and First Philosophy." *Philosophy of Science* 51 (1984): 667–76.

———. "What Is the Question Concerning the Rationality of Science?" *Philosophy of Science* 52 (1985): 517–37.

———. "Relativism, Truth and Incoherence." *Synthese* 68 (1986): 225–59.

———. *Relativism Refuted.* Dordrecht, Holland: D. Reidel Publishing Co., 1987.

———. *Educating Reason.* New York: Routledge, 1988.

Smith, Dorothy E. "Commentary on Sandra Harding's 'The Method Question'." *APA Newsletter* 88, no. 3 (1989): 44–46.

Soble, Alan. Review of *Whose Science? Whose Knowledge? Thinking from Women's Lives* by Sandra Harding. *International Studies in Philosophy of Science* 6, no. 2 (1992): 159–62.

Sommers, Christina Hoff. "Should the Academy Support Academic Feminists?" *Public Affairs Quarterly* 2, no. 3 (July 1988): 97–120.

———. "Feminist Philosophers Are Oddly Unsympathetic to the Women They Claim to Represent." *Chronicle of Higher Education* (October 11, 1989): B2–B3.

———. "Do These Feminists Like Women?" *Journal of Social Philosophy* 21 (1990): 66–74.

———. "The Feminist Revelation." *Social Philosophy and Policy* 8, no. 1 (1990): 141–58.

———. *Who Stole Feminism?* New York: Simon and Schuster, 1994.

Stroud, Barry. "The Significance of Naturalized Epistemology." In *Naturalizing Epistemology*, edited by Hilary Kornblith, 71–90. Cambridge, Mass.: MIT Press, 1979.

Tavris, Carol. *The Mismeasure of Women.* New York: Simon and Schuster, 1992.
Thomson, Judith Jarvis. "A Defense of Abortion." *Philosophy and Public Affairs Quarterly* 1, no. 1 (Fall 1971): 47–66.
Tong, Rosemary. *Feminine and Feminist Ethics.* Belmont, Calif.: Wadsworth, 1993.
Toulmin, Stephen. "The Construal of Reality: Criticism in Modern and Postmodern Science." In *The Politics of Interpretation*, edited by W. J. T. Mitchell, 99–118. Chicago: University of Chicago Press, 1983.
Tuana, Nancy. Review of *Sex and Scientific Inquiry*, edited by Sandra Harding and J. F. O'Barr. *APA Newsletter on Feminism* 89, no. 2 (1990): 61–62.
Tuana, Nancy, and Rosemary Tong, eds. "Introduction." In *Essential Readings in Theory, Reinterpretation, and Application.* Boulder, Colo.: Westview Press, 1995.

Vadas, Melinda. "A First Look at Pornography/Civil Rights Ordinance: Could Pornography Be the Subordination of Women?" *Journal of Philosophy* 89, no. 4 (1987): 487–511.

Waithe, Mary Ellen. "On Not Teaching the History of Philosophy." *Hypatia* 4, no. 1 (1989): 132–38.
Warren, Karen J. "Male-Gender Bias and Western Conceptions of Reasons and Rationality." *APA Newsletter* 8, no. 2 (1989): 48–53.
Wartenberg, Thomas. "Teaching Women Philosophy." *Teaching Philosophy* 11, no. 1 (1988): 15–24.
Weiler, Kathleen, *Women Teaching for Change: Gender, Class and Power.* Massachusetts: Bergin and Garvey, 1988.
White, Morton. *What Is and What Ought to Be Done.* New York: Oxford University Press, 1981.
———. "Normative Ethics, Normative Epistemology, and Quine's Holism." In *The Philosophy of W. V. Quine*, edited by Edwin Hahn and Paul Arthur Schilpp, 649–62. LaSalle, Ill.: Open Court Press, 1986.

Yates, Steven. "Multiculturalism and Epistemology." *Public Affairs Quarterly* 6, no. 4 (1993): 435–56.
Young-Bruehl, Elisabeth. "The Education of Women as Philosophers." *Signs* 12, no. 2 (1987): 207–21.

Zabludowski, Andrzej. "On Quine's Indeterminacy Doctrine." *Philosophical Review* 98 (1989): 35–63.

Index

Abortion, 16–17
Absolutism, 74, 78–82, 87
Addelson, Katherine Pyne, 78, 133 n. 115
Aesthetics, 19
Alcoff, Linda, 79, 133 n. 115, 204
Amt, Emilie, 21 n. 7
Analyticity, 158–64
Androcentrism, 27, 35, 40, 51, 181, 190, 194
Antony, Louise, 96, 104, 117–24, 129, 237 n. 19
Archimedes, 55
Archimedian pt. (first philosophy), 107, 114–15, 123, 125–26, 163, 165–68, 171–73
Aristotle, 9, 58
Atherton, Margaret, 71 n. 45
Atkinson, Camille, 207, 224 n. 14
Augustine, 61

Backlash, 11, 74
Bacon, Francis, 42

Baenninger, Maryanne, 21 n. 10
Barber, Donald, 94 n. 66
Beijing, China, 21
Belenky, Mary F., 71 n. 63
Birke, Lynda, 196 n. 10
Bleier, Ruth, 196 n. 14, 218
Bohr, Niels, 28
Bordo, Susan, 36, 57, 206
Brown, Harold, 27

Campbell, Richard, 47 n. 25, 237 n. 25
Carnap, Rudolph, 105, 131 n. 41, 149, 157, 164
Cartesian (radical) skepticism, 105, 107–108, 118, 168–69, 185
Certainty, 56–58, 105, 136, 186, 190
Child, Julia, 60
Chisholm, Roderick, 197 n. 48
Classical epistemology, 19, 46, 51, 54–68, 104–105, 107, 119, 135–36, 150, 174, 189, 197 n. 47, 230, 235
  caricatured, 51